ON HUMAN RIGHTS

The Oxford Amnesty Lectures
1993

Stephen Shute and
Susan Hurley, EDITORS

BasicBooks
A Division of HarperCollins*Publishers*

Copyright © 1993 by BasicBooks,
A Division of HarperCollins Publishers, Inc.

Designed by Joan Greenfield

Library of Congress Cataloging-in-Publication Data
On human rights / Stephen Shute and Susan Hurley, editors.
     p. cm.—(The Oxford Amnesty Lectures; 1993)
    Includes bibliographical references and index.
    ISBN 0–465–05223–1 (cloth)
    ISBN 0–465–05224–X (paper)
    1. Human rights. 2. Civil rights. I. Shute, Stephen, 1955– .
II. Hurley, S. L. (Susan L.) III. Series.
JC571.05 1993
323—dc20   92–56178
                                           CIP

94 95 96 97 CC/RRD 9 8 7 6 5 4 3 2

CONTENTS

PREFACE TO
THE OXFORD AMNESTY LECTURES

A single idea governs the Oxford Amnesty Lectures. Speakers of international reputation are invited to lecture in Oxford on a subject related to human rights. The public is charged to hear them. In this way funds are raised for Amnesty International, and the profile of human rights is raised in the academic and wider communities.

The organization of the lectures is the work of a group of Amnesty supporters. They act with the approval of Amnesty International, but are independent of it. Neither the themes of the annual series nor the views expressed by the speakers should be confused with the views of Amnesty itself. For each annual series a general theme is proposed, bringing a particular discipline or perspective to bear on human rights. The speakers are invited to submit an unpublished lecture which is delivered in Oxford; the lectures are then published as a book.

Amnesty International is a worldwide human rights movement which is independent of any government, political faction, ideology, economic interest, or religious creed. The Amnesty International mandate is as follows: to seek the release of prisoners of conscience—people imprisoned solely for their beliefs, color, ethnic origin, sex, language, or religion, provided that they have neither used nor advocated the use of violence; to oppose the death penalty, torture, or other cruel, inhuman, or degrading treatment or punishment of all prisoners; to end extrajudicial executions or "disappearances"; to oppose abuses by opposition groups—hostage taking, torture, and killings of prisoners and other arbitrary killings.

Members of the Committee of the Oxford Amnesty Lectures 1993 were Madeleine Forey, John Gardner, Ewen Green, Chris Miller, and Stephen Shute.

ACKNOWLEDGMENTS

We are grateful to the Committee of the Oxford Amnesty Lectures for inviting us to edit the present volume. We owe a special debt of gratitude to John Gardner who, with Stephen Shute, helped to prepare the book proposal that became the starting point for the introduction to this volume. The editors would also like to thank Geoffrey Bennington, Jerry Cohen, Chris Miller, and Robert Smith, as well as the contributors themselves, for their helpful comments on the introduction.

—Stephen Shute and Susan Hurley

INTRODUCTION

Stephen Shute and Susan Hurley

Suppose you are sitting comfortably at your desk editing a volume of essays about human rights, and you come across passages such as these, describing events of a kind that may be occurring as you read, and not too far away:

> On the basis of . . . statements of witnesses and actual raped people, one can confirm that . . . occupying Serbian forces formed special concentration camps for women and children. . . .
>
> [W]ar crimes are being committed in special women's concentration camps where little girls, girls and women are being raped in the presence of their parents, brothers and sisters, husbands or children. After that, according to witnesses' statements, the raped persons are further brutalized and even massacred, their breasts are sliced off and their wombs are ripped out. . . . The young girls couldn't physically survive the rapes and quickly died. . . . [O]ver 300 young girls in The Home for Retarded Children were raped.[1]

Or, from an article in the *International Herald Tribune*, reporting an observer's account:

> Once a young woman with a baby was taken in the middle of the hall. . . . They ordered her to take off her clothes. She put the baby on the floor next to her. Four Chetniks raped her; she was silent, looking at her crying child.
>
> When she was left alone she asked if she could breastfeed the baby. Then a Chetnik cut the child's head off with a knife. He gave the bloody head to the mother. The poor woman screamed. They took her outside and she never came back.[2]

The media assault us with horror stories daily (and we do not intend to imply that only one side in this particular conflict has violated human rights). But some things occurring in our own times still stop us in our tracks. You cannot just go back, whether comfortably or uncomfortably, to whatever you were doing; you feel that something must be done. How should we think about these events? What should we do about them? What is the relationship between these two questions? In particular, what is the relationship between the theory of human rights and the practice of international human rights law? We are troubled not solely by injustice, but also by theoretical scruples about the universality of any given view of justice and human rights as a basis for intervention. The relationship between the theory and practice of human rights is problematic.

Understood as a political tradition, liberalism might be considered to be at ease with the idea, if not the practice, of human rights. Indeed, the idea might be thought of as fundamentally a product of the liberal imagination, reflecting the complacent cultural imperialism of the modern Western world. Or, to put it a little more sympathetically, human rights might be seen as bound up with an individualistic and humanist view of the world, which has become the currency of everyday life in our society. If so, one would expect the theory of human rights to be among the main concerns of liberal political philosophy today.

But it is not. For contemporary liberal philosophers, the theory of human rights presents special problems that discourage straightforward engagement. Although liberal philosophers remain attached, by and large, to their individualist humanism, they are also sensitive to the allegation of cultural imperialism. Nor is this just hand-wringing or intellectual squeamishness. It is a genuinely philosophical sensitivity, born of the recognition that liberalism's core claims may seem to be skeptical claims, claims about the impenetrability or instability of moral argument, which sit unhappily with claims to universal applicability. The theory of human rights is caught up in this conflict between universalism and skepti-

3

cism, becoming uncomfortable territory for liberal philosophical enquiry.

The notable philosophers who have contributed to this volume, which is a record of the 1993 series of Oxford Amnesty Lectures, share an interest in the supposed universality of human rights and their capacity to cross cultural boundaries. Some of the lecturers are well known as staunch defenders of the liberal political tradition; others have made their name by criticizing what they regard as liberalism's vain attempt to divorce politics from ethics and to ground human rights in an ahistorical, unsituated rationality possessed by all human beings.

Steven Lukes is Professor of Political and Social Theory at the European University Institute in Florence. Previously a Fellow of Balliol College, Oxford, he has had a long-standing interest in the conceptual and political implications of value pluralism and conflict. His extensive writings on the subject have recently been brought together in a collection of essays entitled *Moral Conflict and Politics,*[3] which reinforces his reputation as a leading political theorist. One of the persistent targets in this book is Marxist political theory. Lukes regards Marxism as essentially a consequentialist ideology and therefore prepared to countenance the abrogation of human rights wherever a recognition of such rights seems likely to impede its revolutionary goals. Thus the essay "Can a Marxist Believe in Human Rights?" answers its title question firmly in the negative. This still leaves open the positive case for human rights. Why should Marxists be alarmed to discover that their ideology leaves no place for human rights?

Lukes here sheds further light on the significance of talk of human rights by asking us to imagine various societies, conceived as Weberian ideal types, in which human rights are not recognized. "Utilitaria" rejects human rights because such rights conflict with the sovereignty of utilitarian calculation. "Communitaria" rejects human rights because of their abstractness from specific, concrete ways of life and social practices. "Proletaria" rejects human rights because they may soften hearts in the struggle against class enemies and because they are superfluous once that struggle is won and a classless world is born. If we accept human rights we depart from each of these three points of view in a given respect. First, we restrain the pursuit of social advantage, however enlightened or benevolent that pursuit. Second, we accept, and protect, the potential abstraction or distance of persons from their specific, concrete ways of life. Third, we hold that, as a matter of fact, the conditions of human life will never be such that human rights are superfluous.

Lukes imagines two further societies in which it might be thought that human rights are respected, and highlights problems within each. "Libertaria" conceives of human rights within a context of market freedoms, property rights, equality of opportunity, and basic civil rights. Yet the poor, homeless, marginalized persons in this society do not enjoy equal respect, or equal access to and influence within essential political and social institutions. Moreover, the Libertarian conception of human rights never demands a step outside a narrowly self-interested point of view to a recognition of the urgent claims of others. Lukes thus implies that human rights require that certain basic equalities be taken more seriously than Libertaria takes them, and also require the transcendence of self-interest in certain circumstances.

In "Egalitaria," by contrast, we find a positive commitment to rendering civil rights of equal worth to everyone and to maintaining decent minimum standards for all, within the context of a general striving for growth and improvement. Yet there are deep problems that threaten Egalitaria's feasibility and viability. The very incentives that seem to be needed for growth give rise to inequalities. Moreover, there is conflict between the ideal of treating individuals as equal, regardless of their cultural identities, and the communitarian ideal of treating cultural identities as equal. These difficulties lead some away from Egalitaria, back to Libertaria or Communitaria. But Lukes describes an "egalitarian plateau" that respects a short list of human rights on which we may hope to secure agreement, including basic welfare rights and basic civil and political rights. We should not, he recommends, abandon that plateau for any of the other four possibilities described.

John Rawls, Professor of Philosophy at Harvard University, is one of the most celebrated of all political philosophers working in the English language today. To him, indeed, goes much of the credit for the vigorous and innovative state of contemporary Anglo-American work in the field. In the first half of the twentieth century, political philosophy had been placed in mortal danger by the combined assault of linguistic preoccupations and unrefined utilitarian assumptions. In his seminal essay "Two Concepts of Rules,"[4] Rawls set himself against both forces, venturing back into substantive moral philosophy. A larger enterprise, however, was in preparation. It had its first exposure to the light in the essay "Justice as Fairness,"[5] but reached full fruition in *A Theory of Justice,*[6] published in 1971 to unprecedented acclaim. This was a direct attack on the whole utilitarian vision, and not simply a comment on the way that we use moral language. Rawls distinguished, as utilitarians on his view could not, between a theory of the right and a theory of the good, building the former on what looked like principles of universal human rationality, while apparently resisting such rationalization in the case of the latter. Thus Rawls offered an intriguing combination of universalism about one part of morality, on which his political theory rests, and agnosticism about the other.

In later work, beginning in earnest with the important article, "Justice as Fairness: Political Not Metaphysical,"[7] Rawls dilutes the contrast. The theory of the right is not, after all, built on principles of universal human rationality. It is still somewhat more general in application than the theory of the good, which is relative to particular people, but the generality of the right is now within the boundaries of established liberal societies only. It depends on a so-called "overlapping consensus." It may seem that the genuinely universalist strand in liberal politics is thus subverted, and with it the universal human right. In his contribution to this volume, however, Rawls develops his position on these matters further and shows that his theory does have universalist implications.

Whereas Lukes appeals briefly to the need for agreement, Rawls brings issues about agreement to center stage. Rawls aims to show how the law of peoples can be developed from a generalization of liberal ideas of justice and how it extends to nonliberal as well as liberal societies. His constructivist approach does not begin with completely general first principles, but rather takes up a series of subjects in turn, adapting the procedures by which rational parties adopt principles of justice to fit the subject in question at each stage. Rawls describes how the idea of the original position with its veil of ignorance, familiar from his *Theory of Justice*,[8] may be used to model the agreement of representatives of both liberal and nonliberal societies on a law of peoples that respects basic human rights and is universal in its reach without being peculiarly Western or objectionably ethnocentric.

Rawls first considers how, within ideal theory, liberal ideas of justice may be extended to a society of liberal democratic societies. He here appeals to the idea of an original position, conceived as a device which, first, represents the parties fairly; second, represents them as rational; and third, represents them as deciding on the principles of a law of peoples for appropriate reasons. From such a device of representation of liberal societies he believes familiar principles, including principles of human rights, will emerge, and that the resulting society of societies will be stable with respect to justice and its law of peoples will be endorsed on due reflection.

The second and crucial stage of his argument shows how well-ordered but nonliberal, hierarchical societies may also come to accept these principles of the law of peoples. To be well-ordered, a hierarchical society must be peaceful, must be guided by some common good conception of justice that imposes moral duties and obligations on all persons in its territory, and, as a consequence, must respect basic human rights. These conditions do not require that a society be liberal or democratic or egalitarian; they are compatible with many forms of traditional or religious social organizations. Rawls argues that these conditions are nevertheless sufficient to bring the representatives of well-ordered hierarchical societies to accept the same principles of the law of peoples, including respect for basic human rights, that representatives of liberal societies will accept.

Basic human rights are thus conceived by Rawls not to express any foundational philosophical doctrine, but rather to express a minimum standard of well-ordered political societies guided by a common good conception of justice. The law of peoples that emerges from this constructivist conception limits the traditional powers of sovereignty not just with respect to waging war but also with respect to the treatment of people within a state's boundaries. In the world as we know it, the practical implications of these limitations, and especially of the latter limitation, are highly significant. Nevertheless, some of the most horrific violations of human rights have occurred, and are occurring, in the course of "ethnic cleansing" and related operations, in contexts in which state boundaries are ill defined and in dispute. Questions arise about how the theory may apply or guide our responses to such cases.

Catharine MacKinnon has gained an international reputation as a feminist writer who has not been afraid to combine theory with practical proposals for reform, and even polemic. In her books *Feminism Unmodified* and *Towards a Feminist Theory of the State*,[9] MacKinnon's overwhelming concern has been the social condition of women. Highly critical of the liberal tradition, which she condemns as guilty of substantive misogyny, and keen to reorient Marxism's materialist concerns, MacKinnon shifts the focus from the relations of production to gender hierarchy. For MacKinnon, gender is not an apolitical given, but rather a socially constructed manifestation of the power differential between men and women. Men have been able to create this power differential because they have been able to expropriate women's sexuality; and they have been able to sustain their position of domination because they have been able to make that expropriation seem natural. MacKinnon responds to this injustice by using the language of rights and advocating the introduction of an Equal Rights Amendment.

In her contribution to this volume, MacKinnon directs our attention to the pervasive banishment of women from rationality and the widespread exclusion of women from human rights theory and practice. She powerfully illustrates her point by reference to the atrocities currently being committed in Bosnia as part of an official policy of "ethnic cleansing" or liquidation, in camps dedicated to the systematic and mass rape of women and children, where victims may be raped by over thirty men per day for months. She stresses the failure of international law, as developed and understood by men, to recognize thus far that these specifically sexual atrocities are war crimes. Will international human rights laws be interpreted in unprecedented fashion to cover the atrocities in Bosnia or will they be shrugged off, largely by men, as "just war and just life"? If war crimes trials are eventually convened a further question arises: Will there be collective responsibility for these rapes, or will those women who survive be expected to identify each of often hundreds of rapists?

The atrocities in Bosnia are distressing enough in themselves. MacKinnon goes on to argue, however, that they are but an extreme example of a general pattern of oppression of women by men. As with the atrocities in Bosnia, these everyday examples of sexual and reproductive abuse have largely gone unrecognized by traditional human rights law. This failure to address the injustices suffered by women, both in war and in peace, has practical and theoretical roots. On a practical level, international human rights law malfunctions because it is not vigorously enforced. Direct action by one state against another known to have violated the various international conventions on human rights is rare and many human rights abuses, especially those against women, go unremedied. On a theoretical level, the exclusion of women from human rights discourse occurs partly because nongovernmental violations of human rights are overlooked. Thus when individual men use their social dominance to oppress women, this oppression is ignored because it does not fit the human rights model. In addition, the model has, according to MacKinnon, been built around a formal notion of equality that omits or marginalizes women; their claim to human status is denied or seen as tenuous and unprecedented.

To remedy these defects, MacKinnon urges us to replace the formal concept of equality, in terms of which much human rights law has to date been understood, with a richer, substantive concept of equality that refuses "to settle for anything less than a single standard of human dignity and entitlement." With this enriched concept in place, a whole set of further equality rights would be spawned, to empower the powerless, to allow claims against individuals and groups as well as governments, to require governments to act against all forms of exploitation and abuse, and to restrain governments responsible for abuse or exploitation.

Richard Rorty is Professor of Humanities at the University of Virginia. Rorty's work straddles the divide between continental and English-speaking philosophy—as does that of another contributor to this volume, Agnes Heller. Unlike Heller, however, Rorty is drawn to skeptical conclusions, articulated in their most general form in his influential book *Philosophy and the Mirror of Nature.*[10] Rorty attacks the very idea of foundational reasoning about political morality. In his essay "The Priority of Democracy to Philosophy,"[11] Rorty argues that no political philosophy underpins the explicit public culture of the liberal state; there is no foundation, except of the shallow kind that Rawls's "overlapping consensus" is meant to supply. There is only the public culture itself. Rorty elaborates the point further in his controversial recent book *Contingency, Irony, and Solidarity,*[12] in which the task of unpacking the liberal tradition is withdrawn from the philosopher and offered to the artist. This transfer may seem to eliminate the possibility of effective criticism of one's own political environment, let alone those of other regimes. But in his contribution to this volume Rorty claims otherwise.

He explains why the search for a foundation to human rights in facts about the nature of human beings or rationality is misguided. He points out that violations of human rights are often not recognized as such by the violators, because they do not regard their victims as human in the relevant sense: The victims are seen as animals, or children, or mere females, and therefore less than human. The traditional philosophical response to such myopia has been to argue about the essence of humanity. Rorty is scornful of this approach, regarding squabbles about human nature as outmoded and welcoming modernity's loss of interest in them.

He sees the human rights culture as a new fact about the world, which needs no foundation in deeper moral knowledge or knowledge of human nature. He allows the value of a project of summarizing and generalizing intuitions about right and wrong, in the manner, for example, of Rawls's difference principle, but he distinguishes this project sharply from the enterprise of seeking knowledge of a foundational justification for such intuitions. The human rights culture owes more to the progress of sentimental education, made possible by leisure and security, than to any progress of moral knowledge. Knowledge-seekers stand on the sidelines, while those able to manipulate feelings and power do the real work of expanding narrow conceptions of the properly human.

Rorty claims his argument is not metaethical or metaphysical, but pragmatic: The search for knowledge of human nature is far less effective at furthering the human rights culture than is sentimental storytelling, which picks up on little, detailed, superficial similarities. Argument and the force of reason do not expand the sympathies of people who are offended by being grouped with those they regard as less than human. According to Rorty, several reasons prevent us from seeing this. We may, for example, find it politically unacceptable to depend on sentimentality. To depend on sentimentality is to depend on the condescension, the niceness, of the relatively well-off and secure, and we resent this dependence. We are unwilling to rest the hope of women in Bosnia for some decent response to their plight on whether television can induce us to feel about what is being done to them as we should feel if it were done to us, or on whether it can induce thoughts like "she could have been my daughter." Sentimentality may also be resisted out of phallogocentrism: it embarrasses the phallogocentric aspiration to dryness and virile purity. But Rorty sees hope in the force of reason here as illusory. A better hope for further progress in the human rights culture lies in sentimental stories, friendship, intermarriage, and the way we raise our young: in the continued progress of sentimental education.

Jean-François Lyotard has taught at the Sorbonne and at the universities of Nanterre and Vincennes, as well as the University of California at Irvine. Lyotard helped introduce the term "postmodern" into contemporary discourse. He describes the postmodern condition as one in which the failure of various grand narratives of legitimation leaves a dispersion of language games. His early work, which climaxed in the 1974 book *Economie Libidinale*,[13] developed from phenomenology toward a distinctive form of psychoanalysis. In his later work this gave way to a concern to account for the possibility of judgments, both theoretical and practical, in the wake of the perceived collapse of metaphysical absolutes. He also became increasingly critical of Marxism.

An innovation of the continental tradition of philosophy within which Lyotard works is to understand the Kantian transcendental universal in terms of what is called "the other." If something—reason, for instance—enjoins me to act ethically, this is because I already have something of the other in me, an incipient communality or, by extension, universality. The other denotes that fragment of the universal that is already in me; yet it is not quite the same as the universal, since its otherness is also defined by its inaccessibility. The other thus provokes a drive toward universality while depriving it of an accountable legitimating power.

Lyotard, like MacKinnon, is concerned with the possibility of exclusion. Unlike Rorty, he is willing to argue from the nature of humanity. Although rationality is traditionally held to differentiate the human realm from the animal, Lyotard appeals instead to a characteristic of human speech, as distinct from mere animal signaling: interlocution. In interlocution, there is reciprocity: The "I" who speaks can become the "you" who listens. Each subject is the other's other. This equivalence between speaker and hearer is, according to Lyotard, the basis of civic relations of equality. The cultural "demotic" community, by contrast, is exclusive.

Does the interlocutory nature of human speech, with its implication of equal exchange, generate a right to freedom of expression? It appears to do so. Yet Lyotard insists that the right to freedom of expression must be earned. The student on whom the discipline of silence is imposed during the master's exposition acquires the right to speak when he or she has something significant to say, that is, to "announce." In the civic community, the faculty of interlocution and the legitimation of speech are merged into a positive right.

Nevertheless, society maintains the threat of exclusion from the interlocutory community as a sanction to compel respect for the interlocutory rights of the other. Lyotard views such exclusion as always a harm, and a grave wrong if unjustly imposed. It is a kind of exclusion from humanity. The most extreme form of such exclusion is the death penalty. To be unable to declare one's plight and excluded from interlocution altogether, as the victims of concentration camps are, is to plumb depths of abjection that may be impossible to translate into the common discourse of our communities. Abjection is also the state of the child who does not yet possess language. It is a state of suffering at any age. Yet out of it may come speech legitimated by the significance of what is said.

Hungarian-born Agnes Heller was among a group of scholars who were dismissed from their posts at Budapest University on political grounds in 1973. After an intervening decade in Australia, she took up her present post as Hannah Arendt Professor of Philosophy at the New School for Social Research in New York. She has written on diverse topics, from renaissance philosophy to the dismantling of European communism, bridging the divide between continental and Anglo-American thinking. Among her many significant publications of recent years is the monograph *Beyond Justice*,[14] an exploration and critique of the tendency to think of ethics and politics as somehow out of harmony with each other. Hegel regarded this tendency as characteristic of modernity, and Heller identifies it in the work of Rawls, among others. For Heller, however, it is not an inescapable predicament of the modern. Rawls is not necessarily condemned, having separated the right from the good, to make ever more diluted claims concerning the authority of the right. What is required is a recognition of the interdependency of right and good, of politics and ethics. Freedom, the enlightenment discovery that drives modernity, must be accepted as the heart of moral value, not just a political necessity. In a multivolume project, *A Theory of Morals,*[15] Heller aims to explore moral value more fully in the light of this observation. Modern moral philosophy should be done with confidence, as ancient philosophy was. There has been no death of universal moral value.

In this volume, Heller focuses on heinous crimes committed in the name of totalitarian regimes, be they of the right or left, Nazi or Communist. The question Heller asks is whether the perpetrators of these crimes should be punished. Her answer takes her into a general discussion of evil. Following Kant, Heller distinguishes evil (which involves asserting wrong to be right, thus removing our capacity to distinguish good from evil) from the more humdrum moral disvalue that derives from bad desires and weaknesses of character. After placing heinous crimes firmly on the evil side of this divide, Heller considers several arguments that might be used to support the view that even the perpetrators of such evil should not be prosecuted. She attacks these arguments on many fronts, sometimes meeting consequentialist arguments on their own terms, and sometimes, again following Kant, trumping consequentialist arguments with moral ones.

· Once opposition to the general proposition that heinous crimes should be prosecuted is out of the way, Heller concretizes her question by asking what should happen to the evil criminal who seems immune from prosecution because of some legal bar. Heller examines two opposing positions, both of which accept as their starting point that there are good moral reasons for punishing the perpetrators of heinous crimes. The first position claims that whatever its moral desirability, such punishment must be ruled out by scruples about retrospective legislation. The second position dismisses scruples of this kind as relying on an unacceptable form of legal positivism, and argues that the presence of a legal impediment should not prevent the perpetrators of heinous crimes from being punished.

Although the second position accords closely with Heller's own views, Heller is not an unqualified naturalist. She regards natural law as having limits and tries to bring out these limits by examining a third position that claims, at first blush paradoxically, that although the perpetrators of heinous crimes should be punished, they also should not be punished. Heller argues that the tension within this position derives not from a paradox, but from a contextualized moral conflict. At its heart is a breakdown of consensus over whether the perpetrator of a heinous crime should be punished. This loss of consensus may destroy our moral intuitions, and with them the so-called "laws of nature." As new generations forget old crimes, however heinous, no consensus concerning responsibility and war crimes trials can emerge. We must therefore tell and retell in our own times the story of what has happened, so that it is never forgotten and justice can be done.

Jon Elster is Professor of Political Science and Philosophy at the University of Chicago. He has been one of the major figures in a movement known as "analytical Marxism," which approaches Marx's theories using the concepts and methods of modern analytical philosophy and social science. Elster's distinctive contribution to analytical Marxism has been based on his argument that explanations of social change focusing on the desires and beliefs of individual people in complex interaction provide more promising foundations for a Marxist view of history than do attempts to explain social change in terms of long-term dynamics in which individual people are merely swept along. One should think in terms of the theory of individual rationality.

This yields an intriguing juxtaposition of Marxist political ideals with a view of the person similar to that held by liberal economists and bearing marked similarities to the one Rawls uses to develop his theory of justice in its more universalist versions. Could it then be used to achieve, what Lukes and so many others have said cannot be achieved: a reconciliation between Marxism and the ideology of human rights? The idea that human rights stand for an individualist model of the human presents fewer problems for a Marxist if, as Elster suggests, there is a level at which Marxism itself is a version of individualist humanism.

Elster's method is illustrated in his important book *Ulysses and the Sirens,*[16] where he explains how various institutional mechanisms that a democracy might employ to check certain of its own tendencies can be seen in terms of the self-binding or precommitment devices which are commonly presumed to be used by individuals rather than societies. He takes up a related topic here: the rule of law and the threat posed to individual rights by an unchecked majority. To guard against this threat a number of countermajoritarian devices—constitutionalism, judicial review, separation of powers, and checks and balances—have been developed, and much of Elster's essay is devoted to an analysis of these. He concludes by discussing the extent to which these devices have been adopted by the post-Communist regimes in Eastern Europe. Elster's survey confirms that despotism, once overthrown, can give rise to new forms of despotism: Those states that had the most despotic and totalitarian forms of communist rule now seem least inclined to embrace countermajoritarian devices, whereas the state least despotic in its former incarnation is emerging as the one most committed to constitutionalism.

The essays in this volume provide searching and provocative argument as well as disturbing information: they advance human rights theory. But they also demonstrate that it is possible, whether from a liberal perspective or from perspectives critical of liberalism, to advance the theory of human rights in a way that supports rather than inhibits the practice of human rights. The theory of human rights need not be trapped in the conflict between universal aspirations and skeptical or relativist doubts. Our hope is that this volume will be seen not just as a theoretical exercise, but also as informing and motivating appropriate responses to the violations of human rights and consequent suffering that surround us.

FIVE FABLES ABOUT HUMAN RIGHTS

Steven Lukes

I propose to discuss the topic of human rights as seen from the standpoint of five doctrines or outlooks that are dominant in our time. I don't propose to be *fair* to these outlooks. Rather, I shall treat them in the form of Weberian "ideal types" or caricatures—a caricature being an exaggerated and simplified representation that, when it succeeds, captures the essentials of what is represented.

The principle that human rights must be defended has become one of the commonplaces of our age. Sometimes the universality of human rights has been challenged: Those historically proclaimed are said to be Eurocentric and inappropriate, or only partly appropriate, to other cultures and circumstances.[1] Alternative, or partly alternative, lists are therefore proposed. Sometimes the historic lists are said to be too short, and further human rights are proposed, from the second unto the third and fourth generation.[2] Sometimes the appeal to human rights, or the language in which it is couched, is said to be unhelpful or even counterproductive in particular campaigns or struggles—in advancing the condition and position of women,[3] say, or in promoting Third World development.[4] But virtually no one actually rejects the principle of defending human rights.

The principle is accepted virtually everywhere. It is also violated virtually everywhere, though much more in some places than in others. Hence the pressing need for organizations such as Amnesty International and Helsinki Watch. But the virtually universal acceptance, even when hypocritical, is very important. It gives such organizations whatever political leverage they have in otherwise unpromising situations. I want to focus on the significance of that acceptance by asking: What ways of thinking does accepting the principle of defending human rights deny and what ways of thinking does it entail? I shall proceed in two stages, first by asking what it would be like *not* to accept the principle and second what it would be like to take it seriously.

First, then, let us ask: What would a world without the principle of human rights look like? I invite you to join me in a series of thought experiments. Let us imagine a series of places in which the principle in question is unknown—places neither utopian nor dystopian but in other respects as attractive as you like, yet which simply lack this particular feature, whose distinctiveness we may thereby hope to understand better.

I

Let us imagine a society called *Utilitaria*. Utilitarians are public-spirited people who display a strong sense of collective purpose: Their single and exclusive goal, overriding all others, is to maximize the overall utility of everyone. Traditionally this has meant "the Greatest Happiness of the Greatest Number" (which is the national motto) but in more recent times there have been disputes about what utility is. Some say it is the same as welfare, as measured by objective indicators such as income, access to medical facilities, housing, and so on. Others, of a more mystical cast of mind, see it as a kind of inner glow, an indefinable subjective state that everyone aims at. Others say it is just the satisfaction of whatever desires anyone happens to have. Others say it is the satisfaction of the desires people ought to have or of those they would have if they were fully informed and sensible. Yet others, gloomier in disposition, say it is just the avoidance of suffering: For them the "greatest happiness" means the "least unhappiness." Utilitarians are distinctly philistine people, who are disinclined to see utility in high culture and never tire of citing the proverb that "pushpin is as good as poetry," though there is a minority tradition of trying to enrich the idea of utility to include the more imaginative sides of life. Despite these differences, all Utilitarians seem agreed on one principle: What counts is what can be counted. The prized possession of every Utilitarian is a pocket calculator. When faced with the question "What is to be done?" they invariably translate it into the question "Which option will produce the greatest sum of utility?" Calculating is the national obsession.

Technocrats, bureaucrats, and judges are the most powerful people in Utilitaria and are much admired. They are particularly adept at calculating, using state-of-the-art computers of ever-increasing power. There are two political parties that vie for power—the Act Party and the Rule Party. The Act Party (Actors) encourages the use of calculators on all possible occasions, whereas the Rule Party (Rulers) discourages ordinary people from using calculators in everyday life. According to the Rule Utilitarians, people should live by conventions or rules of thumb devised and interpreted by the technocrats, bureaucrats, and judges according to their superior methods of calculation.

Life in Utilitaria has its hazards. Another national proverb is "utilitas populi suprema lex est." The problem is that no one can ever know for sure what sacrifices he or she may be called on to make for the greater benefit of all. The Rule Party's rules of thumb are some protection, since they tend to restrain people from doing one another in, but they can always be overridden if a technocrat or a bureaucrat or a judge makes a calculation that overrides them. Everyone remembers the famous case at the turn of the last century of an army captain from a despised minority group who was tried on a charge of treason and found guilty of passing documents to an enemy power. The captain was innocent of the charge but the judges and the generals agreed that the doctrine of "utilitas populi" must prevail. Some intellectuals tried to make a fuss, but they got nowhere. And recently, six people were found guilty of exploding a bomb at a time of trouble for Utilitaria caused by fanatical terrorists from a neighboring island. It turned out that the six were innocent, but "utilitas populi" prevailed and the six stayed in jail.

These hazards might seem troubling to an outsider, but Utilitarians put up with them. Their public spiritedness is so highly developed that they are ready to sacrifice themselves, and indeed one another, whenever calculations show this to be necessary.

Let us now visit a very different kind of country called *Communitaria*. Communitarians are much friendlier people, at least to one another, than are the Utilitarians, but they also have a high degree of public spiritedness and collective purpose. Perhaps "friendliness" is too superficial a word to describe the way they relate to one another. Their mutual bonds constitute their very being. They cannot imagine themselves unencumbered and apart from them; they call such a nightmarish vision "atomism" and recoil with horror from it. Their selves are, as they say, "embedded" or "situated." They identify with one another and identify themselves as so identifying. Indeed, you could say that the Communitarians' national obsession is identity.

Communitaria used to be a very *gemütlich* place, much given to agricultural metaphors. Communitarians were attached to the *soil*, they cultivated their *roots*, and they felt a truly *organic* connection with one another. They particularly despised the Utilitarians' calculative way of life, relying instead on shared understandings and living according to slowly evolving traditions and customs with which they would identify and by which they would be identified.

Communitaria has undergone great changes, however. Waves of immigration and movements of people and modern communications have unsettled the old *gemütlich* ways, creating a far more heterogeneous and pluralistic society. New Communitaria is a true Community of Communities—a patchwork quilt of subcommunities, each claiming recognition for the peculiar value of its own specific way of life. New Communitarians believe in multiculturalism and practice what they call the "politics of recognition," recognizing each subcommunity's identity with scrupulous fairness in the country's institutions. Positive discrimination is used to encourage those that are disadvantaged or in danger of extinction; quotas ensure that all are fairly represented in institutions and in the professions. The schools and colleges teach curricula that exactly reflect the exactly equal value of those communities' cultures and none (certainly not the old *gemütlich* one) is allowed to predominate.

The new Communitarians feel at home in their subcommunities but also take pride in being Communitarians who recognize one another's subcommunitarian identities. But there are problems. One is the inclusion-exclusion problem, how to decide which subcommunities are included in the overall framework and which are not. Some groups get very angry at being included in subcommunities that recognize them but which they don't recognize; others get angry because they recognize themselves as a subcommunity but are not so recognized by others. Recently, for example, a province of Communitaria in which one subcommunity forms a majority passed a law prohibiting members of their subcommunity and all immigrants from attending schools that teach in the language prevailing in the rest of Communitaria and in which most of its business is conducted. The immigrants in particular are none too pleased. A related problem is the vested interests problem; once on the official list, subcommunities want to stay there for ever and keep others out. Moreover, to get on the list, you have to be, or claim to be, an indigenous people or the victims of colonialism, and preferably both.

Then there is the relativism problem. It is obligatory in Communitaria to treat the beliefs and practices of all recognized subcommunities as equally valid, or rather, none is to be treated as more or less valid than any other. But different subcommunities have incompatible beliefs and some engage in very nasty practices, mistreating, degrading, and persecuting groups and individuals, including their own members. Typically, the definers of subcommunitarian identities are men, and their women are sometimes oppressed, marginalized, and badly abused. Some require their womenfolk to conceal their identities in hooded black shrouds. Some practice female circumcision. Unfortunately, Communitaria's official relativism must allow such practices to continue unmolested. Recently, a famous writer from one subcommunity wrote a satirical novel that was partly about the life of another subcommunity's holy religious prophet and founder. Hotheads from the latter subcommunity became wildly incensed at what they took to be an insult to their faith and publicly burned the book in question. Their fanatical and fiery leader, in the home community from which they came, ordered that the famous writer be killed. Other writers from other subcommunities all over the world signed petitions and manifestoes in the famous writer's defense. Communitaria's government dealt with this tricky situation in a suitably relativistic way, declaring that the practice of writing satirical novels was no more but also no less valid than the practice of protecting one's faith against insults.

And finally there is the deviant problem. Not all Communitarians fit well into the subcommunitarian categories. Recalcitrant individuals have been known to reject the category by which they are identified or to pretend that they don't belong to it. Some cross or refuse to acknowledge identifying boundaries, and some even reject the very idea of such boundaries. Non-, ex-, trans-, and anti-identifiers are not the happiest people in Communitaria. They feel uneasy because they tend to be seen as "not true Communitarians," as disloyal, even as rootless cosmopolitans. Fortunately, however, they are few and unorganized. Least of all are they likely to form another subcommunity.

Now I propose to take you to another place, *Proletaria,* so called, nostalgically, after the social class that brought it into being but that has long since withered away, along with all other social classes. Proletaria has no state; that too has withered away. Indeed, it is not a particular country but embraces the entire world. Human and other rights existed in prehistoric times but these too have withered away. The Proletariat in its struggle sometimes used to appeal to such rights for tactical reasons, but they are no longer needed in Proletaria's truly human communist society.

Proletarians lead extremely varied and fulfilling lives. They hunt in the morning, fish in the afternoon, rear cattle in the evening, and criticize after dinner. They develop an enormous range of skills, and no one has to endure a one-sided, crippled development, to fit into a given job description or role, or an exclusive sphere of activity from which one cannot escape. The division of labor has also withered away: People are no longer identified with the work they do or the functions they fulfill. As the prophet Gramsci put it, no one is even an intellectual, because everyone is (among all the other things he or she is). They organize their factories like orchestras and watch over automated machinery; they organize production as associated producers, rationally regulating their interchange with nature, bringing it under their common control, under conditions most favorable to, and worthy of, human nature; and they elect representatives to communes on an annual basis. As the prophet Engels foretold, the government of persons has been replaced by the administration of things, and by the conduct of processes of production. The distinction between work and leisure has withered away; so also has that between the private and the public spheres of life. Money, according to the prophet Marx, "abases all the gods of mankind and changes them into commodities" and has "deprived the whole world, both the human world and nature, of their own proper value."[5] Now the whole cash nexus has withered away. Now at last, as foretold, "love can only be exchanged for love, trust for trust, etc.," influence can be exercised only through stimulation and encouragement and all relations to man and to nature express one's real individual life.[6] An arcadian abundance exists: All produce what they are able to and get what they need. People identify with one another but not, as among the Communitarians, because they belong to this or that community or subcommunity, but rather because they are equally and fully human. Relations between the sexes are fully reciprocal and prostitution is unknown. In Proletaria there is no single dominating obsession or way of living: Everyone develops his or her rich individuality, as all-sided in its production as in its consumption, free of external impediments. There is no longer any contradiction between the interest of the separate individual or the individual family and the interest of all individuals who have intercourse with one another.

The only problem with Proletarian life is that there are no problems. For with communism, as Marx prophesied, we see

> the *definitive* resolution of the antagonism between man and nature and between man and man. It is the true solution of the conflict between existence and essence, between objectification and self-affirmation, between freedom and necessity, between individual and species. It is the solution of the riddle of history and knows itself to be this solution.[7]

Yet visitors to Proletaria (from other planets) are sometimes disbelieving of what they behold. They find it hard to credit that such perfection could be attained and, moreover, maintained without friction. How, they wonder, can the planning of production run so smoothly without markets to provide information through prices about demand? Why are there no conflicts over allocating resources? Don't differing styles of living get in each other's way? Aren't there personal conflicts, between fathers and sons, say, or lovers? Do Proletarians suffer inner turmoil? No sign of any such problems is visible. Proletarians seem able to combine their rich individuality, developing their gifts in all directions, with fully communal social relations. Only sometimes does it occur to the extraterrestrial visitors that they may have lost their way and landed elsewhere than Earth, and that these are not human beings at all.

Human rights are unknown in the three places we have visited, but for different reasons. Utilitarians have no use for them because those who believe in them are, by definition, disposed to question that Utilitarian calculations should be used in all circumstances. As the Utilitarian state's founder, Jeremy Bentham, famously remarked, the very idea of such rights is not only nonsense but "nonsense on stilts," for "there is no right which, when the abolition of it is advantageous to society, should not be abolished."[8] The Communitarians have always rejected such rights because of their abstractness from real, living, concrete, local ways of life. As that eloquent old Communitarian speechifier Edmund Burke put it, their "abstract perfection" is their "practical defect," for "the liberties and the restrictions vary with times and circumstances, and admit of infinite modifications, that cannot be settled upon any abstract rule."[9] A no less eloquent new Communitarian, Alasdair MacIntyre, broadens the attack: "natural or human rights," he says, "are fictions—just as is utility." They are like "witches and unicorns" for "every attempt to give good reasons for believing that there *are* such rights has failed." According to MacIntyre, forms of behavior that presuppose such rights "always have a highly specific and socially local character, and . . . the existence of particular types of social institution or practice is a necessary condition for the notion of a claim to the possession of a right being an intelligible type of human performance."[10] As for Proletarians, their rejection of human rights goes back to the prophet of their revolution, Karl Marx, who described talk of them as "ideological nonsense" and "obsolete verbal rubbish,"[11] for two reasons. First, they tended to soften hearts in the heat of the class struggle; the point was to win, not feel sympathy for class enemies. It was, as Trotsky used to say, a matter of "our morals" versus "theirs,"[12] and Lenin observed that "our morality is entirely subordinated to the interests of the proletariat's class struggle. . . . To a communist all morality lies in this united discipline and conscious mass struggle against the exploiters. We do not believe in an eternal morality, and we expose the falseness of all the fables about morality."[13] And second, Marx regarded human rights as anachronistic because they had been necessary only in that prehistorical era when individuals needed protection from injuries and dangers generated out of an imperfect, conflictual, class-ridden world. Once that world was transformed and a new world born, emancipated human beings would flourish free from the need for rights, in abundance, communal relations, and real freedom to develop their manifold human powers.

What does our thought experiment so far suggest that we are accepting when we accept the principle of defending human rights? First, that they are restraints on the pursuit of what is held to be "advantageous to society," however enlightened or benevolent that pursuit may be. Second, that they invoke a certain kind of abstraction from "specific and socially local" practices. They involve seeing persons behind their identifying (even their self-identifying) labels and securing them a protected space within which to live their lives from the inside, whether in conformity with or deviation from the life their community requires of or seeks to impose on them. And third, that human rights presuppose a set of permanent existential facts about the human condition: that human beings will always face the malevolence and cruelty of others, that there will always be scarcity of resources, that human beings will always give priority to the interests of themselves and those close to them, that there will always be imperfect rationality in the pursuit of individual and collective aims, and that there will never be an unforced convergence in ways of life and conceptions of what makes it valuable. In the face of these facts, if all individuals are to be equally respected, they will need public protection from injury and degradation, and from unfairness and arbitrariness in the allocation of basic resources and in the operation of the laws and rules of social life. You will not be able to rely on others' altruism or benevolence or paternalism. Even if the values of those others are your own, they can harm you in countless ways, by sheer miscalculation or mistake or misjudgment. Limited rationality puts you in danger from the well meaning no less than from the malevolent and the selfish. But often the values of others will not be your own. You will need protection to live your own life from the inside, pursuing your own conception of what is valuable, rather than a life imposed on you. For this, social and cultural preconditions must exist. Thus Kurds in Turkey must not be treated as "Mountain Turks" but have their own institutions, education, and language. Now we can see the sense in which human rights are individualistic and the sense in which they are not. To defend human rights is to protect individuals from utilitarian sacrifices, communitarian impositions, and from injury, degradation, and arbitrariness, but doing so cannot be viewed independently of economic, legal, political, and cultural conditions and may well involve the protection and even fostering of collective goods, such as the Kurdish language and culture. For to defend human rights is not merely to protect individuals. It is also to protect the activities and relations that make their lives more valuable, activities and relations that cannot be conceived reductively as merely individual goods. Thus the right to free expression and communication protects artistic expression and the communication of information; the right to a fair trial protects a well-functioning legal system; the right to free association protects democratic trade unions, social movements, and political demonstrations, and so on.

II

I turn now to the second stage of my inquiry. What would it be like to take human rights, thus understood, seriously? To approach this question, let me propose a further thought experiment. Let us now imagine worlds with human rights, where they are widely recognized and systematically honored.

One place where some people think rights flourish is *Libertaria*. Libertarian life runs exclusively and entirely on market principles. It is located somewhere in Eastern Europe or maybe in China in the near future. Everything there can be bought and sold; everything of value has a price and is subject to Libertarians' national obsession: cost-benefit analysis. The most basic and prized of all their rights is the right to property, beginning with each Libertarian's ownership of himself or herself and extending (as Libertarians like to say) to whatever they "mix their labor with." They own their talents and abilities and, in developing and deploying these, Libertarians claim the right to whatever rewards the market will bring. They love to tell the story of Wilt Chamberlain, the famous basketball player whom thousands are willing to pay to watch. Would it be just, they ask, to deprive him of these freely given rewards in order to benefit others?

They also attach great importance to the right of engaging in voluntary transfers of what they rightly own—transactions of giving, receiving, and exchanging, which they use to the advantage of their families, through private education and the inheritance of wealth. There is a very low level of regressive taxation which is used only to maintain Libertaria's system of free exchange, the infrastructure of the economy, the army and the police, and the justice system to enforce free contracts. Compulsory redistribution is prohibited since it would violate people's unlimited rights to whatever they can earn. Inequalities are great and growing, based on social class, as well as on differential talents and efforts. There is no public education, no public health system, no public support for the arts or recreation; there are no public libraries, no public transport, roads, parks, or beaches. Water, gas, electricity, nuclear power, garbage disposal, postal services, and telecommunications are all in private hands, as are the prisons. The poor, the ill, the handicapped, the unlucky, and the untalented are given some sympathy and a measure of charity, but Libertarians do not regard their worsening plight as any kind of injustice, since they do not result from anyone's rights being infringed.

No one is tortured in Libertaria. All have the right to vote, the rule of law prevails, there is freedom of expression (in media controlled by the rich) and of association (though trade unions cannot have closed shops or call strikes, since that would violate others' rights). There is equal opportunity in the sense that active discrimination against individuals and groups is prohibited, but there is an unequal start to the race for jobs and rewards; the socially privileged have a considerable advantage stemming from their social backgrounds. All can enter the race but losers fall by the wayside. The successful are fond of quoting the national motto: "The Devil take the hindmost!" The homeless sleeping under bridges and the unemployed are, however, consoled by the thought that they have the same rights as every other Libertarian.

Are human rights taken seriously enough in Libertaria? I believe the answer is no, for two reasons. First, as I said, the basic civil rights are respected there—there is no torture, there is universal franchise, the rule of law, freedom of expression and association and formal equality of opportunity. Yet the possessors of these rights are not equally respected; not all Libertarians are treated as equally human. To adapt a phrase of Anatole France, those who sleep under the bridges have the same rights as those who don't. Though all Libertarians have the right to vote, the worst off, the marginalized and the excluded, do not have equal power to organize and influence political decisions, or equal access to legal processes, or an equal chance to articulate and communicate their points of view, or an equal representation in Libertarian public and institutional life, or an equal chance in the race for qualifications, positions, and rewards.

The second reason for thinking that Libertaria fails to take human rights seriously enough relates to the distinctively Libertarian rights. Libertarians believe that they have an unlimited right to whatever rewards their abilities and efforts can bring in the marketplace and the unlimited right to make voluntary choices that benefit themselves and their families. No Libertarian ever takes a step outside the narrowly self-interested point of view of advancing his own, or at most his family's, interests. He is impervious to the thought that others might have more urgent claims on resources, or that some of his advantages are gained at the expense of others, or that the structure of Libertarian life is a structure of injustice.

Are human rights in better shape elsewhere? Where is the principle of defending them more securely defended? Where are all human beings more securely treated as equally human? Where are they protected against Utilitarian sacrifices for the advantage of society and against Communitarian imposition of a particular way of life, against the Communist illusion that a world beyond rights can be attained and against the Libertarian illusion that a world run entirely on market principles is a world that recognizes them fully?

Is *Egalitaria* such a place? Egalitaria is a one-status society in the sense that all Egalitarians are treated as being of equal worth. One person's well-being and freedom are regarded as just as valuable as any other's. The basic liberties, the rule of law, toleration, equality of opportunity are all constitutionally guaranteed. But they are also made real by Egalitarians' commitment to rendering everyone's conditions of life such that these equal rights are of equal worth to their possessors. They differ about how to do this, but one currently influential view is that a basic economic and political structure can be created to make everyone better off while giving priority to bettering the condition of the worst off. On this view no inequality is justified unless it results in making the worst off better off than they would otherwise be. All agree that progressive taxation and extensive welfare provision should ensure a decent minimum standard of life for all. But there is also within Egalitarian culture a momentum toward raising that minimum through policies that gradually eliminate involuntary disadvantage. That momentum is fueled by a sense of injustice that perpetually tracks further instances of illegitimate inequality, or involuntary disadvantage—whether these result from religion or class or ethnicity or gender, and so on—and seeks policies that will render Egalitarians more equal in their conditions of life.

Could there be such a place as Egalitaria? More precisely, is Egalitaria feasible: Could it be attained anywhere in the present world? And is it viable: Could it be maintained stably over time? Some doubt that it is feasible. Some say that, even if feasible, it is not viable. Some say that it might be viable, if it were feasible, but it is not. Others say that it is neither feasible nor viable. I fear that there are good reasons for these doubts. I shall suggest two major reasons for doubting the attainability and the maintainability of Egalitaria and conclude by suggesting what they imply about how we should view the principle of defending human rights.

The first reason for thinking that Egalitaria may, after all, be a mirage is what we may call the libertarian constraint.

This is found, above all, in the economic sphere. Egalitarians are (or should be) extremely concerned to achieve maximal economic growth. For them equality cannot be traded off against efficiency. Rather, they seek most efficiently to achieve an economy that will attain the highest level of equality of condition at the highest feasible economic level. The worst off (and everyone else) under a more equal system should, they hope, be at least as well off as the worst off (and everyone else) under a less equal system. If the cost of more equality is a lesser prospect of prosperity for everyone or most people, their hopes of attaining, let alone maintaining, Egalitaria, at least under conditions of freedom, are correspondingly dimmed.

Egalitarians these days are (or should be) keen students of Libertarian economics. They know what markets can and cannot do.[14] On the one hand, they know when and how markets can fail. Markets reproduce existing inequalities of endowments, resources, and power; they can generate external diseconomies, such as pollution, which they cannot deal with; they can, when unchecked, lead to oligopolies and monopolies; they can ravage the environment, through deforestation and in other ways; they can produce destabilizing crises of confidence with ramifying effects; they can encourage greed, consumerism, commercialism, opportunism, political passivity, indifference, and anonymity, a world of alienated strangers. They cannot fairly allocate public goods, or foster social accountability in the use of resources or democracy at the workplace, or meet social and individual needs that cannot be expressed in the form of purchasing power, or balance the needs of present and future generations.

On the other hand, they are indispensable and cannot be simulated. There is no alternative to markets as a signaling device for transmitting in a decentralized process information about tastes, productive techniques, resources, and so on, or as a discovery procedure through which restless individuals, in pursuit of entrepreneurial profit, seek new ways of satisfying needs, and even, as the Prophet Marx himself acknowledged, as an arena of freedom and choice. Egalitarians know that command economies can only fail in comparison with market economies, and they know that, even if the market can in various ways be socialized, "market socialism" is, at best, an as yet ill-defined hope.

They also know that no economy can function on altruism and moral incentives alone, and that material incentives, and notably the profit motive, are indispensable to a well-functioning economy. Most work that needs to be done, and in particular entrepreneurial functions, must draw on motives that derive from individuals' pursuit of material advantage for themselves and for their families. They know, in short, that any feasible and viable economy must be based on market processes and material incentives, however controlled and supplemented in order to render them socially accountable,[15] thereby creating and reinforcing the very inequalities they earnestly seek to reduce.

The second major reason for skepticism that Egalitaria can be attained and, if so, maintained we may call the communitarian constraint. This is found primarily in the cultural sphere. Egalitarians hope that everyone can, at least when considering public and political issues, achieve a certain kind of abstraction from their own point of view and circumstances. They hope that they can view anyone, including themselves, impartially, seeing everyone's life as of equal worth and everyone's well-being and freedom as equally valuable. Professor Rawls has modeled such a standpoint in his image of an "Original Position" where individuals reason behind a "veil of ignorance"; others have tried to capture it in other ways.

Yet Egalitarians must admit that this is not a natural attitude in the world in which we live and that it seems in increasingly many places less and less so. Yugoslavs turned almost overnight into Serbs and Croats. It mattered urgently to some Czechoslovaks that they are Slovaks and it matters deeply to some Canadians that they are Québecois. Even Black or Hispanic or Asian Americans are insisting on seeing themselves in politically correct ways. It seems that belonging to certain kinds of encompassing groups with cultures of self-recognition, and identifying and being identified as so belonging, is increasingly essential to many people's well-being.[16] To the extent that this is so, the "politics of equal dignity" that would treat individuals equally, irrespective of their group affiliations, is put in jeopardy.[17]

Consider the idea of fraternity. Unlike liberty and equality, which are conditions to be achieved, who your brothers are is determined by the past. You and they form a collectivity in contradistinction to the rest of mankind, and in particular to that portion of it that you and they see as sources of danger or objects of envy or resentment. The history of fraternity during the course of the French Revolution is instructive.[18] It began with a promise of universal brotherhood; soon it came to mean patriotism; and eventually the idea was used to justify militancy against external enemies and purges of enemies within. The revolutionary slogan "la fraternité ou la mort" thus acquired a new and ominous meaning, promising violence first against nonbrothers and then against false brothers. Collective or communal identity always requires, as they say, an "other"; every affirmation of belonging includes an explicit or implicit exclusion clause. The Egalitarians' problem is to render such exclusions harmless.

The problem is to attain a general acceptance of multiple identities that do not conflict. But how many situations in the present world are favorable to such an outcome? The least promising, and most explosive, seems to be that of formerly communist federal states containing peoples with historical enmities at different levels of economic development. The least unpromising, perhaps, are polyethnic societies composed mainly of various immigrant groups who demand the right freely to express their particularity within the economic and political institutions of the dominant culture. But there, too, wherever that right is interpreted as a collective right to equal recognition, a threat to egalitarian outcomes is raised: that of treating individuals only or mainly as the bearers of their collective identities[19] and thus of building not Egalitaria but Communitaria.

Here, then, are two major reasons for doubting that Egalitaria can be realized anywhere in this world (let alone across it as a whole). They very naturally lead those impressed by them to take up anti-egalitarian political positions. They constitute the two main sources of right wing thinking today—libertarian and communitarian. Both point to severe limitations on the capacity of human beings to achieve that abstraction or impartial regard that could lead them to view all lives as equally valuable.[20] Both are sufficiently powerful and persuasive to convince reasonable people to reject egalitarian politics.

How, in the light of this last fact, should we view human rights? I think it follows that the list of human rights should be kept both reasonably short and reasonably abstract. It should include the basic civil and political rights, the rule of law, freedom of expression and association, equality of opportunity, and the right to some basic level of material well-being, but probably no more. For only these have a prospect of securing agreement across the broad spectrum of contemporary political life, even though disagreement breaks out again once you ask how these abstract rights are to be made concrete, how the formal is to become real. Who are the possessors of civil and political rights? Nationals? Citizens? Guest-workers? Refugees? All who are residents within a given territory? Exactly what does the rule of law require? Does it involve equalizing access to legal advice and representation? Public defenders? The jury system? Equal representation of minorities on juries? The right to challenge jurors without cause? When are freedom of expression and association truly free? Does the former have implications for the distribution and forms of ownership of mass media and the modes and principles of their public regulation? Does the latter entail some form of industrial democracy that goes beyond what currently obtains? What must be equal for opportunities to be equal? Is the issue one of nondiscrimination against an existing background of economic, social, and cultural inequalities or is that background itself the field within which opportunities can be made more equal? What is the basic minimum? Should it be set low to avoid negative incentive effects? If so, how low? Or should there be a basic income for all, and, if so, should that include those who could but don't work, or don't accept work that is on offer? And how is a basic minimum level of material well-being to be conceived and measured—in terms of welfare, or income, or resources, or level of living, or basic capabilities, or in some other way?

To defend these human rights is to defend a kind of "egalitarian plateau" on which such political conflicts and arguments can take place.[21] I hope I have convinced you that there are powerful reasons against abandoning that plateau for any of the first four countries we have visited, even if the principle of defending human rights cannot take us any further toward Egalitaria.

The plateau is under siege. One army flies a communitarian flag and practices "ethnic cleansing." It has already destroyed Mostar and other places and is currently threatening Kosovo and Macedonia. It is laying siege to Sarajevo, slaughtering and starving men, women, and children, and raping women, only because they have the wrong collective identity. We are complicitly allowing this to go on, within the very walls of modern, civilized Europe. The barbarians are within the gates.

I believe that the principle of defending human rights requires an end to our complicity and appeasement. We must raise the siege of Sarajevo and defeat the barbarians by force. Only then can we resume the journey to Egalitaria, which, if it can be reached at all, can only be reached from the plateau of human rights.

THE LAW OF PEOPLES

John Rawls

One aim of this lecture is to sketch—in a short space, I can do no more than that—how the law of peoples[1] may be developed out of liberal ideas of justice similar to but more general than the idea I called justice as fairness and presented in my book *A Theory of Justice* (1971). By the law of peoples I mean a political conception of right and justice[2] that applies to the principles and norms of international law and practice. In section 58 of the above work I indicated how from justice as fairness the law of peoples might be developed for the limited purpose of addressing several questions of just war. In this lecture my sketch of that law covers more ground and includes an account of the role of human rights. Even though the idea of justice I use to do this is more general than justice as fairness, it is still connected with the idea of the social contract: the procedure of construction, and the various steps gone through, are much the same in both cases.

A further aim is to set out the bearing of political liberalism once a liberal political conception of justice is extended to the law of peoples. In particular, we ask: What form does the toleration of nonliberal societies take in this case? Surely tyrannical and dictatorial regimes cannot be accepted as members in good standing of a reasonable society of peoples. But equally not all regimes can reasonably be required to be

---

I am indebted to many people for helping me with this lecture. I have indicated specific debts in notes to the text. More general debts I should like to acknowledge are to Ronald Dworkin and Thomas Nagel for discussions about my earlier attempts to consider the law of peoples at their seminars at New York University in the fall of 1990 and 1991; to T. M. Scanlon and Joshua Cohen for valuable criticism and comments; to Michael Doyle and Philip Soper for instructive correspondence; and as always to Burton Dreben. I am especially indebted to Erin Kelly, who has read all the drafts of this lecture and proposed many improvements, most of which I have adopted. Her criticisms and suggestions have been essential in my getting right, as I hope, the line of reasoning in part IV.

liberal, otherwise the law of peoples itself would not express liberalism's own principle of toleration for other reasonable ways of ordering society nor further its attempt to find a shared basis of agreement among reasonable peoples. Just as a citizen in a liberal society must respect other persons' comprehensive religious, philosophical, and moral doctrines provided they are pursued in accordance with a reasonable political conception of justice, so a liberal society must respect other societies organized by comprehensive doctrines, provided their political and social institutions meet certain conditions that lead the society to adhere to a reasonable law of peoples.

More specifically, we ask: Where are the reasonable limits of toleration to be drawn? It turns out that a well-ordered nonliberal society will accept the same law of peoples that well-ordered liberal societies accept. Here I understand a well-ordered society as being peaceful and not expansionist; its legal system satisfies certain requisite conditions of legitimacy in the eyes of its own people; and, as a consequence of this, it honors basic human rights (part IV). One kind of nonliberal society satisfying these conditions is illustrated by what I call, for lack of a better term, a well-ordered hierarchical society. This example makes the point, central for this argument, that although any society must honor basic human rights, it need not be liberal. It also indicates the role of human rights as part of a reasonable law of peoples.

I. HOW A SOCIAL CONTRACT DOCTRINE IS UNIVERSAL IN ITS REACH

I begin by explaining the way in which a social contract doctrine with its procedure of construction is universal in its reach.

Every society must have a conception of how it is related to other societies and of how it is to conduct itself toward them. It lives with them in the same world and except for the very special case of isolation of a society from all the rest—long in the past now—it must formulate certain ideals and principles for guiding its policies toward other peoples. Like justice as fairness, the more general liberal conception I have in mind—as specified in Part III—begins with the case of a hypothetically closed and self-sufficient liberal democratic society and covers only political values and not all of life. The question now arises as to how that conception can be extended in a convincing way to cover a society's relations with other societies to yield a reasonable law of peoples. In the absence of this extension to the law of peoples, a liberal conception of political justice would appear to be historicist and to apply only to societies whose political institutions and culture are liberal. In making the case for justice as fairness, and for similar more general liberal conceptions, it is essential to show that this is not so.

The problem of the law of peoples is only one of several problems of extension for these ideas of justice. There is the additional problem of extending these ideas to future generations, under which falls the problem of just savings. Also, since the ideas of justice regard persons as normal and fully cooperating members of society over a complete life, and having the requisite capacities to do this, there arises the problem of what is owed to those who fail to meet this condition, either temporarily or permanently, which gives rise to several problems of justice in health care. Finally, there is the problem of what is owed to animals and the rest of nature.

We would eventually like an answer to all these questions, but I doubt that we can find one within the scope of these ideas of justice understood as political conceptions. At best they may yield reasonable answers to the first three problems of extension: to other societies, to future generations, and to certain cases of health care. With regard to the problems which these liberal ideas of justice fail to address, there are several things we might say. One is that the idea of political justice does not cover everything and we should not expect it to. Or the problem may indeed be one of political justice but none of these ideas is correct for the question at hand, however well they may do for other questions. How deep a fault this shows must wait until the question itself can be examined, but we should not expect these ideas, or I think any account of political justice, to handle all these matters.

Let's return to our problem of extending liberal ideas of justice similar to but more general than justice as fairness to the law of peoples. There is a clear contrast between these and other familiar views in the way they are universal in reach. Take, for example, Leibniz's or Locke's doctrines: These are universal both in their source of authority and in their formulation. By that I mean that their source is God's authority or the divine reason, as the case may be; and they are universal in that their principles are stated so as to apply to all reasonable beings everywhere. Leibniz's doctrine is an ethics of creation. It contains the idea of morals as the *imitatio Dei* and applies straightway to us as God's creatures endowed with reason. In Locke's doctrine, God having legitimate authority over all creation, the natural law—that part of God's law that can be known by our natural powers of reason—everywhere has authority and binds us and all peoples.

Most familiar philosophical views—such as rational intuitionism, (classical) utilitarianism, and perfectionism—are also formulated in a general way to apply to us directly in all cases. Although they are not theologically grounded, let's say their source of authority is (human) reason, or an independent realm of moral values, or some other proposed basis of universal validity. In all these views the universality of the doctrine is the direct consequence of its source of authority and of how it is formulated.

By contrast, a constructivist view such as justice as fairness, and more general liberal ideas, do not begin from universal first principles having authority in all cases.[3] In justice as fairness the principles of justice for the basic structure of society are not suitable as fully general principles: They do not apply to all subjects, not to churches and universities, or to the basic structures of all societies, or to the law of peoples. Rather, they are constructed by way of a reasonable procedure in which rational parties adopt principles of justice for each kind of subject as it arises. Typically, a constructivist doctrine proceeds by taking up a series of subjects, starting, say, with principles of political justice for the basic structure of a closed and self-contained democratic society. That done, it then works forward to principles for the claims of future generations, outward to principles for the law of peoples, and inward to principles for special social questions. Each time the constructivist procedure is modified to fit the subject in question. In due course all the main principles are on hand, including those needed for the various political duties and obligations of individuals and associations.[4] Thus, a constructivist liberal doctrine is universal in its reach once it is extended to give principles for all politically relevant subjects, including a law of peoples for the most comprehensive subject, the political society of peoples. Its authority rests on the principles and conceptions of practical reason, but always on these as suitably adjusted to apply to different subjects as they arise in sequence; and always assuming as well that these principles are endorsed on due reflection by the reasonable agents to whom the corresponding principles apply.

At first sight, a constructivist doctrine of this kind appears hopelessly unsystematic. For how are the principles that apply to different cases tied together? And why do we proceed through the series of cases in one order rather than another? Constructivism assumes, however, that there are other forms of unity than that defined by completely general first principles forming a consistent scheme. Unity may also be given by an appropriate sequence of cases and by supposing that the parties in an original position (as I have called it) are to proceed through the sequence with the understanding that the principles for the subject of each later agreement are to be subordinate to those of subjects of all earlier agreements, or else coordinated with and adjusted to them by certain priority rules. I shall try out a particular sequence and point out its merits as we proceed. There is in advance no guarantee that it is the most appropriate sequence and much trial and error may be needed.

In developing a conception of justice for the basic structure or for the law of peoples, or indeed for any subject, constructivism does not view the variation in numbers of people alone as accounting for the appropriateness of different principles in different cases. That families are smaller than constitutional democracies does not explain why different principles apply to them. Rather, it is the distinct structure of the social framework, and the purpose and role of its various parts and how they fit together, that explain why there are different principles for different kinds of subjects. Thus, it is characteristic of a constructivist idea of justice to regard the distinctive nature and purpose of the elements of society, and of the society of peoples, as requiring persons, within a domain where other principles leave them free, to act from principles designed to fit their peculiar roles. As we shall see as we work out the law of peoples, these principles are identified in each case by rational agents fairly, or reasonably, situated given the case at hand. They are not derived from completely general principles such as the principle of utility or the principle of perfectionism.

II.   THREE PRELIMINARY QUESTIONS

Before showing how the extension to the law of peoples can be carried out, I go over three preliminary matters. First, let's distinguish between two parts of justice as fairness, or of any other similar liberal and constructivist conception of justice. One part is worked up to apply to the domestic institutions of democratic societies, their regime and basic structure, and to the duties and obligations of citizens. The other part is worked up to apply to the society of political societies and thus to the political relations between peoples.[5] After the principles of justice have been adopted for domestic justice, the idea of the original position is used again at the next higher level.[6] As before, the parties are representatives, but now they are representatives of peoples whose basic institutions satisfy the principles of justice selected at the first level. We start with the family of societies, each well-ordered by some liberal view meeting certain conditions (justice as fairness is an example), and then work out principles to govern their relations with one another. Here I mention only the first stage of working out the law of peoples. As we shall see in part IV, we must also develop principles which govern the relations between liberal and what I shall call hierarchical societies. It turns out that liberal and hierarchical societies can agree on the same law of peoples and thus this law does not depend on aspects peculiar to the Western tradition.

It may be objected that to proceed in this way is to accept the state as traditionally conceived, with all its familiar powers of sovereignty. These powers include first, the right to go to war in pursuit of state policies—Clausewitz's pursuit of politics by other means—with the aims of politics given by a state's rational prudential interests.[7] They include second, the state's right to do as it likes with people within its own borders. The objection is misapplied for this reason. In the first use of the original position domestic society is seen as closed, since we abstract from relations with other societies. There is no need for armed forces and the question of the government's right to be prepared militarily does not arise, and would be denied if it did. The principles of domestic justice allow a police force to keep domestic order but that is another matter, and although those domestic principles are consistent with a qualified right of war in a society of peoples, they do not of themselves support that right. That is up to the law of peoples itself, still to be constructed. And, as we shall see, this law will also restrict a state's internal sovereignty, its right to do as it likes to people within its borders.

Thus, it is important to see that in this working out of the law of peoples, a government as the political organization of its people is not, as it were, the author of its own power. The war powers of governments, whatever they should be, are only those acceptable within a reasonable law of peoples. Presuming the existence of a government whereby a people is domestically organized with institutions of background justice does not prejudge these questions. We must reformulate the powers of sovereignty in light of a reasonable law of peoples and get rid of the right to war and the right to internal autonomy, which have been part of the (positive) international law for the two and a half centuries following the Thirty Years War, as part of the classical states system.[8]

Moreover, these ideas accord with a dramatic shift in how international law is now understood. Since World War II international law has become far more demanding than in the past. It tends to restrict a state's right to wage war to cases of self-defense (this allows collective security), and it also tends to limit a state's right of internal sovereignty.[9] The role of human rights connects most obviously with the latter change as part of the effort to provide a suitable definition of, and limits on, a government's internal sovereignty, though it is not unconnected with the first. At this point I leave aside the many difficulties of interpreting these rights and limits, and take their general meaning and tendency as clear enough. What is essential is that our elaboration of the law of peoples should fit—as it turns out to do—these two basic changes, and give them a suitable rationale.

The second preliminary matter concerns the question: In working out the law of peoples, why do we start (as I said above) with those societies well-ordered by liberal views somewhat more general than justice as fairness? Wouldn't it be better to start with the world as a whole, with a global original position, so to speak, and discuss the question whether, and in what form, there should be states, or peoples, at all? Some writers (I mention them later) have thought that a social contract constructivist view should proceed in this manner, that it gives an appropriate universality from the start.

I think there is no clear initial answer to this question. We should try various alternatives and weigh their pluses and minuses. Since in working out justice as fairness I begin with domestic society, I shall continue from there as if what has been done so far is more or less sound. Thus I build on the steps taken until now, as this seems to provide a suitable starting point for the extension to the law of peoples. A further reason for proceeding thus is that peoples as corporate bodies organized by their governments now exist in some form all over the world. Historically speaking, all principles and standards proposed for the law of peoples must, to be feasible, prove acceptable to the considered and reflective public opinion of peoples and their governments.

Suppose, then, that we are (even though we are not) members of a well-ordered society. Our convictions about justice are roughly the same as those of citizens (if there are any) in the family of societies well-ordered by liberal conceptions of justice and whose social and historical conditions are similar to ours. They have the same kinds of reasons for affirming their mode of government as we do for affirming ours. This common understanding of liberal societies provides an apt starting point for the extension to the law of peoples.

Finally, I note the distinction between the law of peoples

and the law of nations, or international law. The latter is an existing, or positive, legal order, however incomplete it may be in some ways, lacking, for example, an effective scheme of sanctions such as normally characterizes domestic law. The law of peoples, by contrast, is a family of political concepts with principles of right, justice, and the common good, that specify the content of a liberal conception of justice worked up to extend to and to apply to international law. It provides the concepts and principles by which that law is to be judged.

This distinction between the law of peoples and the law of nations should be straightforward. It is no more obscure than the distinction between the principles of justice that apply to the basic structure of domestic society and the existing political, social, and legal institutions that actually realize that structure.

III. THE EXTENSION TO LIBERAL
SOCIETIES

The three preliminary matters settled, I turn to the extension of liberal ideas of justice to the law of peoples. I understand these ideas of justice to contain three main elements: (i) a list of certain basic rights and liberties and opportunities (familiar from constitutional democratic regimes); (ii) a high priority for these fundamental freedoms, especially with respect to claims of the general good and of perfectionist values; and (iii) measures assuring for all citizens adequate all-purpose means to make effective use of their freedoms. Justice as fairness is typical of these conceptions except that its egalitarian features are stronger. To some degree the more general liberal ideas lack the three egalitarian features of the fair value of the political liberties, of fair equality of opportunity, and of the difference principle. These features are not needed for the construction of a reasonable law of peoples and by not assuming them our account has greater generality.

There are two main stages to the extension to the law of peoples and each stage has two steps. The first stage of the extension I call the ideal, or strict compliance, theory, and unless otherwise stated, we work entirely in this theory. This means that the relevant concepts and principles are strictly complied with by all parties to the agreements made and that the requisite favorable conditions for liberal or hierarchical institutions are on hand. Our first aim is to see what a reasonable law of peoples, fully honored, would require and establish in this case.

To make the account manageable, we suppose there are only two kinds of well-ordered domestic societies, liberal societies and hierarchical societies. I discuss at the first step the case of well-ordered liberal democratic societies. This leads to the idea of a well-ordered political society of societies of democratic peoples. After this I turn to societies that are well-ordered and just, often religious in nature and not characterized by the separation of church and state. Their political institutions specify a just consultation hierarchy, as I shall say, while their basic social institutions satisfy a conception of justice expressing an appropriate conception of the common good. Fundamental for our rendering of the law of peoples is that both liberal and hierarchical societies accept it. Together they are members in good standing of a well-ordered society of the just peoples of the world.

The second stage in working out the law of peoples is that of nonideal theory, and it also includes two steps. The first step is that of noncompliance theory. Here we have the predicament of just societies, both democratic and hierarchical, as they confront states that refuse to comply with a reasonable law of peoples. The second step of this second stage is that of unfavorable conditions. It poses the different problem of how the poorer and less technologically advanced societies of the world can attain historical and social conditions that allow them to establish just and workable institutions, either liberal or hierarchical. In actual affairs, nonideal theory is of first practical importance and deals with problems we face every day. Yet, for reasons of space, I shall say very little about it (parts VI and VII).

Before beginning the extension we need to be sure that the original position with the veil of ignorance is a device of representation for the case of liberal societies. In the first use of the original position, its function as a device of representation means that it models what we regard—you and I, and here and now[10]—as fair conditions for the parties, as representatives of free and equal citizens, to specify the terms of cooperation regulating the basic structure of their society. Since that position includes the veil of ignorance, it also models what we regard as acceptable restrictions on reasons for adopting a political conception of justice. Therefore, the conception the parties would adopt identifies the conception of justice that we regard—you and I, here and now—as fair and supported by the best reasons.

Three conditions are essential: First, the original position represents the parties (or citizens) fairly, or reasonably; second, it represents them as rational; and third, it represents them as deciding between available principles for appropriate reasons. We check that these three conditions are satisfied by observing that citizens are indeed represented fairly, or reasonably, in virtue of the symmetry and equality of their representatives' situation in the original position. Next, citizens are represented as rational in virtue of the aim of their representatives to do the best they can for their essential interests as persons. Finally, they are represented as deciding for appropriate reasons: The veil of ignorance prevents their representatives from invoking reasons deemed unsuitable, given the aim of representing citizens as free and equal persons.

At the next level, when the original position is used to extend a liberal conception to the law of peoples, it is a device of representation because it models what we would regard—you and I, here and now[11]—as fair conditions under which the parties, this time as representatives of societies well-ordered by liberal conceptions of justice, are to specify the law of peoples and the fair terms of their cooperation.

The original position is a device of representation because, as before, free and equal peoples are represented as both reasonably situated and rational, and as deciding in accordance with appropriate reasons. The parties as representatives of democratic peoples are symmetrically situated, and so the peoples they represent are represented reasonably. Moreover, the parties deliberate among available principles for the law of peoples by reference to the fundamental interests of democratic societies in accordance with, or as presupposed by, the liberal principles of domestic justice. And finally, the parties are subject to a veil of ignorance: They do not know, for example, the size of the territory, or the population, or the relative strength of the people whose fundamental interests they represent. Although they know that reasonably favorable conditions obtain that make democracy possible, they do not know the extent of their natural resources, or level of their economic development, or any such related information. These conditions model what we, as members of societies well-ordered by liberal conceptions of justice, would accept as fair—here and now—in specifying the basic terms of cooperation between peoples who, as peoples, regard themselves as free and equal. We use the original position at the second level as a device of representation as we did at the first.

I assume that working out the law of peoples for liberal democratic societies only will result in the adoption of certain familiar principles of justice, and will also allow for various forms of cooperative association among democratic peoples and not for a world state. Here I follow Kant's lead in *Perpetual Peace* (1795) in thinking that a world government—by which I mean a unified political regime with the legal powers normally exercised by central governments—would be either a global despotism or else a fragile empire torn by frequent civil strife as various regions and peoples try to gain political autonomy.[12] On the other hand, it may turn out, as I sketch below, that there will be many different kinds of organizations subject to the judgment of the law of democratic peoples, charged with regulating cooperation between them, and having certain recognized duties. Some of these organizations (like the United Nations) may have the authority to condemn domestic institutions that violate human rights, and in certain severe cases to punish them by imposing economic sanctions, or even by military intervention. The scope of these powers is all peoples' and covers their domestic affairs.

If all this is sound, I believe the principles of justice between free and democratic peoples will include certain familiar principles long recognized as belonging to the law of peoples, among them the following:

1. Peoples (as organized by their governments) are free and independent and their freedom and independence is to be respected by other peoples.
2. Peoples are equal and parties to their own agreements.
3. Peoples have the right of self-defense but no right to war.
4. Peoples are to observe a duty of nonintervention.
5. Peoples are to observe treaties and undertakings.
6. Peoples are to observe certain specified restrictions on the conduct of war (assumed to be in self-defense).
7. Peoples are to honor human rights.

This statement of principles is of course incomplete; other principles would need to be added. Further, they require much explanation and interpretation, and some of them are superfluous in a society of well-ordered democratic peoples, for instance, the sixth regarding the conduct of war and the seventh regarding human rights. The main point is that given the idea of a society of free and independent democratic peoples, who are ready to recognize certain basic principles of political justice governing their conduct, principles of this kind constitute the charter of their association.[13] Obviously, a principle such as the fourth—that of nonintervention—will have to be qualified in the general case. Although suitable for a society of well-ordered democratic peoples who respect human rights, it fails in the case of disordered societies in which wars and serious violations of human rights are endemic. Also, the right to independence, and equally the right to self-determination, hold only within certain limits, to be specified by the law of peoples for the general case. Thus, no people has the right to self-determination, or a right to secession, at the expense of the subjugation of another people;[14] nor can a people protest their condemnation by the world society when their domestic institutions violate the human rights of certain minorities living among them. Their right to independence is no shield from that condemnation, or even from coercive intervention by other peoples in grave cases.

There will also be principles for forming and regulating federations (associations) of peoples, and standards of fairness for trade and other cooperative arrangements. There should be certain provisions for mutual assistance between peoples in times of famine and drought, and were it feasible, as it should be, provisions for ensuring that in all reasonably developed liberal societies people's basic needs are met.[15] These provisions will specify duties of assistance in certain situations, and they will vary in stringency depending on the severity of the case.

An important role of a people's government, however arbitrary a society's boundaries may appear from a historical point of view,[16] is to be the representative and effective agent of a people as they take responsibility for their territory and the size of their population, as well as for maintaining its environmental integrity and its capacity to sustain them. The idea here appeals to the point of the institution of property: Unless a definite agent is given responsibility for maintaining an asset and bears the loss for not doing so, that asset tends to deteriorate. In this case the asset is the people's territory and its capacity to sustain them in perpetuity; the agent is the people themselves as politically organized. They must recognize that they cannot make up for irresponsibility in caring for their land and conserving their natural resources by conquest in war or by migrating into other people's territory without their consent.[17]

These remarks belong to ideal theory and indicate some of the responsibilities of peoples in a just society of well-ordered liberal societies. Since the boundaries of peoples are often historically the outcome of violence and aggression, and some peoples are wrongly subjected to others, the law of peoples in its nonideal part should, as far as possible, contain principles and standards—or at least some guidelines—for coping with these matters.

To complete this sketch of the law of peoples for well-ordered liberal societies only, let's consider under what conditions we can reasonably accept this part of the law of peoples and regard it as justified.

There are two conditions beyond the three requirements earlier noted in discussing the original position as a device of representation. These requirements were: that the parties (as representatives of free and equal peoples) be represented as reasonably situated, as rational, and as deciding in accordance with appropriate reasons. One of the two further conditions is that the political society of well-ordered democratic peoples should itself be stable in the right way.[18] Given the existence of a political society of such peoples, its members will tend increasingly over time to accept its principles and judgments as they come to understand the ideas of justice expressed in the law among them and appreciate its benefits for all liberal peoples.

To say that the society of democratic peoples is stable in the right way is to say that it is stable with respect to justice, that is, that the institutions and practices among peoples always more or less satisfy the relevant principles of justice, although social conditions are presumably always changing. It is further to say that the law of peoples is honored not simply because of a fortunate balance of power—it being in no people's interest to upset it—but because, despite the possibly shifting fortunes of different peoples, all are moved to adhere to their common law accepting it as just and beneficial for all. This means that the justice of the society of democratic peoples is stable with respect to the distribution of fortune among them. Here fortune refers not to a society's military success or the lack of it, but to other kinds of success: its achievement of political and social freedom, the fullness and expressiveness of its culture, the economic well-being of all its citizens.

The historical record suggests that, at least so far as the principle against war is concerned, this condition of stability would be satisfied in a society of just democratic peoples. Although democratic societies have been as often involved in war as nondemocratic states[19] and have often vigorously defended their institutions, since 1800, as Michael Doyle points out, firmly established liberal societies have not gone to war with one another.[20] And in wars in which a number of major powers were engaged, such as the two World Wars, democratic states have fought as allies on the same side. Indeed, the absence of war between democracies is as close as anything we know to an empirical law in relations between societies.[21] This being so, I shall suppose that a society of democratic peoples, all of whose basic institutions are well ordered by liberal conceptions of justice (though not necessarily by the same conception) will be stable in the right way as above specified. The sketch of the law of such peoples therefore seems to meet the condition of political realism given by that of stability for the right reasons.

Observe that I state what I call Doyle's law as holding between well-established and well-ordered liberal democracies that are significant if not major powers. The reasons for this law's holding (supposing it does) are quite compatible with actual democracies, marked as they are by considerable injustice and oligarchic tendencies, intervening, often covertly, in smaller countries whose democracies are less well established and secure. Witness the United States' overturning the democracies of Allende in Chile, Arbenz in Guatemala, Mossadegh in Iran, and, some would add, the Sandinistas in Nicaragua. Whatever the merits of these regimes, covert operations against them can be carried out by a government bureaucracy at the urging of oligarchic interests without the knowledge or criticism of the public, and presenting it with a fait accompli. All this is made easier by the handy appeal to national security given the situation of superpower rivalry in the Cold War, which allowed those democracies, however implausibly, to be cast as a danger. While democratic peoples are not expansionist, they do defend their security interest, and this an oligarchic government can easily manipulate in a time of superpower rivalry to support covert interventions once they are found out.[22]

The last condition for us to accept this sketch of the law of democratic peoples as sound is that we can, as citizens of liberal societies, endorse the principles and judgments of this law on due reflection. We must be able to say that the doctrine of the law of peoples for such societies, more than any other doctrine, ties together our considered political convictions and moral judgments at all levels of generality, from the most general to the more particular, into one coherent view.

IV. EXTENSION TO HIERARCHICAL SOCIETIES

Recall from part III that the extension of liberal ideas of justice to the law of peoples proceeds in two stages, each stage having two steps. The first stage is that of ideal theory and we have just completed the first step of that: the extension of the law of peoples to well-ordered liberal societies only. The second step of ideal theory is more difficult: It requires us to specify a second kind of society—a hierarchical society, as I shall say—and then to state when such a society is well ordered. Our aim is to extend the law of peoples to these well-ordered hierarchical societies and to show that they accept the same law of peoples as liberal societies do. Thus, this shared law of well-ordered peoples, both liberal and hierarchical, specifies the content of ideal theory. It specifies the kind of society of well-ordered peoples all people should want and it sets the regulative end of their foreign policy. Important for us, it has the obvious corollary that nonliberal societies also honor human rights.

To show all this we proceed thus. First, we state three requirements for any well-ordered hierarchical regime. It will be clear that satisfying these requirements does not entail that a regime be liberal. Next, we confirm that, in an original position with a veil of ignorance, the representatives of well-ordered hierarchical regimes are reasonably situated as well as rational, and are moved by appropriate reasons. In this case also, the original position is a device of representation for the adoption of law among hierarchical peoples. Finally, we show that in the original position the representatives of well-ordered hierarchical societies would adopt the same law of peoples that the representatives of liberal societies do. That law thus serves as a common law of a just political society of well-ordered peoples.

The first of the three requirements for a hierarchical society to be well ordered is that it must be peaceful and gain its legitimate aims through diplomacy and trade, and other ways of peace. It follows that its religious doctrine, assumed to be comprehensive and influential in government policy, is not expansionist in the sense that it fully respects the civic order and integrity of other societies. If it seeks wider influence, it does so in ways compatible with the independence of, and the liberties within, other societies. This feature of its religion supports the institutional basis of its peaceful conduct and distinguishes it from leading European states during the religious wars of the sixteenth and seventeenth centuries.

A second fundamental requirement uses an idea of Philip Soper. It has several parts. It requires first, that a hierarchical society's system of law be such as to impose moral duties and obligations on all persons within its territory.[23] It requires further that its system of law be guided by a common good conception of justice, meaning by this a conception that takes impartially into account what it sees not unreasonably as the fundamental interests of all members of society. It is not the case that the interests of some are arbitrarily privileged, while the interests of others go for naught. Finally, there must be sincere and not unreasonable belief on the part of judges and other officials who administer the legal order that the law is indeed guided by a common good conception of justice. This belief must be demonstrated by a willingness to defend publicly the state's injunctions as justified by law. Courts are an efficient way of doing this.[24] These aspects of a legal order are necessary to establish a regime's legitimacy in the eyes of its own people. To sum up the second requirement we say: The system of law is sincerely and not unreasonably believed to be guided by a common good conception of justice. It takes into account people's essential interests and imposes moral duties and obligations on all members of society.

This second requirement can be spelled out further by adding that the political institutions of a well-ordered hierarchical society constitute a reasonable consultation hierarchy. They include a family of representative bodies, or other assemblies, whose task is to look after the important interests of all elements of society. Although in hierarchical societies persons are not regarded as free and equal citizens, as they are in liberal societies, they are seen as responsible members of society who can recognize their moral duties and obligations and play their part in social life.

With a consultation hierarchy there is an opportunity for different voices to be heard, not, to be sure, in a way allowed by democratic institutions, but appropriately in view of the religious and philosophical values of the society in question. Thus, individuals do not have the right of free speech as in a liberal society; but as members of associations and corporate bodies they have the right at some point in the process of consultation to express political dissent and the government has an obligation to take their dissent seriously and to give a conscientious reply. That different voices can be heard is necessary because the sincere belief of judges and other officials has two components: honest belief and respect for the possibility of dissent.[25] Judges and officials must be willing to address objections. They cannot refuse to listen to them on the grounds that they think those expressing them are incompetent and cannot understand. Then we would not have a consultation hierarchy but a purely paternalistic regime.

In view of this account of the institutional basis of a hierarchical society, we can say that its conception of the common good of justice secures for all persons at least certain minimum rights to means of subsistence and security (the right to life),[26] to liberty (freedom from slavery, serfdom, and forced occupations) and (personal) property, as well as to formal equality as expressed by the rules of natural justice[27] (for example, that similar cases be treated similarly). This shows that a well-ordered hierarchical society also meets a third requirement: it respects basic human rights.

The argument for this conclusion is that the second requirement rules out violations of these rights. For to satisfy it, a society's legal order must impose moral duties and obligations on all persons in its territory and it must embody a reasonable consultation hierarchy which will protect human rights. A sincere and reasonable belief on the part of judges and other officials that the system of law is guided by a common good conception of justice has the same result. Such a belief is simply unreasonable, if not irrational, when those rights are infringed.

There is a question about religious toleration that calls for explicit mention. Whereas in hierarchical societies a state religion may be on some questions the ultimate authority within society and control government policy on certain important matters, that authority is not (as I have said) extended politically to other societies. Further, their (comprehensive) religious or philosophical doctrines are not unreasonable: They admit a measure of liberty of conscience and freedom of thought, even if these freedoms are not in general equal for all members of society as they are in liberal regimes.[28] A hierarchical society may have an established religion with certain privileges. Still, it is essential to its being well-ordered that no religions are persecuted, or denied civic and social conditions that permit their practice in peace and without fear.[29] Also essential, and this because of the inequality of religious freedom, if for no other reason, is that a hierarchical society must allow for the right of emigration.[30] The rights noted here are counted as human rights. In part V we return to the role and status of these rights.

An institutional basis that realizes the three requirements can take many forms. This deserves emphasis, as I have indicated only the religious case. We are not trying to describe all possible forms of social order consistent with membership in good standing of a reasonable society of peoples. Rather, we have specified three necessary conditions for membership of a reasonable society of peoples and then shown by example that these conditions do not require a society to be liberal.

This completes the account of the requirements imposed on the basic institutions of a well-ordered hierarchical society. My aim has been to outline a conception of justice that, although distant from liberal conceptions, still has features that give to societies regulated accordingly the moral status required to be members in good standing in a reasonable society of well-ordered peoples. It is important to see, as I have noted, that an agreement on a law of peoples ensuring human rights is not an agreement only liberal societies can make. We must now confirm this.

Hierarchical societies are well-ordered in terms of their own conceptions of justice.[31] This being so, their representatives in an appropriate original position would adopt the same principles as those sketched above that would be adopted by the representatives of liberal societies. Each hierarchical society's interests are understood by its representatives in accordance with or as presupposed by its conception of justice. This enables us to say in this case also that the original position is a device of representation.

Two considerations confirm this. The first is that, in view of the common good conception of justice held in a hierarchical society, the parties care about the good of the society they represent, and so about its security as assured by the laws against war and aggression. They also care about the benefits of trade and assistance between peoples in time of need. All these help protect human rights. In view of this, we can say that the representatives of hierarchical societies are rational. The second consideration is that they do not try to extend their religious and philosophical doctrines to other peoples by war or aggression, and they respect the civic order and integrity of other societies. Hence, they accept—as you and I would accept[32]—the original position as fair between peoples and would endorse the law of peoples adopted by their representatives as specifying fair terms of political cooperation between them and other societies. Thus, the representatives are reasonably situated and this suffices for the use of the original position as a device of representation in extending the law of peoples to hierarchical societies.[33]

Note that I have supposed that the parties as representatives of peoples are to be situated equally, even though the conception of justice of the hierarchical society they represent allows basic inequalities between its members. For example, some of its members are not granted equal liberty of conscience. There is, however, no inconsistency in this: A people sincerely affirming a nonliberal conception of justice may still think their society should be treated equally in a just law of peoples, even though its members accept basic inequalities among themselves. Though a society lacks basic equality, it is not unreasonable for that society to insist on equality in making claims against other societies.

About this last point, two observations. One is that although the original position at the first level, that of domestic justice, incorporates a political conception of the person rooted in the public culture of a liberal society, the original position at the second level, that of the law of peoples, does not. I emphasize this fact, since it enables a liberal conception of justice to be extended to yield a more general law of peoples without prejudging the case against nonliberal societies.

This leads to a second observation. As mentioned earlier, the law of peoples might have been worked out by starting with an all-inclusive original position with representatives of all the individual persons of the world.[34] In this case the question of whether there are to be separate societies and of the relations between them, will be settled by the parties behind a veil of ignorance. Offhand it is not clear why proceeding this way should lead to different results than, as I have done, proceeding from separate societies outward. All things considered, one might reach the same law of peoples in either case. The difficulty with an all-inclusive, or global, original position is that its use of liberal ideas is much more troublesome, for in this case we are treating all persons, regardless of their society and culture, as individuals who are free and equal, and as reasonable and rational, and so according to liberal conceptions. This makes the basis of the law of peoples too narrow.

Hence I think it best to follow the two-level[35] bottom-up procedure, beginning first with the principles of justice for the basic structure of domestic society and then moving upward and outward to the law of peoples. In so doing our knowledge of how peoples and their governments have acted historically gives us guidance in how to proceed and suggests questions and possibilities we might not otherwise have thought of. But this is simply a point of method and settles no questions of substance. These depend on what can actually be worked out.

One might well be skeptical that a liberal social contract and constructivist[36] idea of justice can be worked out to give a conception of the law of peoples universal in its reach and also applying to nonliberal societies. Our discussion of hierarchical societies should put these doubts to rest. I have noted the conditions under which we could accept the law of liberal peoples we had sketched as sound and justified. In this connection we considered whether that law was stable with respect to justice, and whether, on due reflection, we could accept the judgments that its principles and precepts led us to make. If both these things hold, we said, the law of liberal peoples as laid out could, by the criteria we can now apply, be accepted as justified.

Parallel remarks hold for the wider law of peoples including well-ordered hierarchical societies. Here I simply add, without argument or evidence, but hoping it seems plausible, that these societies will honor a just law of peoples for much the same reasons liberal peoples will do so, and that both we and they will find the judgments to which it leads acceptable to our convictions, all things considered. I believe it is of importance here that well-ordered hierarchical societies are not expansionist and their legal order is guided by a common good conception of justice ensuring that it honors human rights. These societies also affirm a peaceful society of peoples and benefit therefrom as liberal societies do. All have a common interest in changing the way in which politics among peoples—war and threats of war—has hitherto been carried on.

We may therefore view this wider law of peoples as sound and justified. This fundamental point deserves emphasis: There is nothing relevantly different between how, say, justice as fairness is worked out for the domestic case in *A Theory of Justice,* and how the law of peoples is worked out from more general liberal ideas of justice. In both cases we use the same fundamental idea of a reasonable procedure of construction in which rational agents fairly situated (the parties as representatives of citizens in one case and of peoples or societies in the other) select principles of justice for the relevant subject, either their separate domestic institutions or the shared law of peoples. As always, the parties are guided by the appropriate reasons as specified by a veil of ignorance. Thus, obligations and duties are not imposed by one society on another; instead, reasonable societies agree on what the bonds will be. Once we confirm that a domestic society, or a society of peoples, when regulated by the corresponding principles of justice, is stable with respect to justice (as previously defined), and once we have checked that we can endorse those principles on due reflection, then in both domains the ideals, laws, and principles of justice are justified in the same way.[37]

V.   HUMAN RIGHTS

A few of the features of human rights as we have described them are these. First, these rights do not depend on any particular comprehensive moral doctrine or philosophical conception of human nature, such as, for example, that human beings are moral persons and have equal worth, or that they have certain particular moral and intellectual powers that entitle them to these rights. This would require a quite deep philosophical theory that many if not most hierarchical societies might reject as liberal or democratic, or in some way distinctive of the Western political tradition and prejudicial to other cultures.

We therefore take a different tack and say that basic human rights express a minimum standard of well-ordered political institutions for all peoples who belong, as members in good standing, to a just political society of peoples.[38] Any systematic violation of these rights is a serious matter and troubling to the society of peoples as a whole, both liberal and hierarchical. Since they must express a minimum standard, the requirements that yield these rights should be quite weak.

Recall that we postulated that a society's system of law must be such as to impose moral duties and obligations on all its members and be regulated by what judges and other officials reasonably and sincerely believe is a common good conception of justice. For this condition to hold, the law must at least uphold such basic rights as the right to life and security, to personal property, and the elements of the rule of law, as well as the right to a certain liberty of conscience and freedom of association, and the right to emigration. These rights we refer to as human rights.

Next we consider what the imposition of these duties and obligations implies, including (1) a common good conception of justice and (2) good faith on the part of officials to explain and justify the legal order to those bound by it. For these things to hold does not require the liberal idea that persons are first citizens and as such free and equal members of society who hold those basic rights as the rights of citizens. It requires only that persons be responsible and cooperating members of society who can recognize and act in accordance with their moral duties and obligations. It would be hard to reject these requirements (a common good conception of justice and a good faith official justification of the law) as too strong for a minimally decent regime. Human rights, understood as resulting from these requirements, could not be rejected as peculiarly liberal or special to our Western tradition. In that sense, they are politically neutral.[39]

To confirm this last point, I consider an alleged difficulty. Many societies have political traditions that are different from Western individualism in its many forms. In considering persons from a political point of view, these traditions are said to regard persons not as citizens first with the rights of citizens but rather as first being members of groups: communities, associations, or corporations.[40] On this alternative, let's say associationist, view, whatever rights persons have arise from this prior membership and are normally enabling rights, that is, rights that enable persons to perform their duties in the groups to which they belong. To illustrate with respect to political rights: Hegel rejects the idea of one person one vote on the grounds that it expresses the democratic and individualistic idea that each person, as an atomic unit, has the basic right to participate equally in political deliberation.[41] By contrast, in the well-ordered rational state, as Hegel presents it in *The Philosophy of Right*, persons belong first to estates, corporations, and associations. Since these social forms represent the rational[42] interests of their members in what Hegel views as a just consultation hierarchy, some persons will take part in politically representing these interests in the consultation process, but they do so as members of estates and corporations and not as individuals, and not all individuals are involved.

The essential point here is that the basic human rights as we have described them can be protected in a well-ordered hierarchical state with its consultation hierarchy; what holds in Hegel's scheme of political rights holds for all rights.[43] Its system of law can fulfill the conditions laid down and ensure the right to life and security, to personal property and the elements of the rule of law, as well as the right to a certain freedom of conscience and freedom of association. Admittedly it ensures these rights to persons as members of estates and corporations and not as citizens. But that does not matter. The rights are guaranteed and the requirement that a system of law must be such as to impose moral rights and duties is met. Human rights understood in the light of that condition cannot be rejected as peculiar to our Western tradition.

Human rights are a special class of rights designed to play a special role in a reasonable law of peoples for the present age. Recall that the accepted ideas about international law changed in two basic ways following World War II, and this change in basic moral beliefs is comparable to other profound historical changes.[44] War is no longer an admissible means of state policy. It is only justified in self-defense and a state's internal sovereignty is now limited. One role of human rights is precisely to specify limits to that sovereignty.

Human rights are thus distinct from, say, constitutional rights, or the rights of democratic citizenship,[45] or from other kinds of rights that belong to certain kinds of political institutions, both individualist and associationist. They are a special class of rights of universal application and hardly controversial in their general intention. They are part of a reasonable law of peoples and specify limits on the domestic institutions required of all peoples by that law. In this sense they specify the outer boundary of admissible domestic law of societies in good standing in a just society of peoples.[46]

Human rights have these three roles:

1. They are a necessary condition of a regime's legitimacy and of the decency of its legal order.
2. By being in place, they are also sufficient to exclude justified and forceful intervention by other peoples, say by economic sanctions, or in grave cases, by military force.
3. They set a limit on pluralism among peoples.[47]

VI. NONIDEAL THEORY: NONCOMPLIANCE

So far we have been concerned solely with ideal theory. By developing a liberal conception of justice we have reviewed the philosophical and moral grounds of an ideal conception of a society of well-ordered peoples and of the principles that apply to its law and practices. That conception is to guide the conduct of peoples toward one another and the design of common institutions for their mutual benefit.

Before our sketch of the law of peoples is complete, however, we must take note of, even though we cannot properly discuss, the questions arising from the highly nonideal conditions of our world with its great injustices and widespread social evils. Nonideal theory asks how the ideal conception of the society of well-ordered peoples might be achieved, or at least worked toward, generally in gradual steps. It looks for policies and courses of action likely to be effective and politically possible as well as morally permissible for that purpose. So conceived, nonideal theory presupposes that ideal theory is already on hand for, until the ideal is identified, at least in outline, nonideal theory lacks an objective by reference to which its questions can be answered. And although the specific conditions of our world at any given time—the status quo—do not determine the ideal conception of the society of well-ordered peoples, those conditions do affect answers to the questions of nonideal theory. They are questions of transition: In any given case, they start from where a society is and seek effective ways permitted by the law of peoples to move the society some distance toward the goal.

We may distinguish two kinds of nonideal theory. One kind deals with conditions of noncompliance, that is, with conditions in which certain regimes refuse to acknowledge a reasonable law of peoples. These we may call outlaw regimes. The other kind of nonideal theory deals with unfavorable conditions, that is, with the conditions of peoples whose historical, social, and economic circumstances make their achieving a well-ordered regime, whether liberal or hierarchical, difficult if not impossible.

I begin with noncompliance theory. As we have said, a reasonable law of peoples guides the well-ordered regimes in facing outlaw regimes by specifying the goal they should always have in mind and indicating the means they may use or must avoid in pursuing that goal.

Outlaw regimes are a varied lot. Some are headed by governments that seem to recognize no conception of right and justice at all; often their legal order is at bottom a system of coercion and terror. The Nazi regime is a demonic example of this. A more common case, philosophically more interesting and historically more respectable, are those societies—they would scoff at being referred to as outlaw regimes—whose rulers affirm comprehensive doctrines that recognize no geographic limits to the legitimate authority of their established religious or philosophical views. Spain, France, and the Hapsburgs all tried at some time to subject much of Europe and the world to their will.[48] They hoped to spread true religion and culture, sought dominion and glory, not to mention wealth and territory. Such societies are checked only by a balance of power, but as this is changing and unstable, the hegemonic theory of war, so-called, fits nicely.[49]

The law-abiding societies—both liberal and hierarchical—can at best establish a modus vivendi with the outlaw expansionist regimes and defend the integrity of their societies as the law of peoples allows. In this situation the law-abiding societies exist in a state of nature with the outlaw regimes, and they have a duty to their own and to one another's societies and well-being, as well as a duty to the well-being of peoples subjected to outlaw regimes, though not to their rulers and elites. These several duties are not all equally strong, but there is always a duty to consider the more extensive long-run aims and to affirm them as overall guides of foreign policy. Thus, the only legitimate grounds of the right to war against outlaw regimes is defense of the society of well-ordered peoples and, in grave cases, of innocent persons subject to outlaw regimes and the protection of their human rights. This accords with Kant's idea that our first political duty is to leave the state of nature and submit ourselves along with others to the rule of a reasonable and just law.[50]

The defense of well-ordered peoples is only the first and most urgent task. Another long-run aim, as specified by the law of peoples, is to bring all societies eventually to honor that law and to be full and self-standing members of the society of well-ordered peoples, and so secure human rights everywhere. How to do this is a question of foreign policy; these things call for political wisdom, and success depends in part on luck. They are not matters to which political philosophy has much to add. I venture several familiar points.

For well-ordered peoples to achieve this long-run aim they should establish among themselves new institutions and practices to serve as a kind of federative center and public forum of their common opinion and policy toward the other regimes. This can either be done separately or within institutions such as the United Nations by forming an alliance of well-ordered peoples on certain issues. This federative center may be used both to formulate and to express the opinion of the well-ordered societies. There they may expose to public view the unjust and cruel institutions of oppressive and expansionist regimes and their violations of human rights.

Even these regimes are not altogether indifferent to this kind of criticism, especially when the basis of it is a reasonable and well-founded law of peoples that cannot be easily dismissed as simply liberal or Western. Gradually over time the well-ordered peoples may pressure the outlaw regimes to change their ways; but by itself this pressure is unlikely to be effective. It must be backed up by the firm denial of all military aid, or economic and other assistance; nor should outlaw regimes be admitted by well-ordered peoples as members in good standing into their mutually beneficial cooperative practices.

VII. NONIDEAL THEORY: UNFAVORABLE CONDITIONS

A few words about the second kind of nonideal theory, that of unfavorable conditions. By these I mean the conditions of societies that lack the political and cultural traditions, the human capital and know-how, and the resources, material and technological, that make well-ordered societies possible. In noncompliance theory we saw that the goal of well-ordered societies is somehow to bring the outlaw states into the society of well-ordered peoples. The outlaw societies in the historical cases we mentioned above were not societies burdened by unfavorable resources, material and technological, or lacking in human capital and know-how; on the contrary, they were among the most politically and socially advanced and economically developed societies of their day. The fault in those societies lay in their political traditions and the background institutions of law, property, and class structure, with their sustaining beliefs and culture. These things must be changed before a reasonable law of peoples can be accepted and supported.

We must ask the parallel question: What is the goal specified by nonideal theory for the case of unfavorable conditions? The answer is clear. Eventually each society now burdened by unfavorable conditions should be raised to, or assisted toward, conditions that make a well-ordered society possible.

Some writers have proposed that the difference principle, or some other liberal principle of distributive justice, be adopted to deal with this problem and to regulate accordingly the economic inequalities in the society of peoples.[51] Although I think the difference principle is reasonable for domestic justice in a democratic society, it is not feasible as a way to deal with the general problem of unfavorable conditions among societies. For one thing, it belongs to the ideal theory for a democratic society and is not framed for our present case. More serious, there are various kinds of societies in the society of peoples and not all of them can reasonably be expected to accept any particular liberal principle of distributive justice; and even different liberal societies adopt different principles for their domestic institutions. For their part, the hierarchical societies reject all liberal principles of domestic justice. We cannot suppose that they will find such principles acceptable in dealing with other peoples. In our construction of the liberal law of peoples, therefore, liberal principles of domestic distributive justice are not generalized to answer questions about unfavorable conditions.

Confirming this is the fact that in a constructivist conception there is no reason to think that the principles that apply to domestic justice are also appropriate for regulating inequalities in a society of peoples. As we saw at the outset, each kind of subject—whether an institution or an individual, whether a political society or a society of political societies—may be governed by its own characteristic principles. What these principles are must be worked out by a suitable procedure beginning from a correct starting point. We ask how rational representatives suitably motivated, and reasonably situated with respect to one another, would be most strongly moved to select among the feasible ideals and principles to apply to the subject in question. Since the problem and subject are different in each case, the ideals and principles adopted may also be different. As always, the whole procedure and the principles it yields must be acceptable on due reflection.

Although no liberal principle of distributive justice would be adopted for dealing with unfavorable conditions, that certainly does not mean that the well-ordered and wealthier societies have no duties and obligations to societies burdened by such conditions. For the ideal conception of the society of peoples that well-ordered societies affirm directs that in due course all societies must reach, or be assisted to, the conditions that make a well-ordered society possible. This implies that human rights are to be recognized and secured everywhere, and that basic human needs are to be met. Thus, the basis of the duty of assistance is not some liberal principle of distributive justice. Rather, it is the ideal conception of the society of peoples itself as consisting of well-ordered societies, with each people, as I have said, a full and self-standing member of the society of peoples, and capable of taking charge of their political life and maintaining decent political and social institutions as specified by the three requirements earlier surveyed.[52]

I shall not attempt to discuss here how this might be done, as the problem of giving economic and technological aid so that it makes a sustained contribution is highly complicated and varies from country to country. Moreover the problem is often not the lack of natural resources. Many societies with unfavorable conditions don't lack for resources. Well-ordered societies can get on with very little; their wealth lies elsewhere: in their political and cultural traditions, in their human capital and knowledge, and in their capacity for political and economic organization. Rather, the problem is commonly the nature of the public political culture and the religious and philosophical traditions that underlie its institutions. The great social evils in poorer societies are likely to be oppressive government and corrupt elites; the subjection of women abetted by unreasonable religion, with the resulting overpopulation relative to what the economy of the society can decently sustain. Perhaps there is no society anywhere in the world whose people, were they reasonably and rationally governed, and their numbers sensibly adjusted to their economy and resources, could not have a decent and worthwhile life.

These general remarks indicate what is so often the source of the problem: the public political culture and its roots in the background social structure. The obligation of wealthier societies to assist in trying to rectify matters is in no way diminished, only made more difficult. Here, too, in ways I need not describe, an emphasis on human rights may work, when backed by other kinds of assistance, to moderate, albeit slowly, oppressive government, the corruption of elites, and the subjection of women.[53]

VIII. CONCLUDING REFLECTIONS

I have not said much about what might be called the philosophical basis of human rights. That is because, despite their name, human rights are a special class of rights explained by their role in a liberal conception of the law of peoples acceptable to both well-ordered liberal and hierarchical societies. I have therefore sketched how such a law of peoples might be worked out on the basis of a liberal conception of justice.[54] Within this framework I have indicated how respect for human rights is one of the conditions imposed on any political regime to be admissible as a member in good standing into a just political society of peoples. Once we understand this, and once we understand how a reasonable law of peoples is developed out of the liberal conception of justice and how this conception can be universal in its reach, it is perfectly clear why those rights hold across cultural and economic boundaries, as well as the boundaries between nation states, or other political units. With our two other conditions, these rights determine the limits of toleration in a reasonable society of peoples.

About these limits, the following observation: If we start with a well-ordered liberal society that realizes an egalitarian conception of justice such as justice as fairness,[55] the members of that society will nevertheless accept into the society of peoples other liberal societies whose institutions are considerably less egalitarian. This is implicit in our beginning with liberal conceptions more general than justice as fairness as defined in part III. But citizens in a well-ordered egalitarian society will still view the domestic regimes of those societies as less congenial to them than the regime of their own society.

This illustrates what happens whenever the scope of toleration is extended: The criteria of reasonableness are relaxed.[56] In the case we have considered, we seek to include other than liberal societies as members in good standing of a reasonable society of peoples. Hence when we move to these societies, their domestic regimes are less, often much less, congenial to us. This poses the problem of the limits of toleration. Where are these limits to be drawn? Clearly, tyrannical and dictatorial regimes must be outlawed, and also, for basic liberal reasons, expansionist states like those of the Wars of Religion. The three necessary conditions for a well-ordered regime—that it respect the principles of peace and not be expansionist, that its system of law meet the essentials of legitimacy in the eyes of its own people, and that it honor basic human rights—are proposed as an answer as to where those limits lie. These conditions indicate the bedrock beyond which we cannot go.

We have discussed how far many societies of the world have always been, and are today, from meeting these three conditions for being a member in good standing of a reasonable society of peoples. The law of peoples provides the basis for judging the conduct of any existing regime, liberal as well as nonliberal. And since our account of the law of peoples was developed out of a liberal conception of justice, we must address the question whether the liberal law of peoples is ethnocentric and merely Western.

To address this question, recall that in working out the law of peoples we assumed that liberal societies conduct themselves toward other societies from the point of view of their own liberal political conception. Regarding this conception as sound, and as meeting all the criteria they are now able to apply, how else are they to proceed? To the objection that to proceed thus is ethnocentric or merely Western, the reply is: no, not necessarily. Whether it is so turns on the content of the political conception that liberal societies embrace once it is worked up to provide at least an outline of the law of peoples.

Looking at the outline of that law, we should note the difference between it and the law of peoples as it might be understood by religious and expansionist states that reject the liberal conception. The liberal conception asks of other societies only what they can reasonably grant without submitting to a position of inferiority, much less to domination. It is crucial that a liberal conception of the law of peoples not ask well-ordered hierarchical societies to abandon their religious institutions and adopt liberal ones. True, in our sketch we supposed that traditional societies would affirm the law of peoples that would hold among just liberal societies. That law is therefore universal in its reach: It asks of other societies only what they can accept once they are prepared to stand in a relation of equality with all other societies and once their regimes accept the criterion of legitimacy in the eyes of their own people. In what other relations can a society and its regime reasonably expect to stand?

Moreover, the liberal law of peoples does not justify economic sanctions or military pressure on well-ordered hierarchical societies to change their ways, provided they respect the rules of peace and their political institutions satisfy the essential conditions we have reviewed. If, however, these conditions are violated, external pressure of one kind or another may be justified depending on the severity and the circumstances of the case. A concern for human rights should be a fixed part of the foreign policy of liberal and hierarchical societies.

Looking back at our discussion, let's recall that besides sketching how the law of peoples might be developed from liberal conceptions of right and justice, a further aim was to set out the bearing of political liberalism for a wider world society once a liberal political conception of justice is extended to the law of peoples. In particular, we asked: What form does the toleration of nonliberal societies take in this case? Although tyrannical and dictatorial regimes cannot be accepted as members in good standing of a reasonable society of peoples, not all regimes can reasonably be required to be liberal. If so, the law of peoples would not express liberalism's own principle of toleration for other reasonable ways of ordering society. A liberal society must respect other societies organized by comprehensive doctrines, provided their political and social institutions meet certain conditions that lead the society to adhere to a reasonable law of peoples.

I did not try to present an argument to this conclusion. I took it as clear that if other nonliberal societies honored certain conditions, such as the three requirements discussed in part IV, they would be accepted by liberal societies as members in good standing of a society of peoples. There would be no political case to attack these nonliberal societies militarily, or to bring economic or other sanctions against them to revise their institutions. Critical commentary in liberal societies would be fully consistent with the civic liberties and integrity of those societies.

What conception of toleration of other societies does the law of peoples express? How is it connected with political liberalism? If it should be asked whether liberal societies are, morally speaking, better than hierarchical societies, and therefore whether the world would be a better place if all societies were liberal, those holding a comprehensive liberal view could think it would be. But that opinion would not support a claim to rid the world of nonliberal regimes. It could have no operative force in what, as a matter of right, they could do politically. The situation is parallel to the toleration of other conceptions of the good in the domestic case. Someone holding a comprehensive liberal view can say that their society would be a better place if every one held such a view. They might be wrong in this judgment even by their own lights, as other doctrines may play a moderating and balancing role given the larger background of belief and conviction, and give society's culture a certain depth and richness. The point is that to affirm the superiority of a particular comprehensive view is fully compatible with affirming a political conception of justice that does not impose it, and thus with political liberalism itself.

Political liberalism holds that comprehensive doctrines have but a restricted place in liberal democratic politics in this sense: Fundamental constitutional questions and matters concerning basic rights and liberties are to be settled by a public political conception of justice, exemplified by the liberal political conceptions, and not by those wider doctrines. For given the pluralism of democratic societies—a pluralism best seen as the outcome of the exercise of human reason under free institutions, and which can only be undone by the oppressive use of state power—affirming such a public conception and the basic political institutions that realize it, is the most reasonable basis of social unity available to us.

The law of peoples, as I have sketched it, is simply the extension of these same ideas to the political society of well-ordered peoples. That law, which settles fundamental constitutional questions and matters of basic justice as they arise for the society of peoples, must also be based on a public political conception of justice and not on a comprehensive religious, philosophical, or moral doctrine. I have sketched the content of such a political conception and tried to explain how it could be endorsed by well-ordered societies, both liberal and hierarchical. Except as a basis of a modus vivendi, expansionist societies of whatever kind could not endorse it; but in principle there is no peaceful solution in their case except the domination of one side or the peace of exhaustion.

CRIMES OF WAR, CRIMES OF PEACE

Catharine A. MacKinnon

Where, after all, do universal human rights begin? In small places, close to home. . .
—Eleanor Roosevelt

I

In reality begins principle. The loftiest legal abstractions, however strenuously empty of social specificity on the surface, are born of social life: amid the intercourse of particular groups, in the presumptive ease of the deciding classes, through the trauma of specific atrocities, at the expense of the silent and excluded, as a victory (usually compromised, often pyrrhic) for the powerless. Law does not grow by syllogistic compulsion; it is pushed by the social logic of domination and challenge to domination, forged in the interaction of change and resistance to change. It is not only in the common law that the life of the law is experience, not logic.[1] Behind all law is someone's story—someone whose blood, if you read closely, leaks through the lines. Text does not beget text; life does. The question—a question of politics and history and therefore law—is whose experience grounds what law.

Human rights principles are based on experience, but not that of women. It is not that women's human rights have not been violated. When women are violated like men who are otherwise like them—when women's arms and legs bleed when severed, when women are shot in pits and gassed in vans, when women's bodies are hidden at the bottom of abandoned mines, when women's skulls are sent from Auschwitz to Strasbourg for experiments—this is not recorded as the history of human rights atrocities to women. They are Argentinian or Honduran or Jewish. When things happen to women that also happen to men,

The help and contributions of Natalie Nenadic, Asja Armanda, Susanne Baer, Jeffrey Masson, Jessica Neuwirth, Joan Fitzpatrick, Cass Sunstein, Andrea Dworkin, Richard Rorty, Kent Harvey, Rita Rendell, and the wonderful staff at the University of Michigan Law Library are gratefully acknowledged.

like being beaten and disappeared and tortured to death, the fact that they happened to women is not counted in, or marked as, human suffering. When no war has been declared and still women are beaten by men with whom they are close, when wives disappear from supermarket parking lots, when prostitutes float up in rivers or turn up under piles of rags in abandoned buildings, this is overlooked entirely in the record of human suffering because the victims are women and it smells of sex. What happens to women is either too particular to be universal or too universal to be particular, meaning either too human to be female or too female to be human.

Women are violated in many ways that men are not, or rarely are; many of these violations are sexual and reproductive.[2] Ranging from objectification to killing,[3] from dehumanization and defilement to mutilation and torture to sexual murder, this abuse occurs in forms and settings and legal postures that overlap every recognized human rights convention but is addressed, effectively and as such, by none. What most often happens to women escapes the human rights net. Something—jurisdictional, evidentiary, substantive, customary, or habitual—is always wrong with it. Abuses of women as women rarely seem to fit what these laws and their enforcing bodies have in mind; the more abuses there are, the more they do not fit. Whether in war or in what is called peacetime, at home or abroad, in private or in public, by our side or the other side, man's inhumanity to woman is ignored.

Women's absence shapes human rights in substance and in form, effectively defining what a human and a right are. What does it mean to recognize a principle called human rights that does not really apply to the systemic and systematic violations of the dignity and integrity and security and life of over half the human race? It means that what violates the dignity of others is dignity for them; what violates the integrity of others is integrity for them; what violates the security of others is as much security as they are going to get. Even death to a full human being is less serious for them. Half of humanity is thus effectively defined as nonhuman, subhuman, properly rightsless creatures, beings whose reality of violation, to the extent it is somehow female, floats beneath international legal space.

For a compressed illustration of some current realities that are at once a hair's breadth and a gendered light-year away from the atrocities that ground human rights principles and fill the factual reports of Amnesty International,[4] consider this communication from an American researcher of Bosnian and Croatian descent gathering information in Croatia and Bosnia-Herzegovina:

> Serbian forces have exterminated over 200,000 Croatians and Muslims thus far in an operation they've coined "ethnic cleansing." In this genocide, in Bosnia-Herzegovina alone over 30,000 Muslim and Croatian girls and women are pregnant from mass rape. Of the 100 Serbian-run concentration camps, about 20 are solely rape/death camps for Muslim and Croatian women and children. . . . [There are] news reports and pictures here of Serbian tanks plastered with pornography . . . [and reports that those who] catch the eye of the men looking at the pornography are killed. . . . Some massacres in villages as well as rapes and/or executions in camps are being videotaped as they're happening. One Croatian woman described being tortured by electric-shocks and gang-raped in a camp by Serbian men dressed in Croatian uniforms who filmed the rapes and forced her to "confess" on film that Croatians raped her. In the streets of Zagreb, UN troops often ask local women how much they cost. . . . There are reports of refugee women being forced to sexually service them to receive aid. . . . Tomorrow I talk to two survivors of mass rape, thirty men per day for over three months. . . . The UN passed a resolution to collect

evidence, a first step for a war crimes trial, but it is said there is no precedent for trying sexual atrocities.[5]

Human rights were born in a cauldron, but it was not this one. Rape, forced motherhood, prostitution, pornography, and sexual murder, on the basis of sex and ethnicity together, have not been the horrors which so "outraged the conscience"[6] of the relevant legal world as to imprint themselves on the international legal order.

Formally illegal or not, as policy or merely as what is systematically done, practices of sexual and reproductive abuse occur not only in wartime but also on a daily basis in one form or another in every country in the world. Under domestic and international law, whether or not prohibited on their face, these practices are widely permitted as the liberties of their perpetrators, understood as excesses of passion or spoils of victory, legally rationalized or officially winked at or formally condoned.[7] Even where international instruments could be interpreted to prohibit such practices, it is telling that their cultural supports are more likely to provide the basis for exempting states from their reach than the foundation for a claim of sex discrimination.[8]

The war against Croatia and Bosnia-Herzegovina exemplifies how existing approaches to human rights can work to cover up and confuse who is doing what to whom and effectively condone atrocities. All state parties are apparently covered by most of the relevant international human rights guarantees and laws of war, certainly by customary international law.[9] But nothing has yet been invoked to stop the abuses described in the communication or to hold the perpetrators accountable.[10] What is the problem? The fact of Serbian aggression is beyond question, just as the fact of male aggression against women is beyond question, here and everywhere. "Ethnic cleansing" is a Serbian policy of extermination of non-Serbs with the goal of "all Serbs in one nation," a "Greater Serbia" encompassing what was called Yugo-slavia.[11] "Ethnic cleansing" is a euphemism for genocide. Yet this genocidal war of aggression has repeatedly been con-strued as bilateral, a civil war or an ethnic conflict, to the accompaniment of much international wonderment that peo-ple cannot get along and pious clucking at the behavior of "all sides"[12] in a manner reminiscent of blaming women for get-ting themselves raped by men they know. To call this a civil war is like calling the Holocaust a civil war between German Aryans and German Jews.

One result of this equalization of aggressor with ag-gressed-against is that these rapes are not grasped either as a strategy in genocide or as a practice of misogyny, far less as both at once, continuous at once with *this* ethnic war of aggression and with *the* gendered war of aggression of every-day life. This war is to everyday rape what the Holocaust was to everyday anti-Semitism. Muslim and Croatian women and girls are raped, then murdered, by Serbian military men, regulars and irregulars, in their homes, in rape/death camps, on hillsides, everywhere. Their corpses are often raped as well.[13] When this is noticed, it is either as genocide or as rape, or as femicide but not genocide, but not as rape as a form of genocide directed specifically at women. It is seen either as part of a campaign of Serbia against non-Serbia or an on-slaught by combatants against civilians, but not an attack by men against women. Or, in the feminist whitewash, it be-comes just another instance of aggression by all men against all women all the time, rather than what it is, which is rape by certain men against certain women. The point seems to be to obscure, by any means available, exactly who is doing what to whom and why.[14]

When the women survive, the rapes tend to be regarded as an inevitability of armed conflict, part of the war of all against all, or as a continuation of the hostilities of civil life, of all men against all women. Rape *does* occur in war among and between all sides; rape is a daily act by men against women and is always an act of domination by men over women. But the fact that these rapes are part of an ethnic war of extermination, being misrepresented as a civil war among equal aggressors,[15] means that Muslim and Croatian women are facing twice as many rapists with twice as many excuses, two layers of men on top of them rather than one, and two layers of impunity serving to justify the rapes: just war and just life.

Like all rapes, these rapes are particular as well as generic, and the particularity matters. This is ethnic rape as an official policy of war:[16] not only a policy of the pleasure of male power unleashed; not only a policy to defile, torture, humiliate, degrade, and demoralize the other side; not only a policy of men posturing to gain advantage and ground over other men. It is rape under orders: not out of control, under control. It is rape unto death, rape as massacre, rape to kill or make the victims wish they were dead. It is rape as an instrument of forced exile, to make you leave your home and never come back. It is rape to be seen and heard by others, rape as spectacle. It is rape to shatter a people, to drive a wedge through a community. It is the rape of misogyny liberated by xenophobia and unleashed by official command.[17]

It is rape made sexy for the perpetrators by the defenselessness and youth of many of the victims and the rapists' absolute power to select victims at will. It is rape made more arousing by ethnic hostility against a designated enemy— "For Serbia"—and made to seem right by lies about the behavior of that enemy. It is rape made exciting by knowing that there are no limits on what can be done, that the women *can* be raped to death. Most of all, it is rape made sexually irresistible by the fact that the women *are* about to be sacrificed, by the ultimate power of reducing a person to a corpse, by the powerlessness of the women and children in the face of their imminent murder at the hands of their rapist. It is murder as the ultimate sexual act. Do not say it is not sex for the men. When the men are told to take the women away and not bring them back, they rape them, *then* kill them, then sometimes rape them again, cut off their breasts, and rip out their wombs.[18] One woman was allowed to live so long as she kept her Serbian captor hard all night orally, night after night after night.[19]

This is rape as torture and rape as extermination. Some women who are not killed speak of wanting to take their own lives. It is at once mass rape and serial rape indistinguishable from prostitution. It is concentration camp as brothel: women impounded to be passed around by men among men.[20] It is also rape as a policy of ethnic uniformity and ethnic conquest, annexation and expansion, acquisition by one nation of others, colonization of women's bodies as colonization of the culture they symbolize and embody as well as of the territory they occupy. It is rape because a Serb wants your apartment. Most distinctively, it is rape for reproduction *as* ethnic liquidation: Croatian and Muslim women are raped to help make a Serbian state by making Serbian babies.[21]

This is ethnic rape. If this were racial rape, it would be pure pollution, the children regarded as dirty and contaminated: their mothers' babies, as in the American South under slavery, Black babies. Because it is ethnic rape, the children are regarded as clean and purified: their fathers' babies, Serbian babies, as clean as anyone with a woman's blood in them and on them can be. The idea seems to be to create a fifth column within Croatian and Muslim society, children (all sons?) who will rise up and join their fathers. Much Serbian ideology and practice takes a page from the Nazi book. Combining with it the archaic view that the sperm carries all the genetic material, the Serbs have achieved the ultimate racialization of culture, the (one hopes) final conclusion of Nazism: now culture is genetic.

The spectacle of the United Nations troops violating the population they are supposed to protect adds a touch of the perverse. My correspondent observes that "there are . . . reports of UN troops participating in raping Muslim and Croatian women from the Serb rape/death camps. Their presence has apparently increased trafficking in women and girls through the opening of brothels, brothel-massage parlors, peep-shows, and the local production of pornographic films."[23] A former United Nations Protection Force (UN-PROFOR) commander reportedly accepted offers from Serbian commanders to bring him Muslim girls from the camps for orgies.[24] This paradigmatic instance of the male bond across official lines pointedly poses, in the gender context, Juvenal's question of who shall guard the guardians—especially when the guardians are already there to guard the other guardians. The Nazis took pictures, but in its sophisticated employment of media technology, in the openness of its use of pornography, in its conscious making of pornography of its atrocities, this is perhaps the first truly modern war.[25]

Where do international human rights and humanitarian law stand on this? In real terms, the rules that govern the law's treatment of women elsewhere pertain here as well: A human is not one who is sexually and reproductively violated. One is not human "down there." Nor is a human right something a man in society or in a state of nature takes away from you and others like you. In fact, there are no others like you, because "a man" defines what "an individual" means, and human rights are mostly "individual" rights. Men have their human rights violated; rather, when someone's human rights are recognized as violated, he is probably a man. Men are permitted to be individuals, so can be violated as individuals. If you are hurt as a member of a group, the odds that the group will be considered human are improved if it includes men. Under guarantees of international human rights, as well as in everyday life, a woman is "not yet a name for a way of being human."[26]

A right, as this legal definition is lived in reality, becomes something no woman, as a member of the group women, has to lose. A right is also something only an entity with the power of a nation can violate; it is a duty of government not to interfere with civil and political liberties as they socially exist. The role of international law has been largely, in Isaiah Berlin's sense,[27] negative. It could be more, but it fosters human rights less through mandating governmental intervention than through enforcing governmental abstinence. In other words, if your human rights are going to be violated, pray it is by someone who looks like a government, and that he already acted, and acted wrong.

In Europe, some basis exists for interpreting international law to require that governments act; the affirmative state is more congenial to the European legal tradition in any case.[28] Sometimes international human rights law is stretched to countenance action against private violations, but this is pursued selectively. Honduras was held responsible for murders by private death squads that both acted as if they were official and were officially permitted to operate.[29] "Mainstream human rights groups have taken on the phenomenon of 'disappearances' in Argentina, murder of indigenous rubber tappers in Brazil, and racially-motivated hate crimes—all abuses perpetrated by private individuals," notes Lori Heise, "but when it comes to the beating and murder of millions of women each year, their hands are tied."[30]

Male reality has become human rights principle, or at least the principle governing human rights practice. Men have and take liberties as a function of their social power as men. Men have often needed state force to get away with subjecting other men; slavery, segregation in the United States, and Hitler's persecutions were explicitly legalized. So the model of human rights violation is based on state action. The result is, when men use their liberties socially to deprive women of theirs, it does not look like a human rights violation. But when men are deprived of theirs by governments, it does. The violations of the human rights of men better fit the paradigm of human rights violations because that paradigm has been based on the experiences of men.

In the case of women, by contrast, because male dominance is built into the social structure, social force is often enough. States collaborate elaborately, not just by abdicating social life but by intervening legally to entitle men to much of the power they socially exercise, legitimating what men can get away with in fact. Even recognizing active state involvement, most women are not directly raped, forcibly impregnated, and trafficked by state policy, at least not most of the time. Although the state in some way stands behind most of what men do to women, men typically have enough power to control and violate women without the state explicitly intervening to allow it. To this extent, women are not seen as subjected by the state as such, so their condition is regarded as prelegal, social hence natural, so outside international human rights accountability.

Now consider that most human rights instruments empower states to act against states, rather than individuals or groups to act on their own behalf. Given that only state violations of human rights are recognized, this is very odd. States are the only ones recognized as violating human rights, yet states are also the only ones empowered to redress them. Not only are men's so-called "private" acts against women left out; power to act against public acts are left exclusively in the hands of those who commit those acts. No state effectively guarantees women's human rights within its borders. No state has an incentive to break ranks by setting a human rights standard for women's status and treatment that no state yet meets. Internationally, men's states protect each other the way men protect each other from accountability for violations of women within states. At least this is one explanation for the failure of international human rights law effectively to empower individuals or groups of women to enforce their own human rights against individuals and states alike.[31] Which state is in a position to challenge another state on women's human rights? Which state ever will?

Wartime is largely exceptional in that atrocities by soldiers against civilians are always state acts. But men do in war what they do in peace, only more so. When it comes to women, at least to civilian casualties, the complacency that surrounds peacetime extends to war, however the laws read. And the more a conflict can be framed as *within* a state, as a civil war, as social, as domestic, the less human rights are recognized as being violated.[32] In other words, the closer a fight comes to home, the more "feminized" the victims become no matter what their gender, and the less likely international human rights will be found to be violated, no matter what was done.[33]

II

The received concepts at work here have a complex history, mostly a Western one, which can be read and compressed as follows. The contractarian liberals, building on Greek and Roman antecedents, opposed medieval status notions that assigned human value within a rigid hierarchy based on birth. Seeking to secure human freedom against state tyranny, they posited the radical notion that each person, qua human, had, meaning had by nature, irrevocable and equal entitlements to life, liberty, security, dignity, property, and so on. Through the American and French revolutions, this idea of inalienable human worth called individual rights was entrenched, checking organized power in the form of government. Subsequently, some transnational agreements further elevated and enshrined the same recognitions as binding among state parties.

Then the Third Reich utterly violated all such rights—inter alia by manipulating the pre-1945 system which left minority protection exclusively to states[33]—isolating and then liquidating those it saw as inferior or polluting or oppositional. In particular, the official attempted extermination of the Jews as a people galvanized the notion of supranational guarantees of human rights with a survival urgency. This organized genocide by government policy indelibly marked and fundamentally shaped the content, priorities, sensitivities, and deep structure of the received law of human rights in our time. In a reading of this reality, more than any other, contemporary human rights finds its principled ground.

Largely beneath notice in this tradition has been the status of women as such, socially subordinated to men and excluded or ignored, marginalized or subjected by state policy. Women's enforced inequality has been a reality on which all these systems are materially predicated, so seamlessly it has been invisible. Women were not citizens in Greek democracy; they were wives, slaves, prostitutes.[34] In this setting, Aristotle formulated his equality principle as treating likes alike and unlikes unalike—a concept fundamentally unquestioned since, including in the international human rights context. In this approach, it does not matter whether one is hurt or helped, permitted to dominate or kept subordinated; all that matters is that empirical condition, no matter how created, fits normative treatment.[35] That women were apparently so different to Aristotle as not to be treated unequally under his principle when excluded from citizenship has not been considered a drawback or an indication that something is amiss.

Building on this tradition, the original liberals formulated their social compacts in and for societies in which women could not even vote. With the exception of John Stuart Mill,[36] they did not see a problem in this, projecting their purportedly universal notions of what have come to be called human rights in ways that did not explicitly include women and effectively kept most women from access to them. Humans own property; women mostly cannot; more often they are property. Humans are equal because they can kill; women are socialized not to kill and are punished, not glorified, when they do. Humans consent to a regime or leave it; women have no voice to dissent, no place to go, and no means of leaving.[37] At the same time, guarantees women specifically need, due to sex inequality in society, in order to live to a standard defined as human—like freedom from being bought and sold as sexual chattel, autonomous economic means, reproductive control, personal security from intimate invasion, a credible voice in public life, a nonderivative place in the world—were not considered at all.

What women need for equality was not only not guaranteed; much of women's inequality was guaranteed in the form of men's individual civil liberties.[38] In these theories, abuses of women were tacitly if not explicitly condoned as individual rights. What were called individual rights have become, in life, rights of men as a group over women individually and as a class. Women's rape becomes men's liberty, gang rape their fraternity, prostitution their property, forced pregnancy their family and their privacy, pornography their speech. Put another way, whatever their rebellions accomplished for human freedom, and it was substantial, the American Revolution did not free the slaves, and the French Revolution did free the Marquis de Sade—facts connected by legitimating a traffic in human beings and the sexual abuse of women for economic gain. Understand: This is what the received concept of equality meant and largely still means.

Because women are a group whose claim to human status is tenuous and denied, the attempt to apply human rights law to women as such makes two more general problems worse. Human rights have no ground and no teeth. As to teeth, human rights are enforced internationally primarily between states, states that agree to them. Many, such as the United States, do not agree to many of them. Enforcement is mainly through reporting, meaning moral force, meaning effective nonenforcement. Signatory countries are even permitted formal excuse from compliance, a practice disproportionately used to evade sex equality provisions.[39] The covenants against trafficking in women, for example, are many and venerable,[40] yet the traffic continues unabated, untouched, flourishing. Thailand even traffics in women by policy.[41] China may officially force abortions and sterilizations,[42] yet nothing is done. Enforcement of human rights against states' lack of action and against private parties may be possible in principle but is virtually absent in practice. For women, international human rights presents the biggest gap between principle and practice in the known legal world.

Many existing international instruments guarantee sex equality.[43] Yet so little of women's experience of violation of human rights has been brought under them that it becomes necessary to inquire into the foundations of human rights to explain why. The primary foundation of human rights has been natural law, a secular religion that moves only those who believe in it. Its content tends to redescribe the social status quo and attribute it to nature. (Emphatic use of the existential verb to affirm loudly and often that women "are" human beings carries only the clout of its speaker's decibel level.) Positive law helps little more, since women have had little voice in its formulation in most places. Morality, an alternative ground, can be moving, but does not mean anyone has to do anything, as illustrated by the use of the phrase "moral victory" to refer to an actual defeat. All these grounds come down to social power in the end. If you have it, you can meet their tests for "human"; but power is exactly what women are socially denied, which is why their human rights can be violated and why they need them recognized.

At its philosophical foundations, the natural law tradition on which human rights remain primarily based has never been clear on whether women are men's natural equals. Rather, to oversimplify a complicated debate, it has been relatively clear that they are not, and has provided no method for resolving different conclusions, each equally firmly said to be predicated on the law of nature. Nor has it reconciled its observation that sex is a natural difference with its view that equality is predicated on natural identity. To those who ground human rights in the opportunity to live out one's life project rationally,[44] it should be pointed out that, socially speaking, women as women have not been permitted a life project[45] and are widely considered as not possessed of rationality, or of what passes for reason among men. Others ground human rights in basic personal liberty[46] or in fundamental human dignity,[47] the problem being that you already have to have them to have a human right violated when you are denied them. So, it's back to nature.

Mortimer Adler exemplifies rather than exposes this circularity: "If there are no natural rights, there are no human rights; if there are no human rights, there cannot be any crimes against humanity."[48] Women's problem has been that society and law do not agree that nature made them human, so nothing that is done to them is a crime against humanity, because they have none. If society gives you no rights, such that a state need never deny them to keep you from having them, it may do you little good to have them formally guaranteed in international law. Free of this essentialist circularity, the task is to ground a claim to crimes against humanity clear of natural rights, which are not recognized to exist in nature unless they are recognized to exist in society. In other words, all discourse about nature is a social discourse.

Horror at the Holocaust grounds modern morality. No one knows what is good, but nearly everyone knows the Holocaust was evil. We may not know what human is; but the Holocaust was inhuman. Jewish women were distinctively abused in ways that connect to anti-Semitic misogyny to this day and startlingly resemble the tortures of Croatian and Muslim women by Serbs. The horrific tortures and extermination of millions of Jews of both sexes because they were Jews has overshadowed everything then and since.

Considered in terms of equality theory, the Third Reich can be seen to follow an unbroken line from Aristotle through American segregation of treating "likes alike and unlikes unalike"—Jews having been rendered "unlike" Aryans.[49] Yet human rights law still uses the same equality concept, without reassessment. The dominant lesson that seems to have been learned is that Jews could be and were annihilated because they were "different," not that something is wrong with an equality standard that permits extermination for "differences." The Jews failed the equality test—not the equality test failed the Jews. Not that a better equality theory would have stopped Hitler. But what is one to make of an equality principle apparently logically consistent with, and undisturbed by, genocide? If equality's abstractions are so receptive to Nazi substance, are they perhaps a flawed vehicle for social justice? The fact that international law pervasively guarantees sex equality, yet there is no sex equality, while mass rape and forced childbearing go on both in peacetime and in war, including in genocidal war, suddenly begins to makes sense.

III

[T]he refusal to demand . . . one absolute standard of human dignity is the greatest triumph of antifeminism over

> the will to liberation. . . . A universal standard of human
> dignity is the only principle that completely repudiates sex-
> class exploitation and also propels all of us into a future
> where the fundamental political question is the quality of life
> for all human beings. —*Andrea Dworkin*[50]

One approach to this problem might be to interpret existing
international sex equality guarantees as grounded in the
global women's movement against sex inequality, including
sexual and reproductive abuses, and apply the resulting concepts in peace and in war. A right to equality, both as a right
in itself and as a basis for equal access to other rights, would
ground its definition of inequality, and by implication its
concept of the human, in the universal—meaning worldwide
and everywhere spontaneously indigenous—movement for
women's rights. The reality recognized by this movement is
generating new principles: new in content, form, reach, operation, and relation to social life.

In law, the principles of this movement are best approx-
imated in North American equality law, pioneered by the
Black movement in the United States in the 1960s and 1970s
and the women's movement in Canada in the 1980s and
1990s. These equality rights are implemented by individuals
and groups against other individuals and groups as well as by
and against governments. They allow governments to proceed but do not limit to governments the ability to act against
discrimination. They allow complaints for indirect and systemic inequality. To be fully realized, they call for relief
against state inaction as well as action. Such devices add
enforcement potential rather than let states off the hook.

In the received international human rights tradition, by
contrast, equality has been more abstract than concrete, more
transcendant than secular, more descended from natural law
than admittedly socially based. The Universal Declaration of
Human Rights grants equality "without distinction of any

kind,"[51] as if distinction were the problem and lack of distinction the solution. The Convention on Elimination of All Forms of Discrimination Against Women defines discrimination against women largely in gender neutral and referential terms, guaranteeing enjoyment of all other rights "on a basis of equality of men and women."[52] This has mostly been interpreted nonsubstantively, has not allowed claims by individuals or groups, claims against government inaction, or against private parties. The Committee that oversees it is coming to recognize, however, that violence against women is a form of sex discrimination and seeks to make states responsible for "private acts" if they fail to prevent, investigate, or punish discriminatory acts of violence.[53] All the Committee does is report.[54]

As a basis for an expanded equality principle, women's resistance to sex inequality is ubiquitous and everywhere concrete and socially specific. It is not based on being the same as men but on resistance to violation and abuse and second-class citizenship because one is a woman. It starts close to home. African women oppose genital mutilation. Philippine, Thai, Japanese, and Swedish women organize against the sex trade. Women in Papua New Guinea, the United States, and workers at the United Nations resist sexual harassment. Brazilian and Italian women protest domestic battery and "honor" as a male excuse for killing them. Indian women protest "dowry" and "suttee" as a male excuse for killing them. American women protest domestic battery and romantic love as a male excuse for killing them. Canadian women protest the use of "feminism" as a male excuse for killing them. Women everywhere rise up against rape, even in cultures where women have recently been regarded as chattel. Women in the United States, Scandinavia, and the Philippines resist pornography. Forced motherhood is opposed from Ireland to Germany to Bangladesh. Female infanticide and objectifying advertising are legislated against in India. Everywhere women seek access to literacy, which they have often been denied as women, and to survival based on the work they do, as well as access to doing all kinds of work.[55]

One feature of this movement is its combination of socially specific comparison—men are not treated this way—with its refusal to be limited to imitating or emulating men. Women's diversity is extraordinary, yet everywhere, with social particularity, below some man. This produces an appreciation for the fact that difference by itself is certainly not the excuse for second-class citizenship it has become, but that imposed inferiority is everything. The movement criticizes socially organized power itself, as well as its excesses.

This movement has produced a rich concept of equality as lack of hierarchy, not sameness. Its everywhere relative universality, its refusal to settle for anything less than a single standard of human dignity and entitlement, and its demand for elevation in that standard have left Aristotle in the dust. The scope and depth of this uprising for social equality offers a neglected ground for sex equality as a human right. The movement provides a principled basis in social reality for women's human rights, for a positive equality. Its principles include: If you do not do it to each other, you cannot do it to us; and ending the subordination of women because they are women.

"Civil rights" has been considered a subprovince of human rights, typically distinguished from political, social, economic, and cultural rights, as well as rights of personhood. A more embracing sense of equality is developing and being applied in North America, originating in the civil rights struggle of Blacks for social equality through legal equality in the United States and extending to its current pinnacle formulation in the Supreme Court of Canada's equality jurisprudence originating in the women's movement. This equality is not confined to equal access to other rights, as it is in international human rights law[56] and most domestic equality law, but is a principle in its own right. This equality looks to social context, broadly and in each particular, to eliminate imposed stratification. It envisions an active role for equality law in implementing the necessary changes.

In Canada, the approach takes the form of requiring that laws "promote equality." This "entails the promotion of a society" of equal dignity and respect. "It has a large remedial component."[57] It recognizes that social inequality *exists* and must be changed, rather than assuming a neutral and equal social world and avoiding legal differentiation to preserve it. It is based on noticing the reality of inequality in order to end it, rather than on enforcing a "color blindness" and gender neutrality, which have often meant a blindness to the unequal realities of color and gender. This mandate is interpreted with particular sensitivity to, and priority upon, eliminating the inequality of groups that have traditionally been socially disadvantaged.

This equality looks to "civil society" on the level of ordinary transactions and interactions: buying and selling, work and education and accommodations, home and the street, communications and insurance, as well as voting, elections, and juries. It encompasses segregated toilets and teaching racial hatred, sexual coercion by doctors, and denial of pregnancy benefits. It is rooted in everyday life, looking beyond the legal formalism of formal equality to social consequences. It understands that although inequality hurts individuals, it only hurts them as members of social groups. It addresses the most systemic inequalities, as well as ones that happen only to a few individuals. It practices a social, contextual, relational, antihierarchical equality jurisprudence.

As currently defined, international human rights are so

abstract that people who concretely believe polar opposites can agree on them on principle and give them equally to no one. Both a Stalin and a Solzhenitsyn can embrace them. That neither would likely favor civil rights as described here suggests the tension between such civil rights and "human rights" as currently conceived, in particular between abstract "human rights" equality and substantive "civil rights" equality. Civil rights begin at home or close to it; human rights seem to improve the further one gets from home. By a preference for direct civil remedies in the hands of the unequal, civil rights distribute power from government to people as they redistribute power among people. Human rights tend to see the state as the enemy of equality; civil rights see it as their potential promoter. Human rights locate equality in eliminating irrational differentiation; civil rights see equality as much in affirmative claims of cultural particularity, in ending oppression whether based on real differences or not, and in altering the mainstream to accommodate an uncompromised diversity.

The current political force of the mainstream human rights view takes its deep text, on my analysis, from a reading of the Nazi experience: Survival lies in blending in, in being indistinguishable from one's surroundings, in nondifferentiation. Cast in equality terms, instead of criticizing the view that killed you for being different, you fight for the right to be recognized as the same and to become the same because it will keep you alive. So many Polish Jews died, it is said, because they only spoke Yiddish. They could not "pass" as not Jews. Aryan-appearing German Jews were more likely to survive. It should follow that assimilation—sameness—guarantees an equal right to live, not to be exterminated because of who you are. This is nonarbitrary recognition for meeting the dominant standard, integration over self-determination. Do not think about whether integration is ultimately possible; do not think about those who will never be permitted to meet the standards; do not challenge the standards themselves.

An analogy could be drawn to the psychology of battered women, which is also a dimension of femininity more generally. The only reality is the power of the abuser; keeping your head low keeps you alive. This, too, acquiesces in the dominant standard and concedes the permanent powerlessness of an underclass. The shame of being who you are—as if that is validly and forever the real reason for subordination—leads to always wanting and trying to become who you are not, which women know as living a lie until you become it. This is the victim-side adaptation to the perpetrator-defined reality. It converges with the final solution to the inequality problem: annihilation.

This is the equality of Aristotle, of the Enlightenment, of the Nazis, of mainstream U.S. equality jurisprudence today, and of international human rights law. It seems rather late in the pursuit of equality to seek fair conditions of extermination on the basis of speaking Polish or looking German. It is like a battered woman seeking not to be beaten by serving dinner on time and providing regular sex. Such equality does nothing about the annihilation machine itself, so long as it sorts likes from unlikes accurately. It may mean survival for some under unequal conditions, but do not call it equality. Such equality means conceding the standards under which one is measured, monitoring only their recognition without irrational distinction. One can understand trying to construct an equality principle to ensure survival under conditions of genocide; yet this is very close to conceding genocidal conditions in the construction of the equality principle, with the result that, so far as the equality principle is concerned, we will never live under any but genocidal conditions.

How equality is defined in the North American movements, by contrast, is self-respecting but not isolationist, self-determinant but not segregationist, uncompromised but not absolutist, solid at the core but forgiving at the edges. Its equality is not absolute but relative to the best society has to offer, insisting on an expanded role for the subordinated in redefining standards from the point of view of those living under them. Such a theory may appear to lack principled definition, grounded as it is in response to an unprincipled social world. Perhaps if white men had been lynched, as Black men were in the American South, this would be more of a problem; the fact is, they were not. Given that no society systematically traffics in men as men for sex, rapes men at will and with impunity, forces men to reproduce, batters men in homes, sometimes to death, on an everyday basis, pays men as a group less than women, or presents male sexuality in demeaned ways for entertainment and profit on a large scale, some comparative dimension to the standard has a lot to offer. It also helps avoid imposing foreign cultural standards in diverse social settings.

In legal practice in Canada, this approach has proven capable of addressing a substantial number of realities of sex inequality that have eluded prior attempts. A woman has been permitted to sue her city police force for failure to warn of a serial rapist.[58] Sexual harassment[59] and pregnancy discrimination[60] have been recognized as human rights violations. Under the tutelage if not the direct control of this approach, common law remedies for sexual abuse have recognized inequalities of power[61] and statutes of limitations for incest have been revised based on the experience of victims.[62] Criminal laws against wife battering have been interpreted to recognize the woman's reality[63] and publication of the names of sexual assault victims has been prohibited.[64] When the Court refused to recognize women's equality right to keep their sexual histories out of rape trials,[65] a whole new rape law was introduced to remedy it.[66] Significant decisions have also been made in light of this approach in the area of reproductive rights, preventing men from gaining a veto over women's abortions[67] and recognizing women's rights in and over their fetuses.[68] Perhaps most tellingly, when the rights to freedom of expression of anti-Semites and pornographers were balanced against the equality rights of their targeted victims, equality won.[69] In Canada, some of the reality of inequality is becoming the basis for the legal equality principle.

IV

Against this backdrop, what will become of the Muslim and Croatian women violated by the Serbs? The basis in a women's movement for a meaningful equality interpretation exists. Since November 1991, feminists in Zagreb in particular have been working with refugee survivors of the sexual atrocities of genocide through war. Their accountability to the victims has been continuous and absolute, their documentation and relief effort committed and accurate.[70] If jurisdiction can be secured, and it should be able to be, laws do exist to cover many of the atrocities.[71] Rape, enforced prostitution, and indecent assault are already recognized as war crimes.[72] There is even precedent for trying them.[73] After World War II, Japanese generals were tried for sexual atrocities committed under their command: rape, imprisonment of girls in hotels and subjecting them to repeated rape, mass rape, cutting off breasts, killing women civilians and raping their corpses.[74] Other than the breeding aspect, this has happened in wars before, right down to tortures of fingers and feet.

There are many more examples in which nothing was done: "the mass rapes of women during the war for independence in Bangladesh, the systematic rape of women suspected of complicity in the insurgency in Kashmir, and the belated but growing scandal concerning the 'comfort women' who were abducted and forced into prostitution by the Japanese army during the Second World War."[75] Evidence on rape was presented by the French and Soviet prosecutors at Nuremburg.[76] Sexual forms of torture were documented,[77] but sexual assault was not charged in the indictments. One can only speculate that it was not seen to be within the tribunal's emphasis "not on individual barbarities and perversions" but only on the Nazi "Common Plan."[78] Rape has so often been treated as extracurricular, as just something men do, as a product rather than a policy of war.

Proceeding through war crimes tribunals on behalf of Muslim and Croatian women would create accountability but it would not redistribute power to women in situations other than war. On the civil side of human rights, these atrocities violate every sex equality guarantee in international law, properly interpreted, and they do not fail to do so because this is wartime. Surely this is a "consistent pattern of mass violation of human rights."[79] Perhaps this would be a good occasion to use equality guarantees to address violence against women; there is no state action problem. Such an approach could establish precedents for use by women in peacetime as well.

As a practical matter, it helps that these incidents happened in a war. Men know men hurt men in war, so maybe there is an analogy? It does not help for recognizing them now, or for creating a precedent that could effect nonwar interpretations, that similar acts are common everywhere in peacetime and are widely understood as sex. Yugoslavia's pornography market was "the freest in the world"[80] before this male population was officially mobilized to commit the atrocities they had already been sexually conditioned to enjoy. It does help that men did these acts in declared military groups, instead of one on one everywhere at once and all the time, or in small packs, murdering, raping, pimping, and breeding but not recognized as an army of occupation. Will there be command responsibility for these rapes? Will women have to identify each individual man, often numbering in the hundreds, who raped them? It does not help that no state raped these women and got them pregnant; it does help that a state's men did.[81]

Will these atrocities be seen as human rights abuses? If the Muslims were Jews, would the world be allowing this to happen? Must a group first survive genocide for it to be recognized next time? Will principle see reality? Will it connect with similar acts in everyday life? The murders maybe; the rapes possibly, and if so, probably because they are ethnic, hurting a group that includes men; the pregnancies, less likely (and what to do with the children?); the prostitution, for all the twenty-two treaties against it, little chance; the pornography never, meaning if ever, probably not soon.

Or will this situation and these women, here and now, be the time and place in which the word "woman," like the word "Jew," will finally come to stand, among its meanings, for a reality of abuse that cannot be forgotten, a triumph of survival against all that wanted you dead, a principle of what cannot be done to a human being? Will women, at last, get amnesty?

HUMAN RIGHTS, RATIONALITY, AND SENTIMENTALITY

Richard Rorty

In a report from Bosnia some months ago,[1] David Rieff said "To the Serbs, the Muslims are no longer human. . . . Muslim prisoners, lying on the ground in rows, awaiting interrogation, were driven over by a Serb guard in a small delivery van." This theme of dehumanization recurs when Rieff says

> A Muslim man in Bosansi Petrovac . . . [was] forced to bite off the penis of a fellow-Muslim. . . . If you say that a man is not human, but the man looks like you and the only way to identify this devil is to make him drop his trousers—Muslim men are circumcised and Serb men are not—it is probably only a short step, psychologically, to cutting off his prick. . . . There has never been a campaign of ethnic cleansing from which sexual sadism has gone missing.

The moral to be drawn from Rieff's stories is that Serbian murderers and rapists do not think of themselves as violating human rights. For they are not doing these things to fellow human beings, but to *Muslims*. They are not being inhuman, but rather are discriminating between the true humans and the pseudohumans. They are making the same sort of distinction as the Crusaders made between humans and infidel dogs, and the Black Muslims make between humans and blue-eyed devils. The founder of my university was able both to own slaves and to think it self-evident that all men were endowed by their creator with certain inalienable rights. He had convinced himself that the consciousness of Blacks, like that of animals, "participate[s] more of sensation than reflection."[2] Like the Serbs, Mr. Jefferson did not think of himself as violating *human* rights.

The Serbs take themselves to be acting in the interests of true humanity by purifying the world of pseudohumanity. In this respect, their self-image resembles that of moral philosophers who hope to cleanse the world of prejudice and superstition. This cleansing will permit us to rise above our animality by becoming, for the first time, wholly rational and thus wholly human. The Serbs, the moralists, Jefferson, and the Black Muslims all use the term "men" to mean "people like us." They think the line between humans and animals is not simply the line between featherless bipeds and all others. They think the line divides some featherless bipeds from others: There are animals walking about in humanoid form. We and those like us are paradigm cases of humanity, but those too different from us in behavior or custom are, at best, borderline cases. As Clifford Geertz puts it, "Men's most importunate claims to humanity are cast in the accents of group pride."[3]

We in the safe, rich, democracies feel about the Serbian torturers and rapists as they feel about their Muslim victims: They are more like animals than like us. But we are not doing anything to help the Muslim women who are being gang raped or the Muslim men who are being castrated, any more than we did anything in the thirties when the Nazis were amusing themselves by torturing Jews. Here in the safe countries we find ourselves saying things like "That's how things have always been in the Balkans," suggesting that, unlike us, those people are used to being raped and castrated. The contempt we always feel for losers—Jews in the thirties, Muslims now—combines with our disgust at the winners' behavior to produce the semiconscious attitude: "a plague on both your houses." We think of the Serbs or the Nazis as animals, because ravenous beasts of prey are animals. We think of the Muslims or the Jews being herded into concentration camps as animals, because cattle are animals. Neither sort of animal is very much like us, and there seems no point in human beings getting involved in quarrels between animals.

The human–animal distinction, however, is only one of the three main ways in which we paradigmatic humans distinguish ourselves from borderline cases. A second is by invoking the distinction between adults and children. Ignorant and superstitious people, we say, are like children; they will attain true humanity only if raised up by proper education. If they seem incapable of absorbing such education, that shows they are not really the same kind of being as we educable people are. Blacks, the whites in the United States and in South Africa used to say, are like children. That is why it is appropriate to address Black males, of whatever age, as "boy." Women, men used to say, are permanently childlike; it is therefore appropriate to spend no money on their education, and to refuse them access to power.

When it comes to women, however, there are simpler ways of excluding them from true humanity: for example, using "man" as a synonym of "human being." As feminists have pointed out, such usages reinforce the average male's thankfulness that he was not born a woman, as well as his fear of the ultimate degradation: feminization. The extent of the latter fear is evidenced by the particular sort of sexual sadism Rieff describes. His point that such sadism is never absent from attempts to purify the species or cleanse the territory confirms Catharine MacKinnon's claim that, for most men, being a woman does not count as a way of being human. Being a nonmale is the third main way of being nonhuman. There are several ways of being nonmale. One is to be born without a penis; another is to have one's penis cut or bitten off; a third is to have been penetrated by a penis. Many men who have been raped are convinced that their manhood, and thus their humanity, has been taken away. Like racists who discover they have Jewish or Black ancestry, they may commit suicide out of sheer shame, shame at no longer being the kind of featherless biped that counts as human.

Philosophers have tried to clear this mess up by spelling out what all and only the featherless bipeds have in common, thereby explaining what is essential to being human. Plato argued that there is a big difference between us and the animals, a difference worthy of respect and cultivation. He thought that human beings have a special added ingredient which puts them in a different ontological category than the brutes. Respect for this ingredient provides a reason for people to be nice to each other. Anti-Platonists like Nietzsche reply that attempts to get people to stop murdering, raping, and castrating each other are, in the long run, doomed to fail—for the real truth about human nature is that we are a uniquely nasty and dangerous kind of animal. When contemporary admirers of Plato claim that all featherless bipeds— even the stupid and childlike, even the women, even the sodomized—have the same inalienable rights, admirers of Nietzsche reply that the the very idea of "inalienable human rights" is, like the idea of a special added ingredient, a laughably feeble attempt by the weaker members of the species to fend off the stronger.

As I see it, one important intellectual advance made in our century is the steady decline in interest in the quarrel between Plato and Nietzsche. There is a growing willingness to neglect the question "What is our nature?" and to substitute the question "What can we make of ourselves?" We are much less inclined than our ancestors were to take "theories of human nature" seriously, much less inclined to take ontology or history as a guide to life. We have come to see that the only lesson of either history or anthropology is our extraordinary malleability. We are coming to think of ourselves as the flexible, protean, self-shaping, animal rather than as the rational animal or the cruel animal.

One of the shapes we have recently assumed is that of a human rights culture. I borrow the term "human rights culture" from the Argentinian jurist and philosopher Eduardo Rabossi. In an article called "Human Rights Naturalized," Rabossi argues that philosophers should think of this culture as a new, welcome fact of the post-Holocaust world. They should stop trying to get behind or beneath this fact, stop trying to detect and defend its so-called "philosophical pre-suppositions." On Rabossi's view, philosophers like Alan Gewirth are wrong to argue that human rights cannot depend on historical facts. "My basic point," Rabossi says, is that "the world has changed, that the human rights phenomenon renders human rights foundationalism outmoded and irrelevant."[4]

Rabossi's claim that human rights foundationalism is *outmoded* seems to me both true and important; it will be my principal topic in this lecture. I shall be enlarging on, and defending, Rabossi's claim that the question whether human beings really have the rights enumerated in the Helsinki Declaration is not worth raising. In particular, I shall be defending the claim that nothing relevant to moral choice separates human beings from animals except historically contingent facts of the world, cultural facts.

This claim is sometimes called "cultural relativism" by those who indignantly reject it. One reason they reject it is that such relativism seems to them incompatible with the fact that our human rights culture, the culture with which we in this democracy identify ourselves, is morally superior to other cultures. I quite agree that ours is morally superior, but I do not think this superiority counts in favor of the existence of a universal human nature. It would only do so if we assumed that a moral claim is ill-founded if not backed up by knowledge of a distinctively human attribute. But it is not clear why "respect for human dignity"—our sense that the differences between Serb and Muslim, Christian and infidel, gay and straight, male and female should not matter—must presuppose the existence of any such attribute.

Traditionally, the name of the shared human attribute which supposedly "grounds" morality is "rationality." Cultural relativism is associated with irrationalism because it denies the existence of morally relevant transcultural facts. To agree with Rabossi one must, indeed, be irrationalist in that sense. But one need not be irrationalist in the sense of ceasing to make one's web of belief as coherent, and as perspicuously structured, as possible. Philosophers like myself, who think of rationality as simply the attempt at such coherence, agree with Rabossi that foundationalist projects are outmoded. We see our task as a matter of making our own culture—the human rights culture—more self-conscious and more powerful, rather than of demonstrating its superiority to other cultures by an appeal to something transcultural.

We think that the most philosophy can hope to do is summarize our culturally influenced intuitions about the right thing to do in various situations. The summary is effected by formulating a generalization from which these intuitions can be deduced, with the help of noncontroversial lemmas. That generalization is not supposed to ground our intuitions, but rather to summarize them. John Rawls's "Difference Principle" and the U.S. Supreme Court's construction, in recent decades, of a constitutional "right to privacy" are examples of this kind of summary. We see the formulation of such summarizing generalizations as increasing the predictability, and thus the power and efficiency, of our institutions, thereby heightening the sense of shared moral identity which brings us together in a moral community.

Foundationalist philosophers, such as Plato, Aquinas, and Kant, have hoped to provide independent support for such summarizing generalizations. They would like to infer these generalizations from further premises, premises capable of being known to be true independently of the truth of the moral intuitions which have been summarized. Such premises are supposed to justify our intuitions, by providing premises from which the content of those intuitions can be deduced. I shall lump all such premises together under the label "claims to knowledge about the nature of human beings." In this broad sense, claims to know that our moral intuitions are recollections of the Form of the Good, or that we are the disobedient children of a loving God, or that human beings differ from other kinds of animals by having dignity rather than mere value, are all claims about human nature. So are such counterclaims as that human beings are merely vehicles for selfish genes, or merely eruptions of the will to power.

To claim such knowledge is to claim to know something which, though not itself a moral intuition, can *correct* moral intuitions. It is essential to this idea of moral knowledge that a whole community might come to know that most of their most salient intuitions about the right thing to do were wrong. But now suppose we ask: *Is* there this sort of knowledge? What kind of question is that? On the traditional view, it is a philosophical question, belonging to a branch of epistemology known as "metaethics." But on the pragmatist view which I favor, it is a question of efficiency, of how best to grab hold of history—how best to bring about the utopia sketched by the Enlightenment. If the activities of those who attempt to achieve this sort of knowledge seem of little use in actualizing this utopia, that is a reason to think there is no such knowledge. If it seems that most of the work of changing moral intuitions is being done by manipulating our feelings rather than increasing our knowledge, that will be a reason to think that there is no knowledge of the sort which philosophers like Plato, Aquinas, and Kant hoped to acquire.

This pragmatist argument against the Platonist has the same form as an argument for cutting off payment to the priests who are performing purportedly war-winning sacrifices—an argument which says that all the real work of winning the war seems to be getting done by the generals and admirals, not to mention the foot soldiers. The argument does not say: Since there seem to be no gods, there is probably no need to support the priests. It says instead: Since there is apparently no need to support the priests, there probably are no gods. We pragmatists argue from the fact that the emergence of the human rights culture seems to owe nothing to increased moral knowledge, and everything to hearing sad and sentimental stories, to the conclusion that there is probably no knowledge of the sort Plato envisaged. We go on to argue: Since no useful work seems to be done by insisting on a purportedly ahistorical human nature, there probably is no such nature, or at least nothing in that nature that is relevant to our moral choices.

In short, my doubts about the effectiveness of appeals to moral knowledge are doubts about causal efficacy, not about epistemic status. My doubts have nothing to do with any of the theoretical questions discussed under the heading of "metaethics," questions about the relation between facts and values, or between reason and passion, or between the cognitive and the noncognitive, or between descriptive statements and action-guiding statements. Nor do they have anything to do with questions about realism and antirealism. The difference between the moral realist and the moral antirealist seems to pragmatists to be a difference which makes no practical difference. Further, such metaethical questions presuppose the Platonic distinction between inquiry which aims at efficient problem-solving and inquiry which aims at a goal called "truth for its own sake." That distinction collapses if one follows Dewey in thinking of all inquiry—in physics as well as in ethics—as practical problem-solving, or if one follows Peirce in seeing every belief as action-guiding.[5]

Even after the priests have been pensioned off, however, the memories of certain priests may still be cherished by the community—especially the memories of their prophecies. We remain profoundly grateful to philosophers like Plato and Kant, not because they discovered truths but because they prophesied cosmopolitan utopias—utopias most of whose details they may have got wrong, but utopias we might never have struggled to reach had we not heard their prophecies. As long as our ability to know, and in particular to discuss the question "What is man?" seemed the most important thing

about us human beings, people like Plato and Kant accompa-
nied utopian prophecies with claims to know something deep
and important—something about the parts of the soul, or the
transcendental status of the common moral consciousness.
But this ability, and those questions, have, in the course of the
last two hundred years, come to seem much less important.
Rabossi summarizes this cultural sea change in his claim that
human rights foundationalism is outmoded. In the remainder
of this lecture, I shall take up the questions: *Why* has knowledge become much less important to our self-image than it
was two hundred years ago? Why does the attempt to found
culture on nature, and moral obligation on knowledge of
transcultural universals, seem so much less important to us
than it seemed in the Enlightenment? Why is there so little
resonance, and so little point, in asking whether human beings in fact have the rights listed in the Helsinki Declaration?
Why, in short, has moral philosophy become such an incon-
spicuous part of our culture?

A simple answer is that between Kant's time and ours
Darwin argued most of the intellectuals out of the view that
human beings contain a special added ingredient. He convinced most of us that we were exceptionally talented animals, animals clever enough to take charge of our own future
evolution. I think this answer is right as far as it goes, but
it leads to a further question: Why did Darwin succeed,
relatively speaking, so very easily? Why did he not cause
the creative philosophical ferment caused by Galileo and
Newton?

The revival by the New Science of the seventeenth century of a Democritean–Lucretian corpuscularian picture of
nature scared Kant into inventing transcendental philosophy,
inventing a brand-new kind of knowledge, which could de-
mote the corpuscularian world picture to the status of "appearance." Kant's example encouraged the idea that the philosopher, as an expert on the nature and limits of knowledge,

can serve as supreme cultural arbiter.[6] By the time of Darwin, however, this idea was already beginning to seem quaint. The historicism which dominated the intellectual world of the early nineteenth century had created an antiessentialist mood. So when Darwin came along, he fitted into the evolutionary niche which Herder and Hegel had begun to colonize. Intellectuals who populate this niche look to the future rather than to eternity. They prefer new ideas about how change can be effected to stable criteria for determining the desirability of change. They are the ones who think both Plato and Nietzsche outmoded.

The best explanation of both Darwin's relatively easy triumph, and our own increasing willingness to substitute hope for knowledge, is that the nineteenth and twentieth centuries saw, among the Europeans and Americans, an extraordinary increase in wealth, literacy, and leisure. This increase made possible an unprecedented acceleration in the rate of moral progress. Such events as the French Revolution and the ending of the trans-Atlantic slave trade prompted nineteenth-century intellectuals in the rich democracies to say: It is enough for us to know that we live in an age in which human beings can make things much better for ourselves.[7] We do not need to dig behind this historical fact to nonhistorical facts about what we really are.

In the two centuries since the French Revolution, we have learned that human beings are far more malleable than Plato or Kant had dreamed. The more we are impressed by this malleability, the less interested we become in questions about our ahistorical nature. The more we see a chance to recreate ourselves, the more we read Darwin not as offering one more theory about what we really are but as providing reasons why we need not ask what we really are. Nowadays, to say that we are clever animals is not to say something philosophical and pessimistic but something political and hopeful, namely: If we can work together, we can make ourselves into whatever we are clever and courageous enough to imagine ourselves becoming. This sets aside Kant's question "What is Man?" and substitutes the question "What sort of world can we prepare for our great-grandchildren?"

The question "What is Man?" in the sense of "What is the deep ahistorical nature of human beings?" owed its popularity to the standard answer to that question: We are the *rational* animal, the one which can know as well as merely feel. The residual popularity of this answer accounts for the residual popularity of Kant's astonishing claim that sentimentality has nothing to do with morality, that there is something distinctively and transculturally human called "the sense of moral obligation" which has nothing to do with love, friendship, trust, or social solidarity. As long as we believe *that,* people like Rabossi are going to have a tough time convincing us that human rights foundationalism is an outmoded project.

To overcome this idea of a *sui generis* sense of moral obligation, it would help to stop answering the question "What makes us different from the other animals?" by saying "We can know, and they can merely feel." We should substitute "We can feel *for each other* to a much greater extent than they can." This substitution would let us disentangle Christ's suggestion that love matters more than knowledge from the neo-Platonic suggestion that knowledge of the truth will make us free. For as long as we think that there is an ahistorical power which makes for righteousness—a power called truth, or rationality—we shall not be able to put foundationalism behind us.

The best, and probably the only, argument for putting foundationalism behind us is the one I have already suggested: It would be more efficient to do so, because it would let us concentrate our energies on manipulating sentiments, on sentimental education. That sort of education sufficiently acquaints people of different kinds with one another so that

they are less tempted to think of those different from themselves as only quasi-human. The goal of this manipulation of
sentiment is to expand the reference of the terms "our kind
of people" and "people like us."

All I can do to supplement this argument from increased
efficiency is to offer a suggestion about how Plato managed
to convince us that knowledge of universal truths mattered as
much as he thought it did. Plato thought that the philosopher's task was to answer questions like "Why should I be
moral? Why is it rational to be moral? Why is it in my interest
to be moral? Why is it in the interest of human beings as such
to be moral?" He thought this because he believed the best
way to deal with people like Thrasymachus and Callicles was
to demonstrate to them that they had an interest of which
they were unaware, an interest in being rational, in acquiring
self-knowledge. Plato thereby saddled us with a distinction
between the true and the false self. That distinction was, by
the time of Kant, transmuted into a distinction between categorical, rigid, moral obligation and flexible, empirically deter-
minable, self-interest. Contemporary moral philosophy is
still lumbered with this opposition between self-interest and
morality, an opposition which makes it hard to realize that
my pride in being a part of the human rights culture is no
more external to my self than my desire for financial success.

It would have been better if Plato had decided, as Aristotle
was to decide, that there was nothing much to be done with
people like Thrasymachus and Callicles, and that the problem was how to avoid having children who would be like
Thrasymachus and Callicles. By insisting that he could re-
educate people who had matured without acquiring appropriate moral sentiments by invoking a higher power than
sentiment, the power of reason, Plato got moral philosophy
off on the wrong foot. He led moral philosophers to concentrate on the rather rare figure of the psychopath, the person
who has no concern for any human being other than himself.

Moral philosophy has systematically neglected the much more common case: the person whose treatment of a rather narrow range of featherless bipeds is morally impeccable, but who remains indifferent to the suffering of those outside this range, the ones he or she thinks of as pseudohumans.[8]

Plato set things up so that moral philosophers think they have failed unless they convince the rational egotist that he should not be an egotist—convince him by telling him about his true, unfortunately neglected, self. But the rational egotist is not the problem. The problem is the gallant and honorable Serb who sees Muslims as circumcised dogs. It is the brave soldier and good comrade who loves and is loved by his mates, but who thinks of women as dangerous, malevolent whores and bitches.

Plato thought that the way to get people to be nicer to each other was to point out what they all had in common—rationality. But it does little good to point out, to the people I have just described, that many Muslims and women are good at mathematics or engineering or jurisprudence. Resentful young Nazi toughs were quite aware that many Jews were clever and learned, but this only added to the pleasure they took in beating them up. Nor does it do much good to get such people to read Kant, and agree that one should not treat rational agents simply as means. For everything turns on who counts as a fellow human being, as a rational agent in the only relevant sense—the sense in which rational agency is synonomous with membership in *our* moral community.

For most white people, until very recently, most Black people did not so count. For most Christians, up until the seventeenth century or so, most heathen did not so count. For the Nazis, Jews did not so count. For most males in countries in which the average annual income is under four thousand dollars, most females still do not so count. Whenever tribal and national rivalries become important, members of rival tribes and nations will not so count. Kant's account of the respect due to rational agents tells you that you should extend the respect you feel for people like yourself to all featherless bipeds. This is an excellent suggestion, a good formula for secularizing the Christian doctrine of the brotherhood of man. But it has never been backed up by an argument based on neutral premises, and it never will be. Outside the circle of post-Enlightenment European culture, the circle of relatively safe and secure people who have been manipulating each others' sentiments for two hundred years, most people are simply unable to understand why membership in a biological species is supposed to suffice for membership in a moral community. This is not because they are insufficiently rational. It is, typically, because they live in a world in which it would be just too risky—indeed, would often be insanely dangerous—to let one's sense of moral community stretch beyond one's family, clan, or tribe.

To get whites to be nicer to Blacks, males to females, Serbs to Muslims, or straights to gays, to help our species link up into what Rabossi calls a "planetary community" dominated by a culture of human rights, it is of no use whatever to say, with Kant: Notice that what you have in common, your humanity, is more important than these trivial differences. For the people we are trying to convince will rejoin that they notice nothing of the sort. Such people are *morally* offended by the suggestion that they should treat someone who is not kin as if he were a brother, or a nigger as if he were white, or a queer as if he were normal, or an infidel as if she were a believer. They are offended by the suggestion that they treat people whom they do not think of as human as if they were human. When utilitarians tell them that all pleasures and pains felt by members of our biological species are equally relevant to moral deliberation, or when Kantians tell them that the ability to engage in such deliberation is sufficient for membership in the moral community, they are incredulous. They rejoin that these philosophers seem oblivious to blatantly obvious moral distinctions, distinctions any decent person will draw.

This rejoinder is not just a rhetorical device, nor is it in any way irrational. It is heartfelt. The identity of these people, the people whom we should like to convince to join our Eurocentric human rights culture, is bound up with their sense of who they are *not*. Most people—especially people relatively untouched by the European Enlightenment—simply do not think of themselves as, first and foremost, a human being. Instead, they think of themselves as being a certain *good* sort of human being—a sort defined by explicit opposition to a particularly bad sort. It is crucial for their sense of who they are that they are *not* an infidel, *not* a queer, *not* a woman, *not* an untouchable. Just insofar as they are impoverished, and as their lives are perpetually at risk, they have little else than pride in not being what they are not to sustain their self-respect. Starting with the days when the term "human being" was synonomous with "member of our tribe," we have always thought of human beings in terms of paradigm members of the species. We have contrasted *us*, the *real* humans, with rudimentary, or perverted, or deformed examples of humanity.

We Eurocentric intellectuals like to suggest that we, the paradigm humans, have overcome this primitive parochialism by using that paradigmatic human faculty, reason. So we say that failure to concur with us is due to "prejudice." Our use of these terms in this way may make us nod in agreement when Colin McGinn tells us, in the introduction to his recent book,[9] that learning to tell right from wrong is not as hard as learning French. The only obstacles to agreeing with his moral views, McGinn explains, are "prejudice, vested interest and laziness."

One can see what McGinn means: If, like many of us, you teach students who have been brought up in the shadow of the Holocaust, brought up believing that prejudice against racial or religious groups is a terrible thing, it is not very hard to convert them to standard liberal views about abortion, gay rights, and the like. You may even get them to stop eating animals. All you have to do is convince them that all the arguments on the other side appeal to "morally irrelevant" considerations. You do this by manipulating their sentiments in such a way that they imagine themselves in the shoes of the despised and oppressed. Such students are already so nice that they are eager to define their identity in nonexclusionary terms. The only people they have trouble being nice to are the ones they consider irrational—the religious fundamentalist, the smirking rapist, or the swaggering skinhead.

Producing generations of nice, tolerant, well-off, secure, other-respecting students of this sort in all parts of the world is just what is needed—indeed *all* that is needed—to achieve an Enlightenment utopia. The more youngsters like this we can raise, the stronger and more global our human rights culture will become. But it is not a good idea to encourage these students to label "irrational" the intolerant people they have trouble tolerating. For that Platonic-Kantian epithet suggests that, with only a little more effort, the good and rational part of these other people's souls could have triumphed over the bad and irrational part. It suggests that we good people know something these bad people do not know, and that it is probably their own silly fault that they do not know it. All they have to do, after all, is to think a little harder, be a little more self-conscious, a little more rational.

But the bad people's beliefs are not more or less "irrational" than the belief that race, religion, gender, and sexual preference are all morally irrelevant—that these are all trumped by membership in the biological species. As used by moral philosophers like McGinn, the term "irrational behavior" means no more than "behavior of which we disapprove so strongly that our spade is turned when asked *why* we disapprove of it." It would be better to teach our students that these bad people are no less rational, no less clearheaded, no more prejudiced, than we good people who respect otherness. The bad people's problem is that they were not so lucky in the circumstances of their upbringing as we were. Instead of treating as irrational all those people out there who are trying to find and kill Salman Rushdie, we should treat them as deprived.

Foundationalists think of these people as deprived of truth, of moral knowledge. But it would be better—more specific, more suggestive of possible remedies—to think of them as deprived of two more concrete things: security and sympathy. By "security" I mean conditions of life sufficiently risk-free as to make one's difference from others inessential to one's self-respect, one's sense of worth. These conditions have been enjoyed by Americans and Europeans—the people who dreamed up the human rights culture—much more than they have been enjoyed by anyone else. By "sympathy" I mean the sort of reaction that the Athenians had more of after seeing Aeschylus' *The Persians* than before, the sort that white Americans had more of after reading *Uncle Tom's Cabin* than before, the sort that we have more of after watching TV programs about the genocide in Bosnia. Security and sympathy go together, for the same reasons that peace and economic productivity go together. The tougher things are, the more you have to be afraid of, the more dangerous your situation, the less you can afford the time or effort to think about what things might be like for people with whom you do not immediately identify. Sentimental education only works on people who can relax long enough to listen.

If Rabossi and I are right in thinking human rights foundationalism outmoded, then Hume is a better advisor than Kant about how we intellectuals can hasten the coming of the Enlightenment utopia for which both men yearned. Among contemporary philosophers, the best advisor seems to me to be Annette Baier. Baier describes Hume as "the woman's moral philosopher" because Hume held that "corrected (sometimes rule-corrected) sympathy, not law-discerning reason, is the fundamental moral capacity".[10] Baier would like us to get rid of both the Platonic idea that we have a true self, and the Kantian idea that it is rational to be moral. In aid of this project, she suggests that we think of "trust" rather than "obligation" as the fundamental moral notion. This substitution would mean thinking of the spread of the human rights culture not as a matter of our becoming more aware of the requirements of the moral law, but rather as what Baier calls "a progress of sentiments."[11] This progress consists in an increasing ability to see the similarities between ourselves and people very unlike us as outweighing the differences. It is the result of what I have been calling "sentimental education." The relevant similarities are not a matter of sharing a deep true self which instantiates true humanity, but are such little, superficial, similarities as cherishing our parents and our children—similarities that do not interestingly distinguish us from many nonhuman animals.

To accept Baier's suggestions, however, we should have to overcome our sense that sentiment is too weak a force, and that something stronger is required. This idea that reason is "stronger" than sentiment, that only an insistence on the unconditionality of moral obligation has the power to change human beings for the better, is very persistent. I think that this persistence is due mainly to a semiconscious realization that, if we hand our hopes for moral progress over to senti-ment, we are in effect handing them over to *condescension*. For we shall be relying on those who have the power to change things—people like the rich New England abolition-ists, or rich bleeding hearts like Robert Owen and Friedrich Engels—rather than on something that has power over *them*. We shall have to accept the fact that the fate of the women of Bosnia depends on whether TV journalists manage to do for them what Harriet Beecher Stowe did for black slaves, whether these journalists can make us, the audience back in the safe countries, feel that these women are more like us, more like real human beings, than we had realized.

To rely on the suggestions of sentiment rather than on the commands of reason is to think of powerful people gradually ceasing to oppress others, or ceasing to countenance the oppression of others, out of mere niceness, rather than out of obedience to the moral law. But it is revolting to think that our only hope for a decent society consists in softening the self-satisfied hearts of a leisure class. We want moral progress to burst up from below, rather than waiting patiently upon condescension from the top. The residual popularity of Kantian ideas of "unconditional moral obligation"—obligation imposed by deep ahistorical noncontingent forces—seems to me almost entirely due to our abhorrence for the idea that the people on top hold the future in their hands, that everything depends on them, that there is nothing more powerful to which we can appeal against them.

Like everyone else, I too should prefer a bottom-up way of achieving utopia, a quick reversal of fortune which will make the last first. But I do not think this is how utopia will in fact come into being. Nor do I think that our preference for this way lends any support to the idea that the Enlightenment project lies in the depths of every human soul. So why does this preference make us resist the thought that sentimentality may be the best weapon we have? I think Nietzsche gave the right answer to this question: We resist out of resentment. We *resent* the idea that we shall have to wait for the strong to turn their piggy little eyes to the suffering of the weak. We desperately hope that there is something stronger and more powerful that will *hurt* the strong if they do *not*—if not a vengeful God, then a vengeful aroused proletariat, or, at least, a vengeful superego, or, at the very least, the offended majesty of Kant's tribunal of pure practical reason. The desperate hope for a noncontingent and powerful ally is, according to Nietzsche, the common core of Platonism, of religious insistence on divine omnipotence, and of Kantian moral philosophy.[12]

Nietzsche was, I think, right on the button when he offered this diagnosis. What Santayana called "supernaturalism," the confusion of ideals and power, is all that lies behind the Kantian claim that it is not only nicer, but more rational, to include strangers within our moral community than to exclude them from it. If we agree with Nietzsche and Santayana on this point, however, we do not thereby acquire any reason to turn our backs on the Enlightenment project, as Nietzsche did. Nor do we acquire any reason to be sardonically pessimistic about the chances of this project, in the manner of admirers of Nietzsche like Santayana, Ortega, Heidegger, Strauss, and Foucault.

For even though Nietzsche was absolutely right to see Kant's insistence on unconditionality as an expression of resentment, he was absolutely wrong to treat Christianity, and the age of the democratic revolutions, as signs of human degeneration. He and Kant, alas, shared something with each other which neither shared with Harriet Beecher Stowe—something which Iris Murdoch has called "dryness" and which Jacques Derrida has called "phallogocentrism." The common element in the thought of both men was a desire for purity. This sort of purity consists in being not only autonomous, in command of oneself, but also in having the kind of self-conscious self-sufficiency which Sartre describes as the perfect synthesis of the in-itself and the for-itself. This synthesis could only be attained, Sartre pointed out, if one could rid oneself of everything sticky, slimy, wet, sentimental, and womanish.

Although this desire for virile purity links Plato to Kant, the desire to bring as many different kinds of people as possible into a cosmopolis links Kant to Stowe. Kant is, in the history of moral thinking, a transitional stage between the hopeless attempt to convict Thrasymachus of irrationality and the hopeful attempt to see every new featherless biped who comes along as one of us. Kant's mistake was to think that the only way to have a modest, damped-down, non-fanatical version of Christian brotherhood after letting go of the Christian faith was to revive the themes of pre-Christian philosophical thought. He wanted to make knowledge of a core self do what can be done only by the continual refreshment and re-creation of the self, through interaction with selves as unlike itself as possible.

Kant performed the sort of awkward balancing act required in transitional periods. His project mediated between a dying rationalist tradition and a vision of a new, democratic world, the world of what Rabossi calls "the human rights phenomenon." With the advent of this phenomenon, Kant's balancing act has become outmoded and irrelevant. We are now in a good position to put aside the last vestiges of the ideas that human beings are distinguished by the capacity to know rather than by the capacities for friendship and inter-marriage, distinguished by rigorous rationality rather than by flexible sentimentality. If we do so, we shall have dropped the idea that assured knowledge of a truth about what we have in common is a prerequisite for moral education, as well as the idea of a specifically moral motivation. If we do all these things, we shall see Kant's *Foundations of the Metaphysics of Morals* as a placeholder for *Uncle Tom's Cabin*—a concession to the expectations of an intellectual epoch in which the quest for quasi-scientific knowledge seemed the only possible response to religious exclusionism.[13]

Unfortunately, many philosophers, especially in the English-speaking world, are still trying to hold on to the Platonic insistence that the principal duty of human beings is to *know*. That insistence was the lifeline to which Kant and Hegel thought we had to cling.[14] Just as German philosophers in the period between Kant and Hegel saw themselves as saving "reason" from Hume, many English-speaking philosophers now see themselves saving reason from Derrida. But with the wisdom of hindsight, and with Baier's help, we have learned to read Hume not as a dangerously frivolous iconoclast but as the wettest, most flexible, least phallogocentric thinker of the Enlightenment. Someday, I suspect, our descendants may wish that Derrida's contemporaries had been able to read him not as a frivolous iconoclast, but rather as a sentimental educator, another of "the women's moral philosophers."[15]

If one follows Baier's advice one will not see it as the moral educator's task to answer the rational egotist's question "Why should I be moral?" but rather to answer the much more frequently posed question "Why should I care about a stranger, a person who is no kin to me, a person whose habits I find disgusting?" The traditional answer to the latter question is "Because kinship and custom are morally irrelevant, irrelevant to the obligations imposed by the recognition of membership in the same species." This has never been very convincing, since it begs the question at issue: whether mere species membership is, in fact, a sufficient surrogate for closer kinship. Furthermore, that answer leaves one wide open to Nietzsche's discomfiting rejoinder: *That* universalistic notion, Nietzsche will sneer, would only have crossed the mind of a slave—or, perhaps, the mind of an intellectual, a priest whose self-esteem and livelihood both depend on getting the rest of us to accept a sacred, unarguable, unchallengeable paradox.

A better sort of answer is the sort of long, sad, sentimental story which begins "Because this is what it is like to be in her situation—to be far from home, among strangers," or "Because she might become your daughter-in-law," or "Because her mother would grieve for her." Such stories, repeated and varied over the centuries, have induced us, the rich, safe, powerful, people, to tolerate, and even to cherish, powerless people—people whose appearance or habits or beliefs at first seemed an insult to our own moral identity, our sense of the limits of permissible human variation.

To people who, like Plato and Kant, believe in a philosophically ascertainable truth about what it is to be a human being, the good work remains incomplete as long as we have not answered the question "Yes, but am I under a *moral obligation* to her?" To people like Hume and Baier, it is a mark of intellectual immaturity to raise that question. But we shall go on asking that question as long as we agree with Plato that it is our ability to know that makes us human.

Plato wrote quite a long time ago, in a time when we intellectuals had to pretend to be successors to the priests, had to pretend to know something rather esoteric. Hume did his best to josh us out of that pretense. Baier, who seems to me both the most original and the most useful of contemporary moral philosophers, is still trying to josh us out of it. I think Baier may eventually succeed, for she has the history of the last two hundred years of moral progress on her side. These two centuries are most easily understood not as a period of deepening understanding of the nature of rationality or of morality, but rather as one in which there occurred an astonishingly rapid progress of sentiments, in which it has become much easier for us to be moved to action by sad and sentimental stories.

This progress has brought us to a moment in human history in which it is plausible for Rabossi to say that the human rights phenomenon is a "fact of the world." This phenomenon may be just a blip. But it may mark the beginning of a time in which gang rape brings forth as strong a response when it happens to women as when it happens to men, or when it happens to foreigners as when it happens to people like us.

THE OTHER'S RIGHTS

Jean-François Lyotard

"It seems that a man who is nothing but a man has lost the very qualities which make it possible for others to treat him as a fellow man."[1] With this sentence, taken from the study on *Imperialism* which forms the second part of *The Origins of Totalitarianism* (1951), Hannah Arendt defines the fundamental condition of human rights: A human being has rights only if he is other than a human being. And if he is to be other than *a* human being, he must in addition become an *other* human being. Then "the others" can treat him as their fellow human being. What makes human beings alike is the fact that every human being carries within him the figure of the other. The likeness that they have in common follows from the difference of each from each.

Thou shalt not kill thy fellow human being: To kill a human being is not to kill an animal of the species Homo sapiens, but to kill the human community present in him as both capacity and promise. And you also kill it in yourself. To banish the stranger is to banish the community, and you banish yourself from the community thereby.

What is this figure of the other in me, on which, it is said, my right to be treated as a human being rests? It is this question to which I devote the rest of my reflections.

"Nothing but a man," writes Hannah Arendt. That is, nothing other than an individual of the species Homo sapiens. A powerful species; in the struggle for life enacted in the theater of the world, Homo sapiens has emerged victorious over all other species. And it continues, successfully, to combat them, using hygiene, sanitary arrangements, the protection of the environment, and so on. Each human being is a specimen of this species. He resembles any other member of the species, as a chimpanzee resembles a chimpanzee.

Is the figure of the other (ape) present in every ape? Apes are able to tell each other apart and to distinguish themselves from other species of animal. They can communicate amongst themselves by systems of sensory signals based on the five senses and motility. These systems constitute a sort of language which endows the animals with a sort of community in which affective states (Aristotle's *pathemata*) are exchanged, along with admonitions as to conduct.

This signal-based language is not wholly lacking in the human species, but its role is confined. Animals' capacity to communicate is determined by the genetic stock common to the species, and is of the order of instinct. Human beings have very few instincts. In comparison with their animal brothers, young human beings are slow to realize their capacity in the language of their fellow. And this human language is not common to the species. It functions not by bodily signals, but by signs. These arbitrary signs, combined according to rules which are also arbitrary, but which are fixed by syntactic structures, make it possible to designate any object, real or not, internal or external, as their referent, and to signify something about that object. Finally, and this is what interests us here, this signification is *addressed*.

It is what we today call the "pragmatic" function of human language which governs the formation of the figure of the other. Explicitly or implicitly, every human sentence is destined to someone or something. Some answer, some response, some link or follow-up is expected. The polarization is marked in our languages by the verbal "persons" and the personal pronouns. *I* is the one who is speaking now; *you* is the one to whom this communication is currently addressed. *You* are silent when *I* speak, but *you* can speak, has spoken, and will speak.

Animal communication is, we might say, homogeneous. By contrast, the distinguishing characteristic of interlocution is the relation of simultaneous similarity and disparity introduced between the speakers. The instances *I* and *you* cannot merge, since while the one speaks the other speaks no longer or not yet. *I* and *you* are deictics, and as such are correlated with *now*, and *now* designates the present of speech. From it, the temporality of past and future unfold. But relative to the capacity to speak, which by definition is not confined to the present but extends to every possible interlocution, *I* and *you* are alike. Persons capable of speech alternately occupy the instance *I* and the instance *you*. When they say *I*, they are a past or future *you*, and when they are in the position of *you*, they are so because they have spoken or will speak as *I*.

Interlocution thus implies that human beings cannot, as animals can, merge into a community based on signals. They do so only when the impossibility of interlocution reduces them to that meager resource. In theory, the human *we* does not precede but results from interlocution. In this *we*, the figure of the other remains clearly present to each, to the extent that the other is his possible interlocutor. The one and the other can come to an agreement, after reasoning and debate, and then establish their community by contract. This is the principle of the Greek *politeia* or the modern *republic*. The citizen is the human individual whose right to address others is recognized by those others.

It is important to distinguish the republican principle from the democratic fact. The *demos* is not a contractual but a natural and cultural community. The individual of the *demos* is recognized as such not for his right to speak, but for his birth, language, and historical heritage. These individuals form a *nation* (in the medieval sense in which one hears *nature*), whose principal characteristic is the homogeneity of its constituents. Interlocution does not engender this community; between the members of the nation, language and mores function as signals of recognition. Though possessed of interlocutory capacity, the demotic individual, whether a serf or a free man, uses the language to signal emotions and actions to other specimens of the variety of *Homines* to which they collectively belong. This relationship to language excludes the alterity implicit in civic interlocution. The other remains alien, and does not enjoy the rights reserved to nationals. The very Greeks who invented the *politeia* excluded *barbaroi*. The right of interlocution is not granted to every human being. The figure of the other is that of a threat weighing on the national community from without, which cannot help but undermine its integrity.

I oversimplify my description to bring out the essential opposition between the *demotic* and the *civic*. The difference between them is the consideration given to interlocution, which modifies the figure of the other. The people keeps the other out; the city interiorizes the other. In contemporary human communities, for various reasons, these two aspects are for the most part not distinguished: more or less nation, more or less republic. For example, the institution of a European community undoubtedly draws its justification exclusively from the civic principle.

In the republic, there is a principle of universalization which relates to the function, inherent in speech, of *addressing* the other. If a human being can speak, he is a possible interlocutor. The principle is not invalidated merely by the fact of his speaking a language foreign to the national language. Homo sapiens has always spoken a multitude of languages. But they are all human languages comprising the structural characteristics I have briefly outlined. These characteristics guarantee that an unknown human language can in principle be translated into a known one. I do not wish to take up here the difficulties and enigmas of translation. The theoretical possibility of translation is quite sufficient to extend interlocution to any human individual whatsoever, regardless of natural or national idiom. Civility may become universal in fact as it promises to do by right.

The form in which civility is in fact extended to national

or demotic communities is a serious question. History offers a profusion of different modes, linguistic as well as political and economic. These include: an obligatory single language, an official language alongside which traditional languages are tolerated, compulsory multilingualism, effective multilingualism, and so on. The pattern established depends on the balance of military, political, economic, and cultural power. These relations determine how interlocution extends, but they cannot curb its extension. There is no limiting the function of destination inherent in the structure of sentences: One may beg a service of a tree or a river, and issue a command to a cat. If the addressee is human, he is immediately vested with the status of interlocutor, capable, in his turn, of addressing the first speaker.

There is no a priori limit to the interlocutory capacity. By its association with the recursiveness and translatability of human language, it cannot help but bind all human speakers in a speech community. From this effective (de facto) power there arises what I shall term an *effect of right (un effet de droit)*. If any human being *can* be an interlocutor for other human beings, he *must be able* to, that is, must be enabled or allowed to. We move from the potential implied by competence to the permission implied by entitlement. We know, however, that capacity does not legitimacy make. But it is tempting to merge the two categories in the case of interlocution, both because the capacity to enter into dialogue with others is possessed equally by everyone, and because interlocution in itself implies reciprocity of speech. Reciprocity respects not only the alterity of interlocution but the parity of the interlocutors. It thus guarantees their respective liberty and their equality before the word. These are the characteristics of justice itself. The slippage here from the fact to the right resembles the contemporary confusion of democracy and republic. But how can we avoid it?

Let us take it that the capacity to speak to others is a

human right, and perhaps the most fundamental human right. If the use of this capacity is forbidden, whether de facto, by some injustice of fate, or on principle, for example as a punishment, a harm is inflicted on the speaker thus constrained. He is set apart from the speech community of interlocutors. To no one is he any longer someone other, nor is anyone now his other. There are many ways of imposing silence. Amnesty International knows them better than anyone. Its vocation is modest but decisive. It is *minimal. Amnestos* meant he who is forgotten. Amnesty does not demand that the judgment be revised or that the convicted man be rehabilitated. It simply asks that the institution that has condemned him to silence forget this decree and restore the victim to the community of speakers.

Amnesty's task is in accordance with the provisions of the public law of the republican democracies. I nevertheless maintain that this legality conceals a confusion between a capacity, the aptitude for speech, and a legitimacy, the authority to speak. In other words, there is, strictly speaking, no natural right. It is of the essence of a right that it be merited; no right without duty. The same goes for the capacity to enter into dialogue. It is not true that it realizes itself spontaneously. It requires care and attention, an entire learning process. It requires precisely what is called civilization. The human being as such is no other than a member of the species Homo: an animal that can speak. It is true that its language is so constituted that it effectively contains the promise of interlocution. But if he is to bring out and respect the figure of the other that this promise bears in it, he must free himself from that in him which will not recognize the figure of the other, that is, his animal nature. Children do not spontaneously enter into dialogue. There is something in us which resists, something which does perhaps "speak," but in signals rather than according to the rules of interlocution.

Civilization, understood here as the process of learning

how to share dialogue with *you,* requires a moment of silence. Aristotle said: The master speaks and the pupil listens. For that moment, the status of *I* is forbidden to me, I am assigned the position of *you* for the master, at the *tacit* pole of destination. *Tacit* does not imply *passive.* The exaltation of interactivity as a pedagogic principle is pure demagogy. The pupil has the capacity to speak; he has to win the right to speak. To do so, he must be silent. The suspension of interlocution imposes a silence and that silence is good. It does not undermine the right to speak. It teaches the value of that right. It is the exercise necessary for excellence in speech. Like the pupil, writers, artists, scholars, and novices must enter into retreat in order to learn what they will have to say to others.

The master, whatever his title, exempts his pupils from the sharing of speech in order to tell them something that they do not know. He may even speak to them in a language that they do not understand. The master is not the figure of the general other, of *you,* but the figure of the *Other* in all its separateness. He is the stranger, the foreigner. How can one dialogue with the foreigner? One would have to learn his language. This question is in some measure analogous with that of literature and the arts, testifying to something that is "present" otherwise than as interlocutory expectation: something opaque, Beckett's the "Unnamable."

The silence that the learning process of civilization imposes is the moment of a labor of *estrangement.* It is a matter of speaking otherwise than is my wont and saying something other than what I know how to say. Through the alterity of the master, the strangeness of another logic is, in silence, imposed. He takes me hostage in order to make me hear and say what I do not know. Emmanuel Levinas has elaborated this theme better than anyone.

From this brief analysis, it follows that the interlocutory capacity changes into a right to speak only if the speech can say something other than the *déjà dit* (what has already been said). The right to speak implies a duty to announce. If our speech announces nothing, it is doomed to repetition and to the conservation of existing meanings. The human community may spread, but it will remain the same, prostrated in the euphoria it feels at being on such very good terms with itself. It is the main function of the media today to reinforce the interlocutory consent of the community. They are boring to the extent that they teach us nothing. Interlocution is not an end in itself. It is legitimate only if, through others, the Other announces to me something which I hear but do not understand.

We should then distinguish three different levels of the "right to speak." First, the faculty of interlocution, a principle factually inherent in human languages; second, the legitimation of speech, due to the fact that it announces something other, which it strives to make us understand; and last, the legitimacy of speech, the positive right to speak, which recognizes in the citizen the right to address the citizen. The latter aspect merges the two former. But this confusion is good. By authorizing every possible speaker to address others, the republic makes it every speaker's duty to announce to those others what they do not know. It encourages announcements; it instructs. And, on the other hand, it forbids that anyone be arbitrarily deprived of speech. It discourages terror. In this way it governs silence in everyone's best interest, authorizing the silence of discipline and outlawing the silence of despotism.

This picture of the republic is idyllic, but the idyll conceals something far from idyllic. The threat of being deprived of speech is not contingent; it weighs constantly on the interlocutory right. This is precisely why the republic is indispensable. The human speaker is always afraid that a "keep quiet" will debar his words. He complains of the precariousness of his membership in the speech community. Even the good silence of the writer, the monk, or the pupil contains an element of suffering. Any banishment is a harm inflicted on those who undergo it, but this harm necessarily changes to a wrong when the victim is excluded from the speech community. For the wrong is the harm to which the victim cannot testify, since he cannot be heard. And this is precisely the case of those to whom the right to speak to others is refused.

The right to impose silence which the community grants itself as a sanction is always dangerous. The death sentence evidently does an irremediable wrong to the condemned man, even if he is guilty of a heinous crime. But in relation to our present topic, death is not necessarily the wrong done to him. There are, as the Greeks put it, "beautiful deaths," of which the citizens continue to speak long afterward. It happens that a speaker is more eloquent dead than alive, and does not therefore die for the community. So we must reverse the relation: It is the wrong which is the cause of death, since it implies the exclusion of the speaker from the speech community. The community will not even speak of this exclusion since the victim will be unable to report it and cannot therefore defend himself or appeal.

Those who escaped extermination in the camps are aware of this. Restored to the community, they can describe and narrate what the administration of death was. But how can they communicate the abjection to which they were reduced? It was first and foremost the severing of communication. How can one communicate by means of interlocution the terror of what it means no longer to be destined to anyone or anything? They were not spoken to, they were treated. They were not enemies. The SS or Kapos who called them dogs, pigs, or vermin did not treat them as animals but as refuse. It is the destiny of refuse to be incinerated. The ordeal of being forgotten is unforgettable. It reveals a truth about our relationship to language that is stifled and repressed by the serene belief in dialogue. Abjection is not merely when we are missing from speech, but when we lack language to excess. Our debt to announcement can never be acquitted. The Other in language, the Other that language is, does not say what must be said. It keeps silent. Does it even wait? Excluded from the speech community, the camp victims were rejected into the poverty, the misery of this secret. In that misery resides the true dignity of speech. Clearly, the ordeal of being forgotten cannot be expressed in the sharing of speech, which is, *ex hypothesi*, ignorant of it. Neither *I* nor *you*, the deportee is present in the language of his lords and in that of the deportees themselves only as the third person, who is to be eliminated. He is superfluous as any speaker is superfluous in relation to the Other. But precisely for that reason, absolutely responsible for himself.

The abjection suffered in the camps horribly illustrates the threat of exclusion which weighs on all interlocution. On the school playground, the child to whom the others say "We're not playing with you" experiences this unspeakable suffering. He suffers a wrong equivalent, on its own scale, to a crime against humanity. Even those who submit themselves to the ascesis of separation in order to exalt the annunciatory power of language run the risk of abjection. True, they forswear the company of others only in order to listen more intently to the foreign master. But this enslavement to the Other is perceived as a suspicious dependence on a power alien to the interlocutory community, as a sort of betrayal. The Latin *sacer* (sacred) expressed the ambivalence of the abject: human refuse excluded from the interests of the speech community, yet a sign, perhaps, in which the Other has left its mark and deserving of respectful fear.

In his analysis of the sublime effect, Edmund Burke termed *horror* the state of mind of a person whose participation in speech is threatened. The power which exceeds the capacity of interlocution resembles night. Though we seek to tame it by dialogue, it does not have the figure of the *you*. It may be well- or ill-disposed. We hear it. We cannot understand it. It may be God, it may be Animal, it may be Satan. In silence we strive to translate its voice in order to announce it to the community of speakers. In this way we seek to make our relation to the Other dialectical. But the strangeness of the other seems to escape any totalization. The effort of translation must be endlessly renewed. It is precisely when we think we have reduced the abject or the sacred to transparent meanings that it becomes most opaque and returns to us from without like an accident. The discontent from which contemporary societies are suffering, the postmodern affliction, is this foreclosure of the Other. It is the reverse of the triumphant identification with the Other which affects modern republics at their birth. Saint-Just enacted law in the name of the Other, and instituted the first totalitarian reign of terror.

Wiser than the dialecticians, the Jacobins, and the deciders, Freud acknowledged that abjection was not an episode but a situation constitutive of the human relation to interlocution. As children, we are kept on the margins of interlocution, and condemned to exile. The situation of *infantia* is that of the incomplete human being who *does not yet* speak. The child is spoken to and spoken of, but is not an interlocutor even though he is plunged into the interlocutory community. The statements that concern him have no value for him except as signals or gestures; they are difficult for him to decipher because they are arbitrary, and he has little instinct. He is affected by them, but has no language in which to articulate his own affective states. These reside within him unconsciously, in a forgetfulness which is always present. They do not enter the temporality associated with the instances of destination *I* and *you*. They loom up in the course of the individual life history in apparently unmotivated ways. They block interlocution. With them, the inevitable wrong and abjection of *infantia* erupt into adult relations.

From our native prematurity a mute distress results. It is to this distress that we owe our capacity to question everything around us. But we also owe to it our need to be welcomed, the request that we be authorized to enter the speech community. In interlocution a drama is played out between *me* and *you;* it is the drama of authorization. The question or assertion that we address to others is invariably coupled with an entreaty: Deliver me from my abandonment, allow me to belong among you. This entreaty allows of a wide variety of modalities: friendship, hatred, love, and even indifference. But in it resides the foundation of the right to speak. For it is this right that assures me that my request will be heard, and that I will not be rejected into the abjection of *infantia*. Yet at the same time, I have to announce to you the opaque Otherness that I have experienced, and still am experiencing, as a child.

The law says: Thou shalt not kill. Which means: you shall not refuse to others the role of interlocutor. But the law that forbids the crime of abjection nonetheless evokes its abiding threat or temptation. Interlocution is authorized only by respect for the Other, in my words and in yours.

—*Translated by Chris Miller and Robert Smith*

THE LIMITS TO NATURAL LAW AND THE PARADOX OF EVIL

Agnes Heller

I

Whether moral decisions are evaluated by universal standards or by those of local traditions, moral conflicts are always contextual. Kant's categorical imperative is absolutely universalistic, but its test cases are concrete and particular. One should, for example, return a deposit even when the depositor alone was aware of the arrangement and has since died. In the same way, when I now raise the question of how we can deal with evil, I do so in a specific context. The moral conflicts I shall discuss are those that occur in the aftermath of the collapse of totalitarian regimes and of military and other dictatorships. The question is whether the evils perpetrated under murderous political regimes can, should, or will be punished; whether those responsible for murder, kidnapping, and mass incarceration and discrimination, can, will, or should be made to pay for what they have done.

"Paying" here means paying a part rather than the whole price for their acts. Even when the indictment is for common murder, the consensus against capital punishment in political cases is very strong, and this is also true in those countries where capital punishment has not been abolished. Hannah Arendt's grave meditations on the justification of capital punishment in the Eichmann case[1] are therefore irrelevant in the current context. The alternative to be faced is not that of life or death, but of prosecution or inaction.

Whether the perpetrators of such crimes will be prosecuted is not itself a theoretical question. In all probability some will be prosecuted, but a majority will not. Thus we are confined to two issues: whether there are legal grounds in the existing constitutions (or laws equivalent to constitutions) for the prosecution of these persons; and whether they should be prosecuted, that is, whether there is a moral obligation to prosecute them.

Each combination of "can" and "should" in relation to

these questions represents a moral standpoint. Political considerations or their own life histories make people incline to one or another of the combinations. In what follows, I address some of the merits and demerits of the arguments and evaluate some of our general intuitions on this subject.

The available options can be defined in terms of six possible combinations of a legal and a moral position. The combinations will become clearer as we proceed. *A:* There should be no prosecution at all, nor can there be. *B:* There should be no prosecution though there is no obstacle to prosecution. *C:* The perpetrators should be prosecuted, but cannot be. *D:* They should and can be prosecuted. *E:* They should be prosecuted for historical justice to be done. Finally, *F:* They should pay for their crimes; they should be prosecuted and yet, at the same time, they should not be prosecuted.

II

In whichever of the four combinations it occurs, the formula that perpetrators of heinous crimes "should be punished" implies that "justice should be done." The other formula, according to which "they should not be punished," can imply one of three things. It can imply, most radically, that "justice should not be done." It can imply resignation: "There is no justice in this matter anyway." Or it can imply a positive moral standpoint: "It would be unjust to punish them."

Let us consider the first formula, according to which justice should be done. In thus subscribing to the injunction that "perpetrators of heinous crimes should be punished," we take responsibility for the punishment of the perpetrators. We do so regardless of whether they can (legally) be punished, and of whether they will in fact be punished. We take that responsibility even if we go on to say "and yet they cannot be punished." We are responsible for their punishment because, irrespective of the ultimate course of events, our injunction is an act equivalent to signing the decree of their punishment. Signing is an act of taking responsibility. Signing and taking responsibility are not acts to be approached lightly. Even in one's capacity as an ordinary citizen, one should take one's responsibility no less seriously than would an appointed judge, a member of a jury, or a member of a political body—of an executive or legislative body.

Those who subscribe to the "ought" sentence, "perpetrators of heinous crimes ought be punished," must consider which crimes are heinous and which persons are to be identified as their perpetrators.

In identifying the perpetrators of politically motivated or conditioned crimes, we can avail ourselves of more than forty years of discussion of the Nuremberg trials. The conclusions of this discussion are fairly clear. If, like Honecker, one gives the order "shoot to kill" in regard to innocent persons who are trying to escape to freedom, one is guilty of murder, whereas the soldier who obeys that order is not. Certainly, the soldier too is responsible for the death of the persons he has shot. One is the author of one's own deeds, good or bad. But one is not necessarily the author of the conditions under which they were committed. In this political context, the accused is guilty of a crime if he or she is not only the author of the crime, but also of the circumstances under which that crime was ordered or encouraged.

Who is to decide which heinous crimes must be punished for justice to be done? Under present conditions, only the population of the country where those crimes were committed has, or can claim to have, the authority to decide. There can be no question of international jurisdiction. (German jurisdiction over the crimes committed in former East Germany is not a counterexample. Germany is in the same position as postwar France, which regarded Vichy as a part of the French state.) Yet the unreflective intuition of the population is unreliable, for it is divided along generational lines. In regimes of long standing, different generations have different life experiences, and in a long era of enforced silence, crimes unmentioned because unmentionable will tend to be forgotten. The politics of repression are the politics of psychological repression; even the guilty begin to forget their guilt. But the suffering of the mourner is not mitigated by the lapse of time. Enforced silence rather deepens the wound. Only now can victims and the families of victims cry out for justice and revenge.

If one subscribes to the sentence "perpetrators of heinous crimes should be punished," one also needs a yardstick more reliable than the intuition of the members of a specific community. Yet it is precisely this intuition that one must rely on, for no one other than the members of this community is entitled to determine which crimes are so heinous as to call for punishment. This remains true even if it is decided that legal action cannot be taken.

Since decision here is a matter of judgment, one stratagem for evaluating our intuition is to replace the current cases with analogous ones from history. These analogous stories should be of a kind we have been familiar with since primary school.

The procedure I recommend here is not a mental experiment, but an exercise in becoming aware of our judgmental intuitions. Let us take well-known historical examples of treason, confiscation of wealth, instigation of civil war, political assassination, and mass extermination—whether or not the latter was committed under forms of legality. Whenever the intuitive consensus is in favor of punishment, the judgment will apply to contemporary cases too. By considering many historical examples, we find out something about our intuitions. For example, in cases of treason, confiscation of wealth, instigation of civil war, or political assassination, our judgment may be divided. A profusion of historical texts exists on which we may base our interpretations and reinterpretations. Sometimes we are uncertain whether the deeds in question were crimes at all. They may also be viewed as virtuous deeds: The prophet Jeremiah committed treason, Judith assassinated Holofernes. And even in those cases where we do intuit a crime, it does not follow that we regard the perpetrator as criminal. Even if we take the execution of Mary Stuart to be a judicial murder, we do not intuitively condemn Elizabeth the First as a murderess. But mass murder, be it an act of collective political proscription (as happened under Sulla), or an act of collective terrorism against the "religious alien" (as happened to the Protestants during the St. Bartholomew's Night Massacre) is not open to a forgiving understanding and interpretation. Such acts are unanimously condemned as evil, at least in the context of the European tradition of the last few centuries, and rightly so, for they are the visible face of evil.

Turning now to the question of historical justice: When we subscribe to the sentiment that justice should be done—irrespective of whether it will be done—it is historical justice of which we speak. The "should" refers to the exclusively moral motivation behind the insistence on historical justice. But history includes the future. In enforcing historical justice, we may not consider the pragmatic consequences of our judgment, but we must take into account the moral judgment of future generations. For this reason only genuinely heinous crimes should be punished, for only in such cases can we be certain that all morally competent future generations will subscribe to our verdict and not interpret the act we punish in a different light. It is an entirely different matter whether future interpreters will consider the perpetrators in the same psychological light as we do, whether they will reinterpret the personhood of the perpetrators. Psychological or phenomenological hermeneutics does not concern the moral judgments of events. Opinions may differ about Hitler's personality, but no morally competent person can ever justify Auschwitz. In short, when we demand that heinous crimes ought to be punished in order for historical justice to be done, we are claiming that all morally competent future generations would consent to the historical justice of our judgment. Whether, in punishing, we punish anything other than the manifestation of evil, is an empirical question, and one which has nothing to do with historical justice. Or if it does, we cannot know this. But it is clear that, for historical crimes, there can be no statute of limitations, precisely because they are heinous in the sense that we have just defined.

III

We conclude: The heinous crimes that should be punished for the spirit of historical justice to prevail are those which count as manifestations of evil. But nothing has, as yet, been said about evil. I hope that my theoretical interpretation of evil will illuminate our problem without shifting the focus of our inquiry. I discern evil in the acts in which others discern it; it is my account of evil that is distinctive.

Evil is not an accumulated or excessive moral badness distinguished from all other categories of badness by quantity. Evil is *qualitatively* different from the morally bad. This qualitative difference has become explicit in modern times, although it had already been discovered by particularly discerning moralists such as certain Jewish prophets and Greek philosophers. The knowledge of moral evil emerges through reflection. Where there is no freedom to choose principles of action, there can be badness but not evil. Moral evil requires a fairly sophisticated and consistent system of self-justification. A bad character chooses to commit injustice rather than suffer it; he makes an exception for himself. He does not, however, invent principles that make the wrong right. A bad character succumbs to base passions such as envy, and behaves in a cowardly fashion. Yet he can feel remorse and may indulge in gestures of disorderly repentance. Our model of evil, by way of contrast, is Satan, not because he does the wrong things, but because he induces others to do the wrong things by persuading them that evil is right. Plato's Thrasymachos or Callicles[2] are devilish, not because they are bad characters, but because they make a strong case for maxims that confuse our capacity to distinguish between good and evil. As Kant pointed out, evil resides in evil maxims, not in desires or weakness of character.

In modernity, where traditional morals have become attenuated, evil maxims easily gain the upper hand. Totalitarianism in particular is morally founded on evil maxims. These evil maxims form the basis of the discourse initiated in a totalitarian regime, a discourse into which the proverbial "man on the street" is drawn. The citizens begin to speak the language of totalitarianism and as a result come to take for granted acts which a year before they would not have accepted, and the endorsement of which would have been entirely out of character. Only through internalizing this discourse can they come to believe that they have an obligation to denounce their parents to the police or to confess to crimes that they never committed.

I once compared totalitarianism to a disease. Normal people—people neither especially good nor especially bad—are exposed to the disease, take the contagion, and become alienated from their previous selves. If one catches the virus of evil, one becomes evil, even if there had been no original evil in one's character. Devils are in fact rare phenomena. Evil characters, if we compare their numbers to those of the wrongdoers who have caught the virus and become evil under its influence, are few and far between.

After the demise of totalitarianism, it is not difficult to distinguish between the originally evil and those who became evil through secondary infection. The former originate the evil maxims, stick to their principles to the last, their consciences unruffled, and ascribe the defeat or failure of their principles to the weakness of their followers. The followers, by contrast, can get confused, rewrite their pasts, forget the evil they have committed and remember only the evils they have suffered; they can slough off their totalitarian self. This is how evil could seem banal to Hannah Arendt.[3] But evil is not banal, even if evil persons become banal after the demise of their power base. The soul is not healed just because the epidemic has passed. The pathetically banal soul does not even feel guilty; he or she feels only the remorse of having bet on the wrong horse. Pangs of conscience or repentance are rare.

There is, moreover, a difference between initial and continuous totalitarianism. In the original or initial state, evil has a high density and visibility; it is demonic. What is merely bad is normally repulsive, but a certain power of attraction emanates from moral evil as such. Evil maxims on the one hand align themselves with the underworld of the human soul, on the other don the garb of high sophistication. Evil in this form is sorcery; it terrifies, demands submission. But in the continuous phase of totalitarianism (we refer here to communist totalitarianism, since Nazism was defeated in its first phase), the density and visibility of evil diminish, and its epidemic effect dies away. The principal victims of the regime were immune from the virus in any case. Others were morally immune and never succumbed. In this later phase, they are joined by those who were only slightly infected, who now shrug off their infection and may even attack evil on its home territory. Since the demon is always associated with (totalitarian) power, the slackening of the regime in the continuous phase necessarily has a therapeutic effect.

The collapse of totalitarianism brings the epidemic to an end. Evil maxims are still around, as they always will be while there are maxims to choose and freedom to choose them. But for the time being the bearers of evil maxims seem to have been marginalized.

This specificity of evil, that it is not necessarily a permanent resident of the souls it inhabits, but may enter a soul and subsequently leave it, obviously complicates the issue of retribution. Let us take an example. We know that X was the author of a heinous crime, and we believe that heinous crimes should be punished in order for historic justice to be done. But perhaps the X of today is not the X who committed the crime; perhaps the virus of evil that inhabited his soul has departed leaving only the empty husk of an elderly body and a banal soul. Puccini's Tosca looks at the dead Scarpia and exclaims "and before this man all Rome trembled!" One could repeat her exclamation with reference to many a person alive today. But those who trembled had, at the time, good reason to do so. Scarpia was an evil, treacherous, political murderer—and there are Scarpias who walk amongst us today, enjoying both their lives and the benefits of their crimes. Should they be allowed to do so with impunity?

IV

Let me summarize our conclusions. At the outset, I specified six combinations of two elements, one of them moral, the other legal. These were the six major recommendations for dealing with the unique issues of justice raised by the collapse of totalitarian and other criminal dictatorial regimes. I then identified two categories of crime, the historical and the heinous. Finally, I identified heinous crimes as manifestations of evil. In returning to these six combinations, I shall now consider only the case of evil. The granting of general amnesties or the application of the statute of limitations to functionaries and high officials of the former regimes presents no grave moral problem in my view. On the contrary, there are good reasons for behaving in this way. The only exception I make is where such officials or functionaries were perpetrators of evil.

Let us now turn to the arguments against punishing the perpetrators of evil. There are several arguments intended to show that not even those guilty of the most heinous crimes should be indicted. I shall consider these point by point. I shall not, however, take into account the view of unreconstructed Stalinists, for in their view, no crimes were committed, and if any were committed, they occurred only as the side effects of an otherwise commendable course of action. Besides, these people have no arguments to offer in the standard language of morals or politics, from which their discourse as much as their actions has excluded them.

In the judgment "perpetrators of heinous crimes should not be punished," "punishment" can refer either to legal punishment alone, that is, to indictment, or to moral punishment.

First proposition: Perpetrators of heinous crimes should not be indicted but only morally censured.

To this I answer: One cannot morally punish a person who is removed from normal moral discourse, who does not experience pangs of conscience, or who has already forgotten his crimes. One cannot morally punish a person who despises morals as "petty bourgeois" or as utterly irrelevant.

Modern society is not a homogeneous community. An evil or infected person can avoid moral censure by choosing to live among those who are morally like themselves. In this community, public censure is dismissed, and the prospect of divine punishment mocked as superstition.

Perpetrators of heinous crimes in a totalitarian regime cannot subsequently be morally punished unless they feel remorse. But if they feel anything approaching adequate remorse, they have already been morally punished, and need no second moral punishment.

Thus we see that the recommendation that perpetrators of heinous crimes should only be morally punished is inconsistent, for in either of the two cases we have raised, those who are only morally punished are not punished at all.

Second proposition: Those guilty of heinous crimes should not be punished at all.

Under this heading there is a single purely moral argument. There are, however, various admixtures of pragmatic and moral reasons that can be adduced in its favor. The purely moral reason is religious, even if it is on occasion found in the mouths of unbelievers. It is the precept love your enemies, forgive those who have wronged you.

But even if I succeed in loving my enemies, should I also love those who have wronged my neighbor beyond repair? Those who have wronged me I can perhaps forgive. There is no need to open secret police files. And if they are opened, and the name of the person who denounced me comes to light, I can perhaps forgive him or her. But one cannot forgive the murder of other people's children, nor should one. One has no moral right to forgive in the name of the dead or of the mourners. For there is a logic in the Christian commandment; you should forgive those who have wronged *you* because the principle is of justice, as distinct from revenge. But others should not forgive on your behalf, nor should you forgive on others' behalf, or there would be no justice. If you forgive in the name of others, you can forgive yourself in their name for the evil you perpetrate, and this is an immoral principle. There is therefore only one purely moral gesture open to us here, the exclamation of the saintly Alyosha Karamazov reacting to an account of barbarity: "Shoot him!"[4] No shooting this time—but moral forgiveness is also excluded.

All the pragmatic arguments in favor of not punishing the guilty in this case boil down to the desire to turn over a new leaf. There are two versions of the argument.

First version: Too much blood has been shed; let us put an end to bloodletting. Everything that has happened until now should be forgotten. We should not poison our souls with the desire for revenge. Revenge calls forth further revenge and there is no end to it.

Second version: National reconciliation requires that the past be buried. For this we need everyone's skill and cooperation. It is useless to concern ourselves with the past, we must look ahead, to the future.

In the first formulation, pragmatic and moral considerations are combined. In the second, the moral motivation is negligible.

Let us first consider the "new leaf" argument. The moral considerations in this position are consequentialist. One might equally maintain that a people can only turn to a new and clean page of history *after* having meted out punishment for heinous crimes; this would not be a consequentialist position. Even if one believes that historical justice must be done for any page of history to be clean, it is not in order to cleanse the pages of history that crimes are punished. The motive for the act of retribution is to restore the balance of justice as far as humanly possible.

In the argument under scrutiny, however, retribution is suspended and the act of justice deliberately forgone because of the fear that this act will itself lead to injustices, indeed to a series of injustices. This fear is not unfounded. Every gesture of retribution carries in it the risk of escalation. It is not an insignificant possibility that the morally right may result in the morally wrong.

Although acknowledging these consequentialist points, we should note that there are also consequentialist arguments in favor of punishment. Among them are the following. There can be no turning over a clean leaf without catharsis, and there can be no catharsis if we simply sweep crimes under the carpet. The idyllic new page of history will not after all be clean. The decision not to prosecute the offenders does not cause hatred, resentment, and personal grievances to be forgotten: They simply resurface at the next suitable occasion.

Those who oppose punishment on moral grounds often do so on the basis of a deterrent theory of punishment. Punishment is no longer necessary, it is argued, because the perpetrators of heinous crimes are no longer in a position to commit such crimes. They cannot repeat their crimes. And no one else can either. In contemporary Argentina, no one can any longer cause people to disappear by kidnap, torture, and murder, as happened in the past. In newly unified Germany, no one can give the order that those who cross the border should be shot. Thus it no longer serves any deterrent function to punish those who committed these heinous crimes.

Let us assume, for the sake of simplicity, what I do not acknowledge in fact, that the main principle of punishment is deterrence. Imagine the situation where veteran mass murderers continue to live in the same conditions as everyone else, or, for that matter, in better ones. What kind of morality would this example suggest to present and future politicians? It would convey a simple message: Whatever they do, however criminal their acts, they will get away with them, provided only that they rule for a sufficiently long time and take pains to hide their crimes under forms of legality. People will be so anxious to turn over a new leaf that the crimes of their rulers will go unpunished in the future as they did in the past. This is what the present and future politicians will conclude.

It is possible that no political crimes could today be of the same magnitude as those of the past. But the principle remains: There are crimes on a smaller scale which can still make people miserable, and one never knows what opportunities for evil will arise in the future. If one accepts the principle of deterrence, the negative formulation "we need not punish where there is no reason to deter" must be balanced by the positive formulation "if we wish to deter, we must punish."

The policy adopted in Spain in the aftermath of the Franco regime may serve as a model for the successful combination of moral and pragmatic considerations. A clean page in the history of Spain was opened and the consequences were morally and pragmatically benign. But it should also be said that the context was unique. The Spanish solution can serve as an example only in countries where decisions take place in a somewhat similar context. The purely moral injunction "love your enemies, forgive those who have wronged you" takes on an aura of truth in the context of the Spanish Civil War, in which both sides committed heinous crimes. Symbolically and in very truth, men and women had to forgive the sins of those who had wronged them, their families or friends. In the ex-communist states, and in post-totalitarian states, the situation is quite other, and the example of Spain not therefore applicable.

Let me turn briefly to a second version of the "new leaf of history" argument. In this version, it is argued that the past should be forgotten in order that the future can begin. This is a technological argument; it treats historical periods as if they were machines. The obsolete appliances have to be thrown away and replaced by new ones. However commendable in the field of technology, this attitude is wholly out of place in relation to a nation's history, which is no less about remembering and hanging on to the past than it is about the projection of the future. A nagging awareness of the past creates the third dimension of history, the dimension of meaning that gives life to any projection of the future, however radical the break with the past. A future that is fabricated *ex nihilo* rests on unsound foundations; there is nothing to underpin it. There can, in short, be no national reconciliation if one forgets the very events that set the nation at odds.

V

"Perpetrators of heinous crimes should be punished, for no counterargument has so far convinced us of the contrary." Anyone subscribing to this verdict thereby signs the decree of punishment, whether or not the punishment will in fact be carried out. To sign it is to be led by the belief that it is wrong to let heinous crimes go unpunished, that justice should be done. The blood of the victims cries out to heaven for punishment to be administered in the next world, but no less to ourselves and to posterity for punishment in this world.

Three persons say in unison: the perpetrators should be punished. The first adds: alas, they cannot be. The second insists: since they should be punished, they can be punished. The third raises her hands in perplexity: they should be punished, and yet, at the same time, they should not. These are the last of the three combinations that we introduced, and I shall analyze them one by one.

The first position is this: Justice requires that we prosecute the perpetrators of heinous crimes, but the legal system does not permit it. Prosecution would, to take an example, require retroactive legislation. Compromises are, alas, necessary in political life, and in this case, justice cannot be done.

The second position denies the relevance of this "cannot." Whatever we should do, we must be able to do. No legal system, not even a brand-new one with its origins in democracy, can be allowed to stand in the way of justice. If there is a consensus that heinous crimes have been committed, the perpetrators have to answer for them. There is no place for legalism here, the argument runs, first and foremost because the brand-new laws should not run counter to our moral intuitions. As Judith Shklar has rightly said: There is a continuum between moral and legal considerations.[5]

The argument, we should but we cannot, is based on principles of legal positivism on two counts. First, it disallows the suspension of our own laws—laws such as the statute of limitations—in certain extraordinary cases, such as the punishment of heinous crimes, and second, it treats the pseudo-laws of totalitarian regimes as if they were real ones. But not everything written on a piece of paper and passed as law by a bunch of murderers, their accomplices, and the agents of their institutions, bullied into obedience, qualifies as law. Thousands of trainloads of kulaks were "lawfully" driven to the taiga and left to starve to death there with their children. The legitimate Prime Minister of Hungary was tried and executed according to laws extant. Where laws were produced according to whim, political convenience, and the dictates of political revenge, there were no laws. We conclude that the position "they should be punished, but cannot be" is a lopsided one; its two components are not equally stable. Morality is on the side of those insisting on punishment, but the legal aspects of the argument are treated as little more than a pragmatic consideration, at very best a token on the altar of national, historical reconciliation. And where morality collides with pragmatic considerations, the old Kantian recipe is still valid; the moral "ought" should have priority. What one ought to do, one can do. That is, despite all pragmatic arguments to the contrary, the morally approved course of action should go ahead. Let us then have a new round of Nuremberg Trials. The Nuremberg Trials are our example, and the example is there to be imitated.

We turn now to the last position. It states that heinous crimes should be punished—and simultaneously insists that its perpetrators should not be punished. This position sounds absurd and paradoxical, but it is neither. It locates a moral conflict. All moral conflicts, like moral choices, are contextual. The context for this position is the same as that for the other two positions. It arises in states where the constitution does not provide for the prosecution of those guilty of heinous crimes.

The moral argument for this position can be summed up as follows: Positions one and two both state that a moral ought (justice should be done) is confronted with a mainly legal and pragmatic consideration which brings into focus certain secondary moral issues. The two positions diverged on one count. For the first position (justice should and cannot be done), the obstacles to justice could not be obviated. For the second (justice should and therefore could be done) the obstacles could be removed. But the second position is essentially wrongheaded, for the suspension of the law for particular cases is not just legally but morally wrong. The maxim that the law should be suspended in particular cases is an evil maxim. Philosophers who locate evil in evil maxims have always counted arguments in favor of its suspension as evil. It was because he could not condone such arguments that Socrates suffered an unjust death rather than attempt to escape the laws of his country, and that Kant made such a strong case not against tyrannicide but against the trial of Louis XVI. And it is also wrong to believe that the maxim cannot be evil simply because no evil consequences have flowed from it in certain cases. It is commonplace that good results may flow from bad intentions or designs, but no commonplace makes good of bad or bad of good.

The maxim that perpetrators of heinous crimes should be punished is transcontextual. Evil should be punished everywhere, under all circumstances, and no less, therefore, in the context we here consider. To this maxim there is no exception. Self-punishment, in the form of repentance or penitence, does not constitute an exception. But if a person can be punished only by suspension of the law, he should not be punished, because the maxim that recommends suspension of the law is itself evil. This does not, of course, affect the principle that evil should be punished. Evil should not go unpunished, but neither should one act upon evil maxims, whatever good consequences may follow. Thus the conclusion: perpetrators of heinous crimes should and at the same time should not be punished. No paradox here, just a moral conflict in context.

If we confront the advocates of the third position with the Nuremberg Trials, they will answer that the context in which they must reach a verdict is entirely different. This is not because the Nazi crimes were of a different degree of heinousness; evil is evil, evil is always infinite, and we can say with Nicolaus of Cusa that in an infinite triangle all sides would always be equal, for all of them would be infinite.[6] But a particularity of the Nazi crimes tried in Nuremberg is that they were committed against many different peoples, so that no existing law could possibly have applied to them. For evil to be punished, a recourse to the fictitious laws of nature was necessary, and this meets with our own intuitive—and retrospective—approval. If there is a procedure based on fictitious natural law, it is the consensus of moral intuition that must guide us in establishing the rightness of the principle. And the arguments we have set out show that there is no consensus at all as to whether people who have committed heinous crimes should now be punished. Where intuition is so disparate in its conclusions, we have no moral justification for recourse to the fictitious laws of nature which must by definition reflect moral intuition.

VI

In our discussion of evil, we concluded that those guilty of heinous crimes should punished, for justice must be done. The discussion was conducted in the abstract, irrespective of context. Then we returned to the context, that is, to the situations in which decisions are now being taken. After looking briefly at the arguments against prosecution, we listened to three groups of people who subscribed to the verdict that the perpetrators of such crimes should be punished. Here we took a context narrower than before; we looked at the hardest cases. We assumed a democratically based legal system that makes no provision for the indictment of the perpetrators and we imagined that the guilty showed no sign of serious moral repentance.

All three positions remain thoroughly problematic. If the first is accepted, heinous crimes remain unpunished. Petty thieves will go to prison in countries where mass murderers will enjoy a peaceful old age.

If the second position is accepted, a procedure that feeds on moral legitimacy will be pushed forward in the absence of any such legitimacy. If there should be a second edition of the Nuremberg Trials without the support of consensual moral intuition, it will cast a retrospective shadow on the Nuremberg Trials themselves. They can remain an exemplary act of justice only on condition they are not copied. The Nuremberg Trials stand as the embodiment of the regulative idea, the "ought" sentence according to which those guilty of heinous crimes ought to be punished. Their context remains forever unique.

The first two positions do have a certain value as recommendations. They at least tell you what to do. The third position, by contrast, is not a recommendation at all; it merely formulates a moral conflict. Where a moral choice is confronted with a pragmatic or consequentialist consideration, the categorical imperative or one of its variants can cut the Gordian knot. But where two moral choices confront one another, no categorical imperative is available. One chooses one principle, and thereby infringes the other; or if one chooses neither, one infringes both. Yet it is impossible to choose both at once—this is the definition of a moral conflict.

One might say here, with Derrida,[7] that justice is always incalculable, that it requires that one calculate the incalculable, that it addresses itself to singularity, that, in deciding, we should give ourselves up to the impossible decision; that we should, while taking account of rules and laws, nevertheless decide. Yet everything that can hamper men and women in the process of decision is here present in the extreme, for there are no laws and no rules, not even the prospect of guidance, to orient those who decide. No new law will be founded, or ancient law revived, by their decision. All that will transpire is the impossibility of founding such laws. On the one hand, the argument runs, those who decide will incur guilt whatever course they fasten on. And on the other, choose we must, at least in the inner fastness of our souls.

But the question whether those guilty of heinous crimes should be punished is, in this way, evacuated of its political and social content, and no longer calls for a straightforward answer even when it is asked in a specific context. The question is simply thrown back to the person who asks it: you choose, you sign, it is your responsibility, only be aware that you choose between two evils. It emerges that the double formula "those guilty of heinous crimes should be punished and at the same time should not be punished," this gesture of throwing the ball back into the court, of informing the decision makers that moral conflict cannot be resolved but only cut off by the leap of choice, is a confession of defeat. It concedes our impotence in the confrontation with evil.

VII

Something must have gone wrong at the outset, for the conclusion is not merely disquieting but downright false. We know from experience that evil can in fact be resisted, that many men and women have resisted evil in dark times. And evil must indeed be resisted while it is in power. But in our context, where the dilemma of punishing evil arises, evil has fallen from power. Evil, as we have seen, is intimately related to power, it thrives on the confidence that its power is irresistible, whether this power is political, social, or psychological. There is no evil without power. Resistance to evil, on the other hand, is found in persons combining two characteristics: good maxims and excellent character. Good maxims immunize them to the attraction of evil; they do not become infected during the epidemic. They know where right ends and wrong begins. Their character makes them stand up to evil and oppose it, and they would rather suffer than commit injustice. In resisting evil, they display courage and decency. Contrast this with the qualities needed to subscribe to the verdict that those guilty of heinous crimes should be punished. No courage and decency are needed here. Quite different moral characters can subscribe to the judgment, not least those cowards who hid in the dark while evil was still in power. We thus conclude that what I called our impotence in facing evil is not the manifestation of general human fragility, but a predicament that follows from the very character of evil.

Let me recapitulate the core of our predicament. There

are evil persons in the world; they originate evil maxims, they are demonic. But the radius of their influence is generally insignificant. Then, for many contingent reasons, social, political, and other, the influence of evil maxims suddenly spreads, mobilizing the worst psychological drives and recruiting to its cause the subtlest intellectual apparatus. The epidemic flourishes, evil gains the upper hand and begins to operate on a grand scale, leaving behind it human hecatombs, misery, and devastation. And then, if there is still a "then," the epidemic recedes, and the evil maxims are replaced by disappointment or cynicism. If a totalitarian regime lasts long enough, the worst of the malefactors are already in their graves, beyond the reach of human retribution.

The obstacles to punishment we have discussed so far have been pragmatic and legalistic. But there is another possible obstacle to punishment. The perpetrators cannot be punished, because the main culprits, the initiators of all the evils, are now beyond the reach of human retribution. And those who created the initial conditions in which heinous crimes were committed are the true perpetrators. A handful of them are alive, but most of them are dead. Can justice still be done?

A repeat of the Nuremberg Trials, we have argued, is morally impossible, given the absence of moral consensus about its desirability. The so-called laws of nature are only the projections of our general moral intuition. In the absence of this consensual intuition, the laws of nature are a mere anachronism. But why is there no moral consensus about the desirability of new Nuremberg Trials?

The Nazis were in power for little more than ten years, ten years characterized by the escalation of evil. It was possible to bring to justice all the perpetrators of Nazi crimes, with the exception of Hitler, Himmler, and Goebbels, who escaped through suicide. Soviet totalitarianism, in contrast, lasted between forty and seventy-five years. After the years of escalation of evil, there was a cyclic diminution of its energy. The regime was the same, heinous crimes were still committed, and the suffering of the victims was no less than it had been at the height of the terror. But the diminishing energy of evil led to a kind of banalization. New generations grew up, and many terrible deeds were simply forgotten. To reawaken memories is not, for the most part, welcome. The moral issue here is not whether this oblivion is a good or a bad thing. It is simply that under these conditions, even if there were a consensus about which crimes were so heinous as to require punishment, no moral consensus about new Nuremberg Trials could possibly emerge.

If evil maxims can establish a power base that lasts long enough, perpetrators of evil will, in all probability, never be punished. Those who commit the most execrable crimes will get away with it. This is why we are impotent against evil. Good can resist evil while evil lasts, but becomes impotent against it after evil's demise.

Evil is active while it holds power, but once its power is gone, evil is just an empty shell, the physical body of a person who was once evil. Can evil be punished while it lasts, while it is evil incarnate? The answer is no, evil cannot be punished, but is self-destructive. It turns against itself. Self-destruction is the inevitable logic of evil however long it is in power, however long it lasts.

The perpetrators of heinous crimes should be punished because justice should be done. The times were out of joint, and we must set them straight. But it is of secondary importance whether the surviving perpetrators of crimes are actually punished. The Claudius with whom we have to deal has already lost both crown and queen. But there are no clean new pages in the book of history, and there is no cleansing to be attained at the price of forgetting. On the contrary, like Horatio "speaking to th' yet unknowing world," we should tell and retell the story of those "carnal, bloody, and unnatural acts," those "accidental judgments, casual slaughters," and "deaths put on by cunning and forced cause,"[8] perpetrated by the hand of evil, in the twentieth century, in our own house, and on such a scale as was never dreamt of in Horatio's or even Hamlet's philosophy.

—Language-edited by Chris Miller

MAJORITY RULE AND INDIVIDUAL RIGHTS

Jon Elster

I. INTRODUCTION

My concern with majority rule[1] and individual rights was spurred by recent developments in Eastern Europe and the former Soviet Union. In this region, majority rule is being adopted across the board. At the same time, individual rights have a precarious existence. To exaggerate somewhat, there has been a shift from the despotism of the Party to the despotism of the majority, both inimical to the protection of minority rights. Although there has been progress of a sort, since the Party did not care for the rights of the majority either, the achievements are decidedly limited. In most countries, constitutional democracy is still in the future.

This story has a precedent, or rather several. In England after 1648, in the United States after 1776, and in France after 1789, the abolition of a despotic regime gave rise to untrammeled majority rule, only to be followed some decades later by a regime subject to constitutional constraints.[2] I shall not discuss the case of England, where the third stage took the form of a constitutional monarchy rather than a democracy, but focus instead on the French and the American experiences. In particular, I have found the debates at the Federal Convention in Philadelphia in 1787 and the Assemblée Constituante in Paris in 1789–91 very useful in illuminating the dangers of majority rule.[3] My strategy in this paper, therefore, is first to use these historical precedents to delineate the range of majoritarian problems and counter-majoritarian solutions, and then to look at some implications for Eastern Europe.

I shall proceed as follows. Section II makes a brief argu-

I am grateful to Stephen Holmes, Bernard Manin, Pasquale Pasquino, Herman Schwartz, and Cass Sunstein for comments on a draft of this paper.

ment for the view that decision by majority vote is the ultimate criterion in any democracy, even in constitutional ones. Section III discusses some of the ways in which majority rule can infringe on individual rights. Section IV introduces four solutions to this conflict: constitutional entrenchment, judicial review, separation of powers, checks and balances. In Sections V through VIII, these solutions are considered separately in more detail. Their undesirable side effects are also canvassed. In these sections I draw extensively, but not exclusively, on materials from the two eighteenth-century debates. I conclude in Section IX with a survey of constitutional developments in Eastern Europe.

II. ARGUMENTS FOR MAJORITY RULE

At an abstract level, one can offer axiomatic arguments for majority rule.[4] Thus majority voting is the only system of preference aggregation that satisfies the conditions of *anonymity* (the outcome should not depend on the naming of the preference holders), *neutrality* (the outcome should not depend on the naming of the alternatives), *positive responsiveness* (a condition related to that of Pareto optimality), and *universal domain* (the aggregation mechanism should work for all possible combinations of individual preferences). At a deeper level, however, these conditions themselves are in need of justification. Consider in particular the crucial notion of anonymity. In predemocratic political systems, the idea that everybody's preferences are on a par as inputs to the social decision-making process would be seen as ludicrous.

How, then, can one argue for the condition of anonymity? There has never been a lack of groups claiming a privileged status. The rich, landed property owners, the old, the educated, the intelligent, the nobility, members of the Aryan race or of other ethnic groups, believers of some given religion, and the male half of society have all claimed to be inherently superior to their complements. None of these groups will accept the condition of anonymity. A key to majority rule is found, however, in the very multiplicity of these privilege-claiming groups. In the presence of many different groups who compete on the basis of their innate *quality,* only *quantity* can emerge as a peaceful focal-point solution.[5] Marx once observed that the only peaceful way to resolve the conflict between two royal pretenders is to have a republic.[6] In the struggle over which tribe in ex-colonial countries is to impose its language as the official one, the only solution acceptable to all has often been to choose the language of the former colonial power. Majority decision is similar to these formal, second-best solutions. Although people are not equal, they have to be treated as if they were.

What I have just said does not amount to an argument for anonymity or, to use the more familiar word, equality. It yields at best an explanation of why the idea of equality was irresistible or, more precisely, why from a certain time onward the only practical choice was between repression and equality.[7] Among the various positive arguments for majority rule[8] I shall (for reasons made clear in the next paragraph) limit myself to its close link to utilitarianism. If more people prefer x to y, then the choice of x is likely to yield more aggregate welfare than would be realized if y were chosen. Although it is easy to think of counterexamples, because preferences can differ in intensity, the general correlation is not invalidated. Similarly, the effect of the Condorcet paradox of cyclical majorities is to weaken the correlation, not to eliminate it.

The link between majority rule and utilitarianism is confirmed by the fact that they have the same opponent: the defender of individual rights. There is a large literature on the relation between utility and rights.[9] The relation between majority rule and individual rights—the topic of the present paper—has also been the topic of an extensive legal literature. (These two bodies of writing are, however, rarely related to each other.) In two closely parallel arguments, defenders of individual rights have argued that they trump, respectively, utility maximization and majority rule.[10] To the greatest good for the greatest number and the rule of the many over the few, they oppose respect and concern for the individual. The connection between the two doctrines is undermined, however, if one reason why majority rule has to be constrained by rights is that the majority in the heat of passion may fail to perceive what is in its true interest. In that case, rights are needed to promote aggregate welfare and majority rule becomes the enemy of utilitarianism rather than its natural ally. We shall see, however, that there are other reasons to fear majority rule that do not turn on this argument.

I conclude this section with two remarks that should be kept in mind in what follows. Although one may believe that majority rule needs to be limited and constrained in various ways, these limits and constraints can ultimately have no other normative foundation than a simple majority decision. Consider the ideal case of a constituent assembly operating in a complete historical and social vacuum, for example, a group of settlers writing a constitution for their new country. Although the assembly may decide that a qualified majority shall be required to change the constitution, that decision itself must be taken by a simple majority. If one required a qualified majority at the constitutional convention, two problems arise. First, the assembly might not be able to produce a constitution at all. In constitutional amendments, the existing document serves as the status quo that remains in force when a proposed amendment fails, but in a creation *ex nihilo* there is no status quo that can serve as fallback position. Second, and more important, the decision to use a qualified majority would itself have to be made by a simple majority, to avoid an infinite regress.[11] Although the relevance of this remark is attenuated in actual instances of constitution making, which always take place in a context that imposes or suggests a structure on the process, the fundamental logic of constitution making remains that of a simple majority deciding that a simple majority may not be the best way to decide some issues.

A second, related remark concerns the effects of majoritarian decision making at a constitutional convention when that assembly also serves as an ordinary legislature, as was the case at the Assemblée Constituante. That combination obviously may be undesirable. A main task of a constituent assembly is to strike the proper balance of power between the legislative and the executive branches of government. To assign that task to an assembly that also serves as a legislative body would be to ask it to act as judge in its own cause. A constitution written by a legislative assembly might be expected to give excessive powers to the legislature. In the abstract, this problem could be solved by means similar to the ones used in legislative bodies, by checks and balances. A royal veto over the constitution might, for instance, have kept the legislative tendency to self-aggrandizement in check. However, even those who argued for extensive checks and balances *in* the constitution, did not believe in a similar system for deciding *on* the constitution. Mounier, for instance, argued that the strong unicameral assembly necessary to create the constitution, would be inappropriate for ordinary lawmaking. Similarly, Mirabeau argued that the King should have a veto in the constitution, but not over the constitution itself. Summarizing both points, Clermont-Tonnerre observed that the "three-headed hydra"—king, first chamber, and second chamber—that the constitution should create could not itself have created a constitution. To get around the problem of self-interested framers, the Assemblée Constituante adopted another solution, voting its members ineligible to the first ordinary legislature. Robespierre,[12] in his first great speech, won the assembly for this "self-denying ordinance."[13] Although sometimes viewed by posterity as a disastrous piece of populist overkill,[14] Robespierre's solution did correspond to a genuine difficulty.

III. HOW MAJORITY RULE MAY INFRINGE ON INDIVIDUAL RIGHTS

For the purposes of this paper, I need not discuss what rights are, nor which rights individuals have. It is sufficient to consider principles claimed as rights, and how they might be endangered by majority rule. I shall not consider the inappropriately named "positive rights" that entitle the individual to have part of the social product spent on activities that directly enhance his material welfare, such as the right to work, to welfare, or to a clean environment. Instead I shall limit myself to the traditional rights, such as civil liberties, political liberties, property rights, and the freedom of contract.

A tripartite division of rights will prove convenient. First, there are the rights that enable real and equal political participation, notably the right to vote and freedom of speech and association. Second, there are rights that promote the rule of law, such as a prohibition of bills of attainder, a ban on retroactive legislation or retroactive taxation, a guarantee of full or fair compensation for confiscation of property, a ban on arbitrary search and seizure, and the right to a fair trial. Under this category, I also include the right to be able to count on the laws being reasonably stable.[15] Third, there are rights that protect religious and ethnic groups, by guaranteeing freedom of worship or the right to use and be educated in one's own language. This particular way of classifying rights has no intrinsic merit, except that it is usefully correlated with ways in which—and motives for which—majority rule might possibly infringe on the exercise and the value of rights.

First, a majority government will always be tempted to manipulate political rights to increase its chances of reelection. If it is free to change the timing of the election, it may choose a moment when economic conjunctures are favorable.[16] If electoral district boundaries have to be redrawn because of population changes, the government may try to do so to its advantage. If the majority is free to change the electoral system—for example, proportional representation versus single-member districts—it may exploit this possibility for strategic purposes. If voters have to be registered before they can vote, the government may have an incentive to make registration more difficult to disenfranchise de facto some of those who would have voted for the opposition. In countries with state-owned radio and television, the government may give itself disproportionate time. We may note for later reference that in these cases the attack on rights comes from the majority in parliament, not from the majority in the population. The danger is precisely that the parliamentary majority may have means at its disposal to prevent the popular majority from putting a new government in place.

Second, a majority may set aside the rule of law under the sway of a standing interest or a momentary passion. This was Madison's main worry. "In all cases where a majority are united by a common interest or passion, the rights of the minority are in danger."[17] This distinction between interest and passion is crucial.[18] If the poor or relatively propertyless form a majority, their interest might induce them to enact laws that are contrary to the rights of property, by creating paper money, legislating debtor relief, and so on. A quite different danger arises if the majority is animated by a sudden passion that makes it deaf to the demands of the rule of law. The impulse may originate either in a majority in parliament or in a popular majority that manages to impose its will on

Jon Elster

parliament by nonelectoral methods. The risk of such legislation being passed is especially great in wartime and other
emergency situations, a famous case being the internment of
Japanese-Americans during World War II.

Third, a majority may set aside the rights of an ethnic or
religious minority under the sway of what one might call a
standing passion. In earlier centuries, religious fanaticism has
been the mainspring of this form of majoritarian domination.
Today, ethnic hatred, sometimes combined with religious
differences, is proving a horribly potent source of oppression.

Two distinctions are implicit in what I have said. On the
one hand, we have to identify the relevant majority, and
notably whether it is parliamentary or popular. On the other
hand we have to identify the motives which move the members of the majority to infringe on the rights of the minority.
Here I have discussed three cases: standing interests, standing passions, and momentary passions. Although all six combinations of actors and motives might be relevant, I shall limit
myself to five.

First, there is the case of a parliamentary majority that acts
to preserve itself as a majority, by the various procedural
stratagems mentioned earlier, or to promote such other interests as it might have. Madison, for instance, noted that "It
had often happened that men who had acquired landed property on credit, got into the Legislatures with a view of promoting an unjust protection agst. their Creditors."[19]

Second, there is the case of a parliamentary majority
being swayed by the (standing) passion of *amour-propre*, that
is, vanity or self-love. Although virtually absent at the Federal
Convention, the fear that political agents might act on such
motives was often expressed in the Assemblée Constituante.
Bergasse argued, for instance, that a suspensive veto of the
King would not have the intended effect of making the assembly reconsider its vote, because its *amour-propre* would
prevent it from backing down.[20]

Third, there is the case of a popular majority acting (through its representatives) to further its economic interest. A special case is that in which this interest is defined in terms of present value of future income, discounted by some positive factor. If the discount rate is high, members of the majority might find it in their interest to take confiscatory measures against property owners, even if they know that in the long run they or their descendants would be better off respecting property.

Fourth, there is the case of a popular majority acting (through its representatives) under a sudden impulse, a momentary passion. The founders in Philadelphia and the constituants in Paris constantly referred to this danger. In Philadelphia, we find references to "the turbulence and follies of democracy," "the fury of democracy," "the popular passions [which] spread like wild fire, and become irresistable," "fickleness and passion," "the turbulency and violence of unruly passion," and to the "precipitation, changeableness, and excesses of the first branch." In Paris, Lally-Tollendal referred to the assembly being "entraînée par l'éloquence, séduite par des sophismes, égarée par des intrigues, enflammée par des passions qu'on lui fait partager, emportée par des mouvements soudains qu'on lui communique, arrêtée par des terreurs qu'on lui inspire." Others warned against "les prestiges de l'éloquence, l'effervescence de l'enthousiasme," "les causes d'erreur, de précipitation ou de séduction oratoire," or "l'erreur, la précipitation, l'ambition."[21]

Fifth, there is the case of a popular majority acting (through its representatives) from a standing, permanent passion. A perusal of the quotations in the previous paragraph brings out the predominance of terms such as "sudden," "fickle," "unruly," "precipitation," "changeableness," and the like. By contrast, there were few references in the two eighteenth-century assemblies to more permanent passions and prejudices that might fashion the will of the majority. In

Philadelphia, for instance, nobody mentioned racism or religious sectarianism as potential threats to individual rights.[22] In the late twentieth century, these problems of ethnicity and religion may prove to be the outstanding danger of majority rule. In addition to the problems in Eastern Europe that I discuss in the concluding section, the specter of Islamic majoritarianism in Algeria offers a striking example.

I should add a nuance to this somewhat mechanical presentation. Although I believe that the distinction between interest and passion is of fundamental analytical importance, they often go together in practical politics. On the one hand, passion often makes us believe that something is in our interest which really is not. What Tocqueville called "the democratic sentiment of envy" may dress itself up as a theory that the rich, if not restricted, will use their wealth to subvert the polity. On the other hand, an interest, to be effective in politics, often has to take on the garb of passion. Norms of equality and other social norms can impart a passionate tone to claims that otherwise might be seen as mere expressions of self-interest.[23] In practice, therefore, people will not acknowledge a conflict between interest and passion. But this need not prevent the outside observer from being able to identify one of them as the causally efficacious motive, and the other as its dupe or handmaiden.

IV. COUNTERMAJORITARIAN DEVICES: AN OVERVIEW

In the following sections I discuss what I believe to be the four main countermajoritarian devices used in modern societies. In this section I offer a broader perspective, by attempting to relate the four devices to each other. First, however, I shall briefly comment on a proposal that, although not immediately relevant for current events, was an important background element for the eighteenth-century assemblies.[24] This is the view that when the polity is too large for direct democracy one can reduce the dangers of representative democracy by a system of bound mandates, perhaps combined with the possibility of recalling delegates at any time if they exceed their briefs. In both Philadelphia and Paris, there was general agreement that this system was undesirable. It would reduce democracy to a mere system of preference aggregation, and leave no room for the transformation of preferences through rational deliberation.[25] For many writers, from Aristotle to the present, majority rule is in fact justified by the opportunity it offers for the exchange of ideas and discussion.[26] In a small polity, this ideal can be realized without creating a legislative body with interests of its own. In a large polity, which requires a representative democracy, the latter danger is an unavoidable concomitant of any attempt to realize the deliberative ideal. Independence inevitably cuts both ways. At the same time, direct democracy is more vulnerable to violent popular passions. Whereas both the town meeting and an assembly of (unbound) representatives allow for discussion, the former is vulnerable to the problem of passionate popular majorities and the latter to the problem of self-interested legislative majorities. A representative system constrained by bound mandates may limit both majoritarian dangers, but at the cost of giving up the benefits of deliberation.[27] If the only purpose of representation was to protect individual rights, this system might be optimal. But an assembly is also created to get things done, to work out compromises, and to make good decisions.

The four devices I shall discuss are, to repeat, constitutionalism, judicial review, separation of powers, and checks and balances. In some political systems, these form a tightly knit whole. Judicial review, separation of powers, and checks and balances are all written into the constitution. Judicial review is a mechanism to interpret and enforce the constitution. In doing so, it also serves to prevent usurpation of power by the other organs of state. It can only perform that function, however, if it is reasonably independent of those organs. More generally, checks and balances presupposes some separation of powers: If A is to act as a check on B, it must have some degree of independence from B.

In other systems, these elements are decoupled from each other to a larger extent. England, for instance, does not even have a written constitution, and yet there are limits on majority rule that form part of what has been called the unwritten constitution.[28] Judicial review may go beyond the constitution and consider rights not specifically enumerated in that document. Also, the institution of judicial review may not itself be specifically mentioned in the constitution. This is the case in the United States. Although checks and balances presupposes a separation of powers, the converse is not true. The French constitution of 1789, which was "based on an extreme version of the doctrine of the separation of powers,"[29] had no checks and balances beyond the suspensive veto of the King. In the constitution of the Fifth French Republic, the Conseil Constitutionnel was originally created to strengthen the executive against the legislature. It was only fifteen years later that it was made into (and made itself into) an institution for independent judicial review.[30]

V. CONSTITUTIONALISM AS A CONSTRAINT ON MAJORITY RULE

Majority rule can be restrained by the constitution, both directly and indirectly. In this section I discuss the direct influence that derives from the combination of the constitutionalization of certain laws and procedures that make it difficult to amend the constitution. In later sections I discuss other restraining devices that may or may not be explicitly mentioned in the constitution but that, if they are, operate in a different manner.

A constitution can affect behavior by acting on the desire of the majority to change the law or on its opportunities to do so.[31] The first mechanism operates by making the process of constitutional amendment very slow and time-consuming, so that impulsive passions can cool down and reason (or interest!) reinstate itself. The second operates by requiring qualified majorities for changing the constitution or, at the limit, declaring some clauses unamendable. Some constitutions (such as the Norwegian one) impose both qualified majorities and delays; others (such as the Swedish one) require only delays.[32] Still others (such as the Hungarian one) require only qualified majorities; New Zealand appears to be unique in that "only ordinary legislative efforts are required to supplement, modify or repeal the Constitution."[33]

Delaying devices are designed to counteract sudden impulses and momentary passions among the majority. Qualified majorities are intended to protect individual rights against the standing interests and passions of the majority. It is easily seen that these two mechanisms must differ fundamentally in their mode of adoption. If we focus on delays, the following description is indeed appropriate: "Constitutions are chains with which men bind themselves in their sane moments that they may not die by a suicidal hand in the day of their frenzy."[34] It is in the straightforward interest of the majority to prevent itself from making rash decisions under the sway of passion. However, the use of qualified majorities cannot be explained or justified by the idea that Peter when sober acts to bind Peter when drunk.[35] If a majority among the founders has a standing interest on some particular issue, that interest will not induce them to set it aside. If they are moved by religious fanaticism, this is a passion they embrace rather than fear. In the eighteenth century the question did not have the importance it assumes today. The founders as a whole, and a fortiori a majority among them, represented a minority elite within the population that could impose its views on the rest. In the United States, for instance, today's majority is bound by a founding minority.

As with the other countermajoritarian devices discussed below, constitutionalism has a potential for creating problems as well as solving them. One should keep in mind a dictum of constitutional lawyers, due to Justice Robert Jackson: The constitution is not a suicide pact. It must be possible to unbind oneself in an emergency. Society must not be confined too tightly.[36] In the debates over the constitutional ban on paper money at the Federal Convention, George Mason said that "Though he had a mortal hatred to paper money, yet as he could not foresee all emergencies, he was unwilling to tie the hands of the Legislature. He observed that the late war could not have been carried on, had such a prohibition existed."[37] The ensuing dilemma is very tight. On the one hand, one might wish for the constitution to allow for unforeseen and unforeseeable emergencies. On the other hand, some of the occasions that will be claimed to have emergency status will be the very situations in which the constitution was supposed to act as a protection. An alcoholic will always be able to specify some way in which today is special and exceptional.[38]

VI. JUDICIAL REVIEW AS A COUNTERMAJORITARIAN DEVICE

The dilemma has been solved by judicial review. Let me first note that having a constitution by itself does not solve anything, unless an apparatus of interpretation and enforcement is in place. Sieyès' claim that the constitution did away with the need for executive veto or similar devices[39] had no force as long as he did not specify a practical mechanism by which violations of the constitution would trigger the necessary corrections. He asserted that in such cases one would have to appeal to an extraordinary constitutional convention, but said nothing about who should have the right to call it. And in any case it is obviously impractical to have to go back to the constituent power to decide charges of unconstitutionality. One needs a less cumbersome way, such as judicial review.

In the two eighteenth-century assemblies, this solution was not a central issue. Other solutions to the problems of majority rule, such as bicameralism and executive veto, had a much more important role.[40] At the Federal Convention, ideas related to judicial review were, nevertheless, considered. On the one hand, the framers distinguished between ex ante control and review ex post. On the other hand, they drew a distinction between the control of the constitutionality of the laws and scrutiny on broader grounds. These issues were mainly discussed in the context of the proposal of instituting a Council of Revision, which would have the power to veto state and federal laws. In the Virginia proposal, the council was supposed to contain, besides the President, "a convenient number of the National Judiciary."

Some speakers argued against any form of ex ante involvement of the judges. Gerry, for instance, expressed "doubts whether the Judiciary ought to form a part of [the Council of Revision], as they will have a sufficient check agst. encroachments on their own department by their exposition of the laws, which involved a power of deciding on their Constitutionality." King similarly "was of the opinion that the Judicial ought not to join in the expounding of a Law, because the Judges will have the expounding of those Laws when they come before them; and they will no doubt stop the operation of such as shall appear repugnant to the constitution."[41]

Others argued that ex post judicial review was insufficient

because constitutionality was not all that was at stake. "Laws may be unjust, may be unwise, may be dangerous, may be destructive, and yet not be so unconstitutional as to justify the Judges in refusing to give them effect." Madison referred to the need for "an additional check agst. a pursuit of those unwise and unjust measures which constituted so great a portion of our calamities." Mason observed that although judges "could declare an unconstitutional law void . . . , with regard to every law, however unjust, oppressive or pernicious, which did not come plainly under this description, they would be under the necessity as Judges to give it a free course."[42]

In a letter of 1817, Madison pointed to a third possibility. Referring to "the attempts in the Convention to vest in the Judiciary Dept. a qualified negative on Legislative *bills,*" he commented that "Such a Controul, *restricted to constitutional points,* besides giving greater stability & system to the rules of expounding the Instrument, would have precluded the question of a Judiciary annulment of Legislative *Acts.*"[43]

Of these various proposals, two correspond to contemporary forms of judicial review. In the United States and Norway, the Supreme Court assesses the constitutionality of laws ex post, if seized by a case that turns on this issue. In much of the European continent, Constitutional Courts may scrutinize the law ex ante, before it is promulgated. These continental systems differ among themselves in important ways, notably with respect to the assignment of the right to bring a law before the Court. I conjecture that ex post review offers a better protection of individual rights, for two reasons. First, ex ante review may create a dangerous complicity between the legislative and the judicial branches of government.[44] Second, a law may have a rights-violating potential that is difficult to anticipate until an actual case has been brought.[45]

Judicial review is basically an answer to the need for an

enforcement mechanism. Even when a law is obviously un-constitutional, someone must be assigned the right to assess it as such and to set in motion the machinery that will over-turn it. The institution to which this right is assigned can then also address the problem mentioned at the end of the previous section, by providing a method for avoiding the absurd consequences that a literal interpretation of the con-stitution would sometimes entail. The Court can apply an old constitution to new circumstances by supplementing or even violating its letter as long as it remains faithful to the spirit.

It is immediately clear that this solution, too, involves problems of its own. If the courts are allowed to decide what is absurd and what is not, or what violates the spirit of the constitution and what does not, the door is wide open for judicial rule rather than mere judicial review. Instead of being a constraint on majority rule, an unelected court will supplant the majority as the main legislator. In theory, therefore, we are confronted with an impossible choice between textualism and originalism on the one hand, and unconstrained activism on the other. In practice, the existence of a legal culture with shared norms of interpretation keep courts from behaving in a totally arbitrary and unpredictable fashion. But if that is the case, isn't there a danger that the courts will be agents of the majority rather than a constraint on what it can do? The steady constitutional erosion of property rights, for instance, has probably occurred because changing attitudes toward property in the population at large eventually found their way into the legal culture as well. But isn't that precisely what the constitution was supposed to prevent?

This objection rests on a misunderstanding. Ultimately, as I said, the constitutional protection of rights must be an-chored in a simple majority. It makes no difference in princi-ple whether the views of the majority are directly expressed in the constitution or in later reinterpretations of the constitution. What matters is that laws reflect the considered opinion of the majority rather than a passing whim or aberration. In this perspective it is actually more reasonable to put one's trust in a slowly evolving legal culture than in a constituent assembly, the members of which are in no way immune to the influence of passion and interest. It remains true, nevertheless, that legal culture can never be more than a soft constraint on the decision of the courts, and that it will always leave some scope for decisions that reflect neither the views of the founding generation nor the considered views of a current majority. Instead, the court may be swayed by minoritarian ideologies—or even by the majoritarian passions of the moment. An example of the latter is the decision of the U.S. Supreme Court that upheld the internment order of American Japanese, even though it was based on little more than collective suspicion.[46]

VII. SEPARATION OF POWERS

In this section and the following I discuss how the relations among state institutions may be organized so as to reduce the dangers of majority rule. This effect can be obtained in two apparently opposed ways: by making the institutions more independent of each other, or by making them more dependent on each other. The former technique is that of the separation of powers, the latter that of checks and balances.

Let me make a preliminary remark about the relationship between the legislative and the executive powers. In the following section, when I discuss executive veto as a constraint on majority rule, I shall assume something like a monarchical or presidential system. In much of the present section, however, I shall assume a parliamentary system in which the executive springs directly from the legislative majority. In such cases, limits on legislative majority rule take the form of limits on the executive.

For present purposes, the most important part of the separation of powers lies in the independence of the judiciary, both as a guarantee of the rule of law and as a protection of judicial review. One aspect of this independence relates to the mode of appointment, tenure and remuneration[47] of judges. Another aspect concerns the organization of the judicial system, such as the selection of jurors and, especially, the assignment of judges to cases. To prevent the government from selecting "reliable" judges to preside over "delicate" cases, many countries have adopted the practice of assigning judges by lot or some other mechanical procedure.

In addition to the traditional trio of executive, legislative, and judiciary, the press and more generally the media are sometimes said to constitute a "fourth power," with the task (among others) of drawing attention to majoritarian abuses. We may understand this idea in a literal way or in a more extended sense. In the literal interpretation we may see public media, such as state-owned radio and television companies, as subject to the principle of the separation of powers. Their independence can be assured partly through the appointment, tenure, and remuneration of the Director General, partly by some degree of budgetary autonomy. In the extended interpretation, privately owned newspapers and broadcasting companies can also be seen to perform the same functions of control and deterrence. To ensure their independence, freedom of speech must have vigorous legal protection against government interference. In addition, government should not be allowed to hold monopolies on paper, printer's ink, and the like.

The independence of a Central Bank falls in the same conceptual category. If politicians have direct control over monetary policy, the temptation to use this tool for short-term or partisan purposes may become irresistible. To see the connection with the topic of this paper, it is sufficient to note that inflation—a frequent outcome of such manipulations—was traditionally seen as a violation of property rights. Again, appointment, tenure, remuneration, and budgetary autonomy are key variables in ensuring independence. As before, this solution to the problem of majority rule may give rise to new problems. Earlier, I referred to George Mason's hesitation with regard to a constitutional prohibition of paper money. Two centuries later, William Nordhaus noted that a similar dilemma arises if one takes the more indirect route of creating an independent Central Bank. To prevent "political business cycles" one might, he observes,

> entrust economic policy to persons that will not be tempted by the Sirens of partisan politics. This procedure is typical for monetary policy, which for historical reasons is lodged in the central bank (as in the independent Federal Reserve System in the US or the Bank of England). A similar possibility is to turn fiscal policy over to a Treasury dominated by civil servants. It may be objected, however, that delegating responsibility to an agency that is not politically responsive to legitimate needs is even more dangerous than a few cycles. This danger is frequently alleged regarding central banks which pay more attention to the "soundness of the dollar" or the latest monetarist craze than to fundamental policy problems.[48]

If for "soundness of the dollar" we substitute "respect for the text of the Constitution" and instead of "monetarist craze" we read "noninterventionist ideology," these remarks also apply to an independent judiciary. But who, then, shall guard these guardians? The generic answer lies in a system of checks and balances, in which the guardians are kept in check by those over whom they keep guard.

VIII.   CHECKS AND BALANCES

In a system of checks and balances, the political institutions are limited by each other, not only in the weak sense that each has its circumscribed sphere of power, but in the stronger sense that even within that sphere it is not omnipotent. The legislative power can be overridden by executive veto and by judicial review, whereas an activist court may be controlled by the threat of new appointments or by the threat to limit the reviewing powers of the court. I shall focus on two devices that act as checks on majority rule: bicameralism and executive veto. Very roughly speaking, the two checks correspond to two of the majoritarian dangers identified above. The existence of a second chamber can by a number of mechanisms counteract the (momentary) passions of the majority. The executive veto can block the tendency toward legislative tyranny. But these stark statements need nuances and qualifications. In fact, both devices have been offered as solutions to both problems, as indicated by the following table:

	Problem of passionate majorities	Problem of self-interested legislators
Bicameralism is the solution	Upper house will slow down the process, and also through wealth or wisdom resist a passionate majority	A divided assembly less likely to become an aristocracy
Executive veto is the solution	Veto can serve as an additional check on dangerous impulses	The executive will resist any legislative self-aggrandizement

Bicameralism is the solution to the problem of passionate majorities. This proposition has several aspects. In the first place, bicameralism simply makes for a slower and more cumbersome process, giving hot spirits time to cool down. When Thomas Jefferson asked George Washington why the Convention had established a Senate, Washington replied by asking, "Why do you pour your coffee into your saucer?" "To cool it," Jefferson replied. "Even so," Washington said. "We pour legislation into the Senatorial saucer to cool it." In France, Mounier observed that the majority might need a cooling-off period to protect itself against the temptation to abdicate from power in favor of a strong man.[49]

This argument does not rely on any special virtues possessed by the senators as compared to the members of the lower house, but appeals merely to the virtues of slowness. It carries over, therefore, to any other delaying or cooling device, such as the need for constitutional changes to be approved by two successive legislatures or the King's suspensive veto. Most bicameral systems, however, have posited some qualitative difference between the senators and the representatives by virtue of which the upper house would be more prudent and conservative and thus act as a brake on the more impetuous lower house. A number of screening mechanisms were envisaged. The lower age limit for senators could be set higher.[50] Senators could be chosen by indirect elections (the original American solution). They could be made subject to longer periods of office, with staggered renewals (also part of the American solution). More controversially, they may be subject to different eligibility requirements with regard to property or income.

In a passage that for me represents the intellectual high point of the Convention, Madison offered a veil-of-ignorance argument for the Senate which serves, he asserted, first to protect the people against their rulers: secondly to protect the people agst. the transient impressions into which they themselves might be led. A people deliberating in a temperate moment, and with the experience of other nations before them, on the plan of Govt, most likely to secure their happiness, would first be aware, that those chargd. with the public happiness, might betray their trust. An obvious precaution agst. this danger wd. be to divide the trust between different bodies of men, who might watch & check each other. . . . It would next occur to such a people, that they themselves were liable to temporary errors, thro' want of information as to their true interest, and that men chosen for a short term, & employed but a small portion of that in public affairs, might err from the same cause. This reflection wd. naturally suggest that the Govt. be so constituted, as that one of its branches might have an oppy. of acquiring a competent knowledge of the public interests. Another reflection equally becoming a people on such an occasion, wd. be that they themselves, as well as a numerous body of Representatives, were liable to err also, from fickleness and passion. A necessary fence agst. this danger would be to select a portion of enlightened citizens, whose limited number and firmness might seasonably interpose agst. impetuous counsels. It ought finally to occur to a people deliberating on a Govt. for themselves, that as different interests necessarily result from the liberty meant to be secured, the major interests might under sudden impulses be tempted to commit injustice on the minority.[51]

Bicameralism is the solution to the problem of self-interested legislators. The mechanism behind this argument is a form of "divide and rule": A homogeneous assembly is more likely to form a united front against the executive than an internally divided one. At the Convention, "Mr. Dickinson was not apprehensive that the Legislature composed of different branches constructed on such different principles, would improperly unite for the purpose of displacing a judge." Mason claimed that a single legislature, as proposed in the New Jersey plan, contained the seeds of "Legislative despotism." In the Assemblée Constituante, Lally-Tollendal stated the matter quite generally: A single power will devour everything, two will fight each other to death, whereas three will maintain a perfect equilibrium.[52]

In both assemblies there was apprehension that an upper house might turn into an aristocracy. In Philadelphia, Gerry said that as "[the new system] now stands it is as compleat an aristocracy as ever was framed. If great powers should be given to the Senate we shall be governed in reality by a Junto as has been apprehended." Wilson said that "he was obliged to consider the whole as having a dangerous tendency to aristocracy; as throwing a dangerous power into the hands of the Senate." This argument had an even stronger appeal in Paris, where the very idea of an upper house powerfully reminded people of the old system of orders. However, the argument can be turned on its head. It is precisely in order to prevent the formation of the *legislature as aristocracy* that one has to accept an *aristocracy within the legislature*. Although a longer term in office for the Senate may turn their members into an aristocracy, that longer tenure is also needed if it is to be a proper check against the lower branch.[53]

The role of bicameralism in checking legislative tyranny was not uncontroversial. Gouverneur Morris argued that "The check provided in the 2d. branch was not meant as a check on Legislative usurpation of power, but on the abuse of lawful powers, on the propensity of the 1st. branch to legislate too much to run into projects of paper money & similar expedients. It is no check on Legislative Tyranny. On the contrary it may favor it, and if the 1st. branch can be seduced may find the means of success."[54] The idea that internal division in the legislature might not reduce—might in fact increase—the tendency to legislative tyranny is not one I have encountered elsewhere in the debates. Nor is it particularly plausible. The idea that internal legislative division might not be a sufficient deterrent to legislative tyranny is more attractive. Executive veto may also be required.

Executive veto is the solution to the problem of passionate majorities. An absolute veto for the executive was not seriously discussed in the American assembly. In the French assembly, it was strongly advocated by some of the "monarchiens," but in the end overwhelmingly defeated. There are two main ways of retaining a form of executive veto even if an absolute veto is rejected. On the one hand, one can allow the assembly to overrule the veto, but require a qualified majority. This was the solution adopted in Philadelphia. On the other hand, one can allow the assembly to overrule the executive by an ordinary majority, but require that the decision be delayed until a later legislature.[55] This was the solution adopted in Paris, allowing the King to veto a proposal in two successive legislatures before the third one could overrule him. In both cases, the solution was defended, among other reasons, for its beneficial impact on passionate majorities.

This argument was made several times in the American debates. According to Madison, "a negative in the Ex: is not only necessary for its own safety, but for the safety of a minority in Danger of oppression from an unjust and interested Majority." Gouverneur Morris was more specific. On July 19 he argued that the upper house is needed as a check "on the propensity in the 1st branch to legislate too much to run into projects of paper money and similar expedients." Two days later he cited the same phenomena—"Emissions of paper money, largesses to the people—a remission of debts and similar measures"—as reasons for a strong executive check. Mason similarly argued that "Notwithstanding the precautions taken in the Constitution of the Legislature, it would so much resemble that of the individual States, that it must be expected frequently to pass unjust and pernicious laws."⁵⁶ In other words, the tripartite system provided a *double check on majority rule*.⁵⁷

In the Assemblée Constituante, the argument took different forms.⁵⁸ For most deputies, executive veto was simply seen as a delaying and cooling device, a brake on passionate majorities. For the radical members of the assembly, it was rather a device that allowed the nation to act as a check on its representatives. After the first veto, the nation could express its opinion through an election. As La Salle put it, "Le veto suspensif est comme une sorte d'appel à la nation, qui la fait intervenir comme juge à la première session, entre le Roi et ses représentants." The argument came in two versions. Some delegates wanted to leave the decision to the legislature following the final veto. Others wanted primary assemblies to vote directly on the motion that had been opposed by the royal veto.⁵⁹

Executive veto is the solution to the problem of self-interested legislators. The role of the executive veto as a check on the tendency toward legislative tyranny was a permanent theme in the two assemblies. In Paris, Lally-Tollendal, citing England as a precedent, claimed that in 1688 the two chambers of Parliament abdicated some of their powers to the executive in order to prevent legislative tyranny. Many other speakers in the Assemblée Constituante argued for the need for a royal veto to check the tendency toward legislative domination. In doing so, they indulged in considerable amounts of cant, imputing either a perfect harmony of interest between the King and the people that would enable him to check the aristocratic tendencies of the legislature, or a perfect coincidence between the will of the King and the general happiness. In the fall of 1789, nobody said outright that even a weak or depraved King would be a useful check on legislative tyranny. After the King's flight to Varenne, it became more difficult to uphold the illusion of his benevolence and wisdom. In the debates on the King's immunity, Duport and Barnave argued that the King could not serve his constitutional function as check on the legislature unless his person was inviolable. "Si le monarque était dépendant du Corps législatif, il en résulterait que celui-ci pourrait détruire son propre frein."[60] I return to this theme below.

The Americans also referred to the British experience: "Where the Executive really was the palladium of liberty, *King* and *Tyrant,* were naturally associated in the minds of people; not *legislature and* tyranny. But where the Executive was not formidable, the two last were most properly associated. After the destruction of the King in Britain, a more pure and unmixed tyranny sprang up in parliament than had been exercised by the monarch."[61] Other historical precedents were cited by Gouverneur Morris. Having first reiterated his motion for an absolute veto, defeated a week previously, he went on to say that

> The most virtuous citizens will often as members of a legislative body concur in measures which afterwards in their private capacity they will be ashamed of. Encroachments of the popular branch of the Government ought to be guarded agst. The Ephori at Sparta became in the end absolute. . . . If the Executive be overturned by the popular branch, as happened in England, the tyranny of one man will ensue—In Rome where the Aristocracy overturned the throne, the consequence was different. He enlarged on the tendency of the legislative Authority to usurp on the Executive and wished the section to be postponed, in order to consider some more effectual check than requiring 2/3 only to overrule the negative of the Executive.[62]

The checks must themselves be kept in check, otherwise there would not be a system of checks *and balances.* In

Paris, defenders of an absolute veto for the King argued that the assembly could always overrule him by refusing to pay taxes. Several delegates responded that in refusing to vote taxes, the assembly would be cutting off its nose to spite its face: "faire cesser le payement de l'impôt, c'est se couper la gorge pour guérir une plaie à la jambe."[63] In Philadelphia, checks on the executive included overruling his veto by a two thirds majority, impeachment, and the incentives provided by reeligibility. The question of checks on the Senate did not arise.

Moreover, the checks must be genuinely independent of the institutions on which they are supposed to provide a check. I have already cited Duport's observation in the Assemblée Constituante, that the King cannot serve as a brake on the legislature if the assembly can remove him at will. At the Federal Convention, the question arose with regard to both the executive and the upper house. Regarding the latter, Sherman argued against Randolph's proposal [that "the first branch of the fœderal Legislature should have the appointment of the Senators"] on the plausible grounds that "if the Senate was to be appointed by the first Branch and out of that Body . . . it would make them too dependent, and thereby destroy the end for which the Senate ought to be appointed." Regarding the former, Gouverneur Morris asserted that if the executive is chosen by Congress, "He will be the mere creature of the Legisl: if appointed & impeachable by that body." Also arguing against selection of the executive by the legislature, Madison asserted that "the candidate would intrigue with the legislature, would derive his appointment from the predominant faction, and be apt to render his administration subservient to its views."[64]

The negative side effects of a system of checks and balances are obvious: The institutions might balance each other so effectively that nothing can be achieved, leading to paralysis rather than responsible government. Admittedly, devices that merely serve to slow down the legislative process do not present this danger, but neither do they offer a response to all problems of majority rule. To counteract the tendency toward legislative tyranny one might need an absolute veto, which might in turn reduce the ability of the system to respond effectively to urgent problems. The stronger the countermajoritarian remedies, the greater the risk of serious side effects. At the Federal Convention, the trade-off was discussed in the debate on the Senate majority needed to overrule a presidential veto. Gouverneur Morris, arguing for a three fourths majority, said that "The excess rather than the deficiency of laws is to be dreaded." Gerry, arguing for a two thirds majority, countered that "If 3/4 be required, a few Senators having hopes from the nomination of the President to offices, will combine with him and impede proper laws."[65]

IX. CONCLUSION

I conclude by applying these analytical categories to recent developments in Eastern Europe.[66] After the fall of the Communist regimes in 1989, entirely new constitutions have been adopted in Bulgaria, the Czech Republic, Croatia, Romania, Slovakia, and Slovenia. The Hungarian constitution has been totally transformed by piecewise amendments, whereas the process remains unfinished in Albania and Poland. In the latter country, however, a "little constitution" that regulates the relation among the main powers of state was adopted on November 17, 1992. Before the breakup of Czechoslovakia, that country, too, saw three years of intense constitutional debates. Although the details vary, two common features can be singled out.

First, most developments took place within the framework of the existing communist constitutions, thus effectively giving them a life after death—in fact *only* after death, since they never mattered before the fall of Communism. In Czechoslovakia, for instance, constitutional reform was arguably blocked by the structure of the 1968 constitution, which gave effective veto power to Slovakian nationalists. Although Czechs outnumber Slovaks two to one, constitutional changes needed three fifth majorities both in the proportionally elected lower house and in each of the equal-sized Czech and Slovak sections of the upper house. In Poland, the situation is even more ironic. As part of the compromise of the Round Table Talks between Solidarity and the government, an upper house with strong veto powers was introduced into the constitution. Although neither side cared about the Senate in itself, or thought that it would become a major political actor, it turned out to be a crucial force (or impediment) in the working out of a new constitution.[67] In Hungary, the thoroughgoing revision of the constitution that took place in the fall of 1989 was facilitated by the simple amendment procedures.

Second, all the constituent assemblies have at the same time served as ordinary legislatures. As mentioned earlier, one would expect this to result in constitutions that give large powers to the legislature at the expense of the executive and the judiciary. More specifically, one would expect bicameral constituent assemblies to adopt bicameralism in the constitution. The latter prediction has been confirmed in Romania and in Poland, the only countries with bicameral constituent assemblies.[68] By and large, the former, more general prediction has also been confirmed, but the picture is somewhat blurred. We would expect, for instance, legislature-oriented constitution makers to propose indirect elections of the President. Although this is indeed the case in Hungary and in the Czech and Slovak Republics, the Bulgarian and Romanian assemblies chose to have direct elections of the President. Except in Poland the directly elected presidents are not vested with large powers in the constitution, yet the moral legitimacy they derive from the popular vote could give them considerable de facto influence, especially in a crisis.

I shall now briefly survey the role in Eastern Europe of the four countermajoritarian, rights-protecting devices I discussed earlier: constitutionalism, judicial review, separation of powers, and checks and balances.

Constitutionalism. For our purposes there are two relevant questions. What rights are included in the constitution? How well does the constitution protect them? Concerning the first question, limitations of space prevent me from offering a full answer. Instead, I shall simply point to some anomalies or other salient features, limiting myself to the countries that have completed the constitution-making process.

Although all countries have constitutional provisions guaranteeing the rights of ethnic minorities, the force of this protection differs widely. The Bulgarian constitution offers by far the weakest protection. For one thing, it contains a ban on political parties formed along "ethnic, racial or religious lines" (Art. 11.4). For another, the Bulgarian constitution is special in that it offers to ethnic minorities only the right to study their own language (Art. 36.2), not the right to study (all subjects) in their own language. It has a general ban on reverse discrimination, on grounds of race, nationality, ethnic self-identity, sex, origin, religion, education, opinion, political affiliation, personal or social status, property status (Art. 6.2). The Romanian constitution contains a limited ban in Article 6.2, requiring the protection of national minorities to "conform to the principles of equality and non-discrimination in relation to the other Romanian citizens." Presumably this excludes affirmative action for the purpose, say, of promoting the situation of Gypsies. The Slovakian constitution contains both a general ban on reverse discrimination and a specific ban on affirmative action in favor of ethnic minorities. It is probably not far-fetched to see these provisions as directly aimed at the Hungarian minority.

In the constitutions of Croatia (Art. 18 of the Constitutional Law of Human Rights and Freedoms), Romania (Art. 59.2), and Slovenia (Art. 64), the political rights of minorities are protected by clauses ensuring their representation in parliament. (One might wonder if this does not contradict Article 6.2 of the Romanian constitution and indeed the more general principle of political equality.) In Slovenia, Article 80 requiring a two thirds majority of all elected deputies for changes in the electoral law may also be seen as protecting political rights, making it more difficult for the majority to manipulate the system to its advantage. Article 71.3 of the Hungarian constitution similarly requires a two thirds majority of the deputies present for the adoption of electoral laws. With two exceptions, the electoral law itself is not constitutionalized. In Poland, the "little constitution" lays down the principle of proportional elections. In the Czech Republic, the lower house is to be elected by the proportional system and the Senate by the majority system. These broad guidelines, however, still leave plenty of room for majoritarian manipulation of thresholds and districts.

The difficulty of changing the constitutions varies considerably. In what must be among the least restrictive provisions in the world, Slovakia requires only a three fifths majority in parliament. In the Czech Republic, amendments require a three fifths majority in each of the two houses. In Hungary, Poland, Slovenia, and Croatia, the basic principle is that two thirds of all deputies must vote in favor of a proposed amendment, but in each country there are some additional stipulations. In Croatia and Slovenia, constitutional amendments may also be adopted by simple majority vote in a referendum. The Hungarian constitution specifies that statutory legislation in a number of specific domains, for example electoral laws, also requires a two thirds majority. The Polish constitution adds that the constitution may not be changed during a state of emergency. In Romania, there must either be a two thirds majority in each chamber or a three quarters majority in a joint session of the two chambers, followed by approval in a referendum. In addition, parliament can amend the constitution by a backdoor procedure to be discussed below. Here, too, the constitution cannot be changed in a state of emergency.

In Bulgaria, the procedure is more complicated. A "minor" constitutional change can be adopted by parliament in one of two ways: by three quarters of the deputies voting for it in three ballots on three different days, or by two thirds voting in favor on two occasions with an interval of no less than two and no more than five months. Fundamental changes have to be approved by a two thirds majority of a special constituent assembly, elections to which will take place if two thirds of the deputies call for them. The most important fundamental changes are those which "resolve on any changes in the form of state structure or form of government" or which call for a change in Article 57.1 of the constitution asserting that "The fundamental civil rights shall be irrevocable."

With the exception of the Bulgarian provisions for major constitutional changes, these systems offer a relatively weak protection against the impulses of passionate majorities. The protection of rights may also be undermined, perhaps more seriously, by the fact that the relevant constitutional clauses are often circumscribed by clauses that render their import somewhat uncertain. On the one hand, there are many references to further regulation by statute.[69] For instance, Article 30.2 of the Bulgarian constitution says that "No one shall be detained or subjected to inspection, search or any other infringement of his personal inviolability, except on the conditions and in a manner established by a law." Similarly, Article 30.8 of the Romanian constitution says that "Indictable offenses of the press shall be established by law." Although the Hungarian constitution contains similar clauses, their sting is drawn by Article 8.2 which asserts that statutes "shall not limit the essential content of fundamental rights," leaving the parliament free to expand the scope of rights but not to shrink them.[70] On the other hand, many rights are limited by public or even private interests. To take a typical example, Article 37.2 of the Bulgarian constitution says that "The freedom of conscience and religion shall not be practiced to the detriment of national security, public order, public health and morals."[71] Whereas many constitutions assert that rights can be limited by the rights of others, the Bulgarian constitution asserts that they shall not be exercised to the detriment of the "legitimate interests" of others. To have rights limited by the public interest is no doubt inevitable.[72] If they can also be overridden by private interests, however, the trumplike character of rights disappears entirely.

Judicial review. All countries in the region practice ex ante or ex post reviews of legislation by constitutional courts.[73] This was also a provision in many of the communist constitutions, with the special feature, however, that decisions by the court could be annulled by parliament. In Poland, this over-ruling mechanism still obtains, although it is rarely utilized. It is more surprising to see that it is also incorporated in the newly enacted constitution of Romania (Art. 145.1). This is the "backdoor" technique referred to above, by which the assembly may enact de facto amendments of the constitution without going to a referendum. One can imagine circumstances in which the rights-protecting function of judicial review would be undermined by this procedure. One might also view it, however, as part of a system of checks and balances, that is, as preventing an undemocratic rule by the judiciary.

The Hungarian court has been by far the most active one. In the last few years it has emerged as a major political force, characterized as the most powerful constitutional court in the world.[74] Two sets of decisions that have been especially important concern legal reactions to acts committed under the communist regime. In three cases the court was asked to assess the constitutionality of laws regarding restitution of nationalized land to its precommunist owners.[75] The court decided that the only reason for discriminating between former landowners and owners of other types of confiscated property or, more crucially, between former owners and "non-former owners" (meaning those who did not formerly hold any kind of property), would be a forward-looking one. If such discrimination would facilitate the transition to a market economy or otherwise have good social results, it was allowable; if not, not. In particular, the pattern of former property holdings was irrelevant. In a recent decision[76] the court struck down as unconstitutional a law extending the statute of limitations for crimes committed during the old regime that, "for political reasons," had not been prosecuted. In the first set of decisions, the court let utilitarian considerations take precedence over backward-looking considerations of abstract justice, on the grounds that the latter did not give rise to any subjective rights to restitution. In the more recent decision, the basic premise of the court was the principle of legal certainty, which was violated both by the element of retroactivity inherent in the law and by the vagueness of the phrase "for political reasons."

The Bulgarian constitutional court has emerged as a weak defender of minority rights against the illiberal provisions in the constitution. On the basis of Articles 11.4 and 44.2 of the constitution, deputies of the former communist party asked that the Movement for Rights and Freedom—the de facto party for the Turkish and Moslem minorities—be declared unconstitutional. Although six of twelve judges found in favor of the petition and only five were against (one was sick), the petition was rejected on the basis of Article 151.1 which requires "a majority of more than half of all justices" for a binding decision.[77] The reasoning of the five judges was too tenuous and fragile, however, to provide a very solid guarantee. We may note, moreover, that the party that was created to serve the interests of the Bulgarian Gypsies *was* declared unconstitutional.

Separation of powers. In spite of its extensive powers—or perhaps because of them—the Hungarian constitutional court has actively sought to limit its own jurisdiction. Although the law authorizes the court to emit advisory opinions on drafts of bills, the court has on several occasions refused to do so on the grounds that it would violate the principle of the separation of powers. The task of the court, it has argued, must be the purely negative one of voiding unconstitutional laws, and it must never get involved in positive lawmaking. One might ask, however, whether the latter danger is not almost unavoidable in systems of ex ante judicial review such as the Hungarian or German ones. This being said, this threat, if it is one, to the separation of powers does not detract from the protection of rights.

Much more serious than the infringement of the judiciary on the other powers of state is the opposite problem, the dependency of the judiciary on the executive. By all accounts, mental habits created under Communism still make judges, especially in lower courts, look to government for advice and guidance. Most of them are, in fact, incapable of independent application of the law because of the abysmally low level of legal education and training under Communism. Conversely, governmental habits of steering the outcome are slow in withering away. The former Hungarian Minister of Justice Kálmán Kulcsár has described (in a personal communication to the author) his difficulties in persuading his officials not to interfere with the assignment of judges to cases. The mode of appointment of judges varies widely.[78] Suffice it to say here that it does not seem to pose any obvious threats to the separation of powers. In particular, fixity of tenure is expressly stipulated in most of the constitutions.

An independent Central Bank has not been a goal for the constitution makers in Eastern Europe, with two exceptions. The main exception is the Czech Republic, where the Hayekian inspiration behind the constitution shows itself in Article 98.1, which protects the bank from intervention by the executive. In Hungary, Article 32.D of the constitution stipulates that the president of the National Bank is appointed by the president of the Republic for a term of six years. Both the fixity of tenure and the fact that the president rather than the government has the appointment power might seem to indicate an intention to keep the bank out of day-to-day politics. In the ongoing turf battles between president and government in Hungary, however, the appointment powers of the former are now degenerating into a mere formality. The Slovenian constitution says (Art. 152) that the governor of the Central Bank shall be appointed by the national assembly, whereas the Bulgarian one (Art. 84.11) says that he shall be elected *and dismissed* by the assembly. Article 40 of the Polish constitution requires that the president present to the Sejm a motion for the appointment *or recall* of the president of the National Bank; once again, there is not the fixity of tenure which would be a minimal condition for independence.

The need for a provision guaranteeing the independence of state-owned media has been made strikingly clear in several countries, notably Hungary and more recently Slovakia. Nevertheless it is a striking fact that none of the constitutions in the region makes any reference to the mode of governance of state-owned radio or television.

Checks and balances. We can distinguish among a number of versions of the idea of checks and balances. The textbook idea posits three main institutions—the executive, the legislative, and the judiciary—which must be so organized as to neutralize any tendency by any one of them to usurp power.

In the two eighteenth-century debates, however, the three parties involved in checks and balances were rather the two houses of the legislature and the executive. Today's Eastern Europe, differs from the textbook scheme in a different way, not in the division of the legislature into two houses, but in the bifurcation of the executive in president and government. If the president has some nontrivial powers, derived from the text of the constitution or from the legitimacy conferred by direct elections, and if the government has some independence from the parliamentary majority that brought it to power, we obtain a new trinity of checks and balances: parliament, government, and president. Such independence can be obtained by the German system of a constructive vote of no confidence, requiring that parliament designate a new prime minister as it simultaneously censures the government in place. An alternative is the French system that allows the government to present bills that are automatically adopted as laws unless parliament brings a vote of no confidence within a specified time limit. Under these systems, government has the same relation to parliament as parliament has to the electorate: It is a trustee, not simply a delegate.

The system with the fewest checks and balances is the Bulgarian one. There is a unicameral assembly, a weak presidential veto (it can be overruled by a simple majority of all elected deputies), and no device that ensures the independence of the government from the parliamentary majority. Institutionally, the constitutional court is the only counterweight to majoritarian assembly rule. De facto, a popular president may also be able to act as an independent force.

Slovakia is more or less in the same position. Although the president is endowed with substantial powers, he can be dismissed by parliament with a three fifths majority on political grounds, without any formal impeachment procedure. The assembly is unicameral, and there is no device to ensure the independence of government.

Romania does not fare much better. Here the constitution has adopted a solution that was previously found only in Italy, a bicameral assembly with two essentially identical chambers. It is hard to see how this arrangement can serve in a system of checks and balances, or for any other purpose. Although the adoption in Article 113 of the French system of "governmental legislation" ensures some independence of government from parliament, this provision has rarely been used so far. The right of the president to call a referendum (Art. 90) offers him some independence from the other powers of state. As noted above, the role of the constitutional court in acting as a brake on parliament is limited by the right of the assembly to overrule the decisions of the court.

Hungary has a unicameral assembly and a largely formal presidency. Although the rule of a constructive vote of no confidence ensures that government has some independence from parliament, the strongest constraint on the legislature is provided by the constitutional court. Slovenia has a somewhat similar system: a second chamber that is essentially consultative, a presidency with few formal powers, the rule of a constructive vote of no confidence, and a potentially powerful constitutional court. Much the same applies to Croatia, except that there is no constructive vote of confidence or any other device to ensure the independence of government.

The Czech Republic has a bicameral system, in which the upper house can force the lower house to adopt a bill by absolute rather than simple majority. In addition, the upper house has to approve changes in the constitution by a three fifths majority. The president, elected by parliament, has little real power. Nor is there any device to ensure the independence of government from parliament.

Poland is the country with the most extensive system of checks and balances, with an upper house and a president that have the power to force the lower house to adopt laws with, respectively, an absolute and a two thirds majority. However, the Sejm can set aside the decisions of the constitutional court by a simple majority. This embarrassing survival from the communist era lingers on mainly because the Sejm is in no hurry to abolish a provision that confers great powers on itself.

Broadly speaking, this overview confirms the idea stated at the outset: Despotism, when overthrown, gives rise to new forms of despotism. Among the countries I have surveyed, Romania, Slovakia, and Bulgaria had the most despotic and totalitarian forms of communist rule. They also seem least inclined to embrace countermajoritarian devices. At the other extreme, the least despotic country—Hungary—is emerging as the one most strongly wedded to the principles of constitutionalism.

I distinguished earlier between the dangers of majority rule arising from three sources: standing interests, standing passions, and momentary passions. I also observed that these dangers can arise in either a parliamentary or a popular majority. In Eastern Europe, the two most acute dangers arise from the standing interest of the parliamentary majority in preserving its power and from the standing passions in the population, notably with regard to ethnic divisions and to backward-looking demands for restitution and retribution. Civil society is not yet sufficiently well-organized to give rise to well-defined interest groups that might threaten the rights of minority property owners or creditors. Momentary passions are, almost by definition, unpredictable.

The emerging constitutional courts hold out the promise of being able to restrain standing and temporary passions. By contrast, the system of checks and balances is not, by and large, well designed to counteract self-interested legislators. As noted, this observation applies not only to ordinary legislation, but to the constitution-making process itself. In fact, the deepest flaw in the political processes in Eastern

Europe is perhaps the constant intermingling of *la politique politisée* and *la politique politisante*. Almost everywhere, the constitutions emerge as the outcome of bargaining for tactical or partisan purposes. Their clauses are viewed as policy instruments, not as providing a relatively fixed framework for policy. In a period of rapid economic and social transformation, this is not unambiguously a bad thing. But there is a price to be paid for flexibility, and some day the bill will come due.

NOTES

Stephen Shute and Susan Hurley:
Introduction

1. Quoted from a translation by Natalie Nenadic of an article that appeared in *Večernji List,* a Zagreb daily, on November 25, 1992. Nenadic is a University of Michigan Law School student who spent five weeks in Bosnia and Croatia in the autumn of 1992 helping groups there to document such events.

2. Quoted from an article by Slavenka Drakulic, printed in the *International Herald Tribune,* December 14, 1992, reprinted from the *New York Times,* December 13, 1992.

3. Steven Lukes, *Moral Conflict and Politics* (Oxford: Clarendon Press, 1991).

4. John Rawls, "Two Concepts of Rules," *The Philosophical Review* 64 (1955): 3.

5. Rawls, "Justice as Fairness," *The Philosophical Review* 67 (1958): 164.

6. Rawls, *A Theory of Justice* (Cambridge, Mass.: Belknap Press, 1971).

7. Rawls, "Justice as Fairness: Political Not Metaphysical," *Philosophy and Public Affairs* 14 (1985): 225.

8. See, especially, chap. 1, pt. 4, and chap. 3. The original position is a purely hypothetical situation corresponding to the state of nature in traditional social contract theory. The veil of ignorance ensures that any bargain reached by contracting parties is fair. In its initial formulation in *A Theory of Justice* this was achieved by denying the contracting parties knowledge of their own abilities, knowledge of their place in the world, and even knowledge of their own conception of the good life (see chap. 1, pt. 3).

9. Catharine A. MacKinnon, *Feminism Unmodified* (Cambridge, Mass.: Harvard University Press, 1987), and *Towards a*

Feminist Theory of the State (Cambridge, Mass.: Harvard University Press, 1989).

10. Richard Rorty, *Philosophy and the Mirror of Nature* (Princeton, N.J.: Princeton University Press, 1979).

11. Rorty, "The Priority of Democracy to Philosophy," in his *Objectivity, Relativism, and Truth: Philosophical Papers,* vol. 1 (Cambridge, England: Cambridge University Press, 1991).

12. Rorty, *Contingency, Irony, and Solidarity* (Cambridge, England: Cambridge University Press, 1989).

13. Jean-François Lyotard, *Economie Libidinale* (Paris: Minuit, 1974).

14. Agnes Heller, *Beyond Justice* (Oxford: Blackwell, 1987).

15. The first two parts of this work have been published and are called *General Ethics* (Oxford: Blackwell, 1988) and *A Philosophy of Morals* (Oxford: Blackwell, 1990). The third part, provisionally entitled *A Theory of Proper Conduct*, is as yet unwritten.

16. Jon Elster, *Ulysses and the Sirens,* rev. ed. (Cambridge, England: Cambridge University Press, 1984).

Steven Lukes: Five Fables about Human Rights

1. See " 'La Conception occidentale des droits de l'homme renforce le malentendu avec l'Islam': un entretien avec Mohamed Arkoun," *Le Monde,* March 15, 1989, 2; and the essays in Adamantia Pollis and Peter Schwab, eds., *Human Rights: Cultural and Ideological Perspectives* (New York: Praeger, 1979), esp. chap. 1, 14ff.

2. See D. D. Raphael, ed., *Political Theory and the Rights of Man* (London: Macmillan, 1967).

3. See Elizabeth Kingdom, *What's Wrong with Rights? Problems for Feminist Politics of Law* (Edinburgh: Edinburgh University Press, 1991).

4. Reginald Herbold Green, *Human Rights, Human Conditions and Law: Some Explorations towards Interaction* (Brighton: IDS, 1989), Discussion Paper no. 267.

5. Karl Marx, "Bruno Bauer: The Capacity of the Present-

day Jews and Christians to Become Free," translated in T. B. Bottomore, ed., *Karl Marx: Early Writings* (London: Watts, 1963), 37.

6. Marx, "Money," translated in Bottomore, *Karl Marx,* 193–94.

7. Marx, "Private Property and Communism," translated in Bottomore, *Karl Marx,* 155.

8. J. Bentham, *Anarchical Fallacies,* reproduced in Jeremy Waldron, ed., *Nonsense on Stilts: Bentham, Burke and Marx on the Rights of Man* (London and New York: Methuen, 1987), 53.

9. Edmund Burke, *Reflections on the Revolution in France,* reproduced in Waldron, *Nonsense,* 105, 106.

10. Alasdair MacIntyre, *After Virtue: A Study in Moral Theory* (London: Duckworth, 1981), 65–67.

11. Marx, *Critique of the Gotha Programme,* in Marx and Friedrich Engels, *Selected Works,* vol. 2 (Moscow: Foreign Languages Publishing House, 1962), 25.

12. Leon Trotsky, "Their Morals and Ours," *The New International,* June 1938, reproduced in *Their Morals and Ours: Marxist versus Liberal Views on Morality: Four Essays by Leon Trotsky, John Dewey and George Novack,* 4th ed. (New York: Pathfinder Press: 1969).

13. V. I. Lenin, "Speech at Third Komsomol Congress, 2 October 1920," in V. I. Lenin, *Collected Works* (Moscow: Foreign Languages Publishing House, 1960–1963), vol. 31, 291, 294.

14. See Samuel Bowles, "What Markets Can—and Cannot—Do," *Challenge: The Magazine of Economic Affairs,* July–August 1991, 11–16.

15. See Diane Elson, "The Economics of a Socialised Market" in Robin Blackburn, ed., *After the Fall: The Failure of Communism and the Future of Socialism* (London: Verso, 1991).

16. See Avishai Margalit and Joseph Raz, "National Self-determination," *Journal of Philosophy* 87 (1990): 441–61.

17. See Charles Taylor, *Multiculturalism and "The Politics of Recognition,"* with commentary by Amy Gutmann (ed.), Steven C. Rockefeller, Michael Walzer, and Susan Wolf (Princeton, N.J.: Princeton University Press, 1992).

18. See the entry on "Fraternité" (by Mona Ozouf) in Fran-

çois Furet and Mona Ozouf, eds., *Dictionnaire critique de la Révolution française* (Paris: Flammarion, 1988), 731–40.

19. See Stephen L. Carter, *Reflections of an Affirmative Action Baby* (New York: Basic Books, 1991), and Will Kymlicka, "Liberalism and the Politization of Ethnicity," *The Canadian Journal of Law and Jurisprudence* 4 (1991): 239–56. Kymlicka makes an interesting distinction between two kinds of cultural pluralism: one associated with multination states, the other with polyethnic immigrant societies.

20. See Thomas Nagel, *Equality and Partiality* (New York: Oxford University Press, 1991).

21. The idea of the egalitarian plateau is Ronald Dworkin's. See his "What Is Equality?" Part 1: "Equality of Welfare"; Part 2: "Equality of Resources," *Philosophy and Public Affairs* 10 (1981): 185–246, 283–345; Part 3: "The Place of Liberty," *Iowa Law Review* 73 (1987): 1–54; Part 4: "Political Equality," *University of San Francisco Law Review* 22 (1988): 1–30, and *A Matter of Principle* (Cambridge, Mass.: Harvard University Press, 1985). See also the discussion in Kymlicka, *Contemporary Political Philosophy: An Introduction* (Oxford: Clarendon Press, 1990).

John Rawls: The Law of Peoples

1. The name "law of peoples" derives from the traditional *ius gentium,* and the way I use it is closest to its meaning in the phrase "ius gentium intra se" (laws of peoples among themselves). In this meaning it refers to what the laws of all peoples had in common. See R. J. Vincent, *Human Rights and International Relations* (Cambridge, England: Cambridge University Press, 1986), 27. Taking these laws to be a core paired with principles of justice applying to the laws of peoples everywhere gives a meaning related to my use of the law of peoples.

2. A political conception of justice has the following three features: (1) it is framed to apply to basic political, economic, and social institutions; in the case of domestic society, to its basic structure, in the present case to the law and practices of the society of

political peoples; (2) it is presented independently of any particular comprehensive religious, philosophical, or moral doctrine, and though it may be derived from or related to several such doctrines, it is not worked out in that way; (3) its content is expressed in terms of certain fundamental ideas seen as implicit in the public political culture of a liberal society. See my *Political Liberalism* (New York: Columbia University Press, 1993), 11–15.

3. In this and the next two paragraphs I draw on the first section of "Basic Structure as Subject" (1978), reprinted in *Political Liberalism.*

4. For a detailed example of how this is done in the case of the four-stage sequence of original position, constitutional convention, the legislature, and the courts, see *A Theory of Justice* (Cambridge, Mass.: Harvard University Press, 1971), 195–201. A briefer statement is found in "Basic Liberties and Their Priority" (1982), reprinted in *Political Liberalism.*

5. By peoples I mean persons and their dependents seen as a corporate body and as organized by their political institutions, which establish the powers of government. In democratic societies persons will be citizens, while in hierarchical and other societies they will be members.

6. See *Theory,* 378ff., where this process is very briefly described.

7. It would be unfair to Clausewitz not to add that for him the state's interests can include regulative moral aims of whatever kind, and thus the aims of war may be to defend democratic societies against tyrannical regimes, somewhat as in World War II. For him the aims of politics are not part of the theory of war, although they are ever present and may properly affect the conduct of war. On this, see the instructive remarks of Peter Paret, "Clausewitz," in Peter Paret, ed., *The Makers of Modern Strategy* (Princeton, N.J.: Princeton University Press, 1986), 209–213. The view in my text characterizes the *raison d'état* as pursued by Frederick the Great. Or so Gerhard Ritter says in *Frederick the Great,* trans. Peter Paret (Berkeley: California University Press, 1968). See chap. 10, and the statement on p. 197.

8. These powers Charles Beitz characterizes as belonging to

what he calls the morality of states in pt. II of his *Political Theory and International Relations* (Princeton, N.J.: Princeton University Press, 1980). They depend, he argues, on a mistaken analogy between individuals and states.

9. Stanley Hoffman, *Janus and Minerva* (Boulder, Colo. and London: Westview Press, 1987), 374.

10. Note: "You and I" are "here and now" citizens of the same liberal democratic society and we are working out the liberal conception of justice in question.

11. In this case "you and I" are citizens of liberal democratic societies but not of the same one.

12. Kant says at Ak: VIII:367: "The idea of international law presupposes the separate existence of independent neighboring states. Although this condition is itself a state of war (unless federative union prevents the outbreak of hostilities), this is rationally preferable to the amalgamation of states under one superior power, as this would end in one universal monarchy, and laws always lose in vigor what government gains in extent; hence a condition of soulless despotism falls into anarchy after stifling seeds of good." This attitude to universal monarchy was shared by other writers of the eighteenth century. See, for example, Hume's "Of the Balance of Power" (1752). F. H. Hinsley, *Power and the Pursuit of Peace* (Cambridge, England: Cambridge University Press, 1966), 162ff., also mentions Montesquieu, Voltaire, and Gibbon. Hinsley also has an instructive discussion of Kant's ideas in chap. 4. See also Patrick Riley, *Kant's Political Philosophy* (Towanda, Pa.: Rowman and Littlefield, 1983), chaps. 5 and 6. Thomas Nagel, in his *Equality and Partiality* (New York: Oxford University Press, 1991), 169 ff., 174, gives strong reasons supporting the same conclusion.

13. See Terry Nardin, *Law, Morality and the Relations of States* (Princeton, N.J.: Princeton University Press, 1983), 269 ff., who stresses this point.

14. A clear example regarding secession is whether the South had a right to secede from 1860 to 1861. By this test it had no such right, since it seceded to perpetuate its domestic institution of slavery. This is as severe a violation of human rights as any, and it extended to nearly half the population.

15. By basic needs I mean roughly those that must be met if citizens are to be in a position to take advantage of the rights, liberties, and opportunities of their society. They include economic means as well as institutional rights and freedoms.

16. From the fact that boundaries are historically arbitrary it does not follow that their role in the law of peoples cannot be justified. To wit: that the boundaries between the several states of the United States are historically arbitrary does not argue to the elimination of our federal system, one way or the other. To fix on their arbitrariness is to fix on the wrong thing. The right question concerns the political values served by the several states in a federal system as compared with the values served by a central system. The answer is given by states' function and role: by the political values they serve as subunits, and whether their boundaries can be, or need to be, redrawn, and much else.

17. This remark implies that a people has at least a qualified right to limit immigration. I leave aside here what these qualifications might be.

18. See "The Domain of the Political and Overlapping Consensus," *New York University Law School Review* 64 (1989): 245, sec. VII.

19. See Jack S. Levy, "Domestic Politics and War," an essay in Robert Rotberg and Theodore Rabb, eds., *The Origin and Prevention of Major Wars* (Cambridge, England: Cambridge University Press, 1989), 87. Levy refers to several historical studies that have confirmed the finding of Small and Singer in the *Jerusalem Journal of International Relations,* vol. 1, 1976, mentioned in note 21 below.

20. See Doyle's two-part article, "Kant, Liberal Legacies, and Foreign Affairs," *Philosophy and Public Affairs* 12 (1983): 205, 323. A survey of the evidence is in the first part, 206–32. Doyle says: "These conventions [those based on the international implications of liberal principles and institutions] of mutual respect have formed a cooperative foundation for relations among liberal democracies of a remarkably effective kind. *Even though liberal states have become involved in numerous wars with nonliberal states, constitutionally secure liberal states have yet to engage in war with one another.* [Italicized in the original.] No one should argue that such wars are impossible;

but preliminary evidence does appear to indicate . . . a significant predisposition against warfare between liberal states" (213).

21. See Levy, "Domestic Politics," 88. In these studies most definitions of democracy are comparable to that of Small and Singer as listed by Levy in a footnote: (1) regular elections and the participation of opposition parties, (2) at least 10 percent of the adult population being able to vote for a (3) parliament that either controlled or shared parity with the executive branch (ibid., 88). Our definition of a liberal democratic regime goes well beyond this definition.

22. On this see Alan Gilbert, "Power-Rivalry Motivated Democracy," *Political Theory* 20 (1992): 681, and esp. 684 ff.

23. Here I draw upon Philip Soper's *A Theory of Law* (Cambridge, Mass.: Harvard University Press, 1984), esp. 125–47. Soper holds that a system of law, as distinct from a system of mere commands coercively enforced, must be such as to give rise, as I have indicated, to moral duties and obligations on all members of society, and judges and other officials must sincerely and reasonably believe that the law is guided by a common good conception of justice. The content of a common good conception of justice is such as to impose morally binding obligations on all members of society. I mention some of the details of Soper's view here, but I do so rather freely and not with the intent of explaining his thought. As the text shows, my aim is to indicate a conception of justice that, while not a liberal conception, still has features that give to societies regulated accordingly the moral standing required to be members of a political society adhering to a reasonable law of peoples. However, we must be careful in understanding this second requirement. For Soper it is part of the definition of a system of law. It is a requirement which a scheme of rules must satisfy to be a system of law properly thus called. See chap. 4, 91–100. I don't follow Soper in this respect; nor do I reject this idea either, as Soper makes a strong case for it. Rather, it is put aside and the requirement is adopted as a substantive moral principle explicable as part of the law of peoples worked up from a liberal conception of justice. The reason for doing this is to avoid the long debated jurisprudential problem of the definition of law. Also, I don't want to have to argue that the

antebellum South, say, didn't have a system of law. I am indebted to Samuel Freeman for valuable discussion of these points.

24. Soper, *A Theory of Law*, 112, 118.

25. Ibid., 141.

26. Henry Shue, *Basic Rights: Substance, Affluence, and U.S. Foreign Policy* (Princeton, N.J.: Princeton University Press, 1980). Shue, p. 23, and Vincent, *Human Rights*, interpret subsistence as including certain minimum economic security, and both hold that subsistence rights are basic. One must agree with this since the reasonable and rational exercise of all liberties, of whatever kind, as well as the intelligent use of property, always implies having certain general all-purpose economic means.

27. On the rules of natural justice, see H. L. A. Hart, *The Concept of Law* (Oxford: Clarendon Press), 156 ff.

28. One might raise the question here as to why religious or philosophical doctrines that deny full and equal liberty of conscience are not unreasonable. I did not say, however, that they are reasonable, but rather that they are not unreasonable. One should allow, I think, a space between the reasonable or the fully reasonable, which requires full and equal liberty of conscience, and the unreasonable, which denies it entirely. Traditional doctrines that allow a measure of liberty of conscience but do not allow it fully are views that lie in that space and are not unreasonable. On this see my *Political Liberalism*, Lecture II, sec. 3.

29. On the importance of this, see Judith Shklar's *Ordinary Vices* (Cambridge, Mass.: Harvard University Press, 1984), in which she presents what she calls the "liberalism of fear." See especially the introduction and chaps. 1 and 6. She once called this kind of liberalism that of "permanent minorities." See her *Legalism* (Cambridge, Mass.: Harvard University Press, 1963), 224.

30. Subject to certain qualifications, liberal societies must also allow for this right.

31. These are not political conceptions of justice in my sense; see note 2 above.

32. Here "you and I" are members of hierarchical societies but again not the same one.

33. Here I am indebted to Lea Brilmayer of New York Univer-

sity for pointing out to me that in my sketch of the law of peoples (October 1990) I failed to state these conditions satisfactorily.

34. Brian Barry, in his splendid *Theories of Justice* (Berkeley: University of California Press, 1989), discusses the merits of doing this. See 183–89 ff. Along the way he raises serious objections to what he takes to be my view of the principles of distributive justice for the law of peoples. I do not discuss these important criticisms here, but I do mention questions related to them hereafter.

35. We can go on to third and later stages once we think of groups of societies joining together into regional associations or federations of some kind, such as the European Community, or a commonwealth of the republics in the former Soviet Union. It is natural to envisage future world society as in good part comprised of such federations together with certain institutions, such as the United Nations, capable of speaking for all the societies of the world.

36. Justice as fairness is such an idea. For our purposes other more general liberal ideas of justice fit the same description. Their lacking the three egalitarian elements of justice as fairness noted in the first paragraph of part 3 does not affect this.

37. There are, however, some differences. The three requirements of legitimacy discussed in this section are to be seen as necessary conditions for a society to be a member in good standing of a reasonable society of peoples; and many religious and philosophical doctrines with their different conceptions of justice may lead to institutions satisfying these conditions. In specifying a reasonable law of peoples, societies with such institutions are viewed as well ordered. However, those requirements do not specify a political conception of justice in my sense (see note 2 above). For one thing, I suppose that a society's common good conception of justice is understood as part of its comprehensive religious or philosophical doctrine. Nor have I suggested that such a conception of justice is constructivist, and I assume it is not. Whether the three requirements for legitimacy can themselves be constructed within a social contract view is another question. I leave it open here. The point, though, is that none of these differences affect the claim in the text

that in both domains the ideals and principles of justice are justified in the same way.

38. Here I draw upon T. M. Scanlon's instructive discussion in "Human Rights as a Neutral Concern," in P. Brown and D. MacLean, eds., *Human Rights and U.S. Foreign Policy* (Lexington, Mass.: Lexington Books, 1979).

39. Scanlon emphasizes this point in "Human Rights," 83, 89–92. It is relevant when we note later in parts 6 and 7 that support for human rights should be part of the foreign policy of well-ordered societies.

40. See R. J. Vincent, "The Idea of Rights in International Ethics," in Terry Nardin, ed. with David Mapel, *Traditions of International Ethics* (Cambridge, England: Cambridge University Press, 1992), 262–65.

41. Hegel, *The Philosophy of Right* (1821); section 308.

42. The meaning of *rational* here is closer to *reasonable* than to *rational* as I have used these terms. The German is *vernünftig,* and this has the full force of reason in the German philosophical tradition. It is far from the economist's meaning of *rational,* given by *zweckmässig* or *rationell.*

43. There is a complication about Hegel's view in that some rights are indeed rights of individuals. For him the rights to life, security, and (personal) property are grounded in personhood; and liberty of conscience follows from being a moral subject with the freedom of subjectivity. I am indebted to Frederick Neuhouser for discussion of these points.

44. See Keith Thomas, *Man and the Natural World* (New York: Pantheon Books, 1983) for an account of the historical change in attitudes toward animals and nature.

45. See Judith Shklar's illuminating discussion of these in her *American Citizenship* (Cambridge, Mass.: Harvard University Press, 1991), with her emphasis on the historical significance of slavery.

46. This fact about human rights can be clarified by distinguishing among the rights that have been listed as human rights in various international declarations. Consider the Universal Declaration of Human Rights of 1948. First, there are human rights proper,

illustrated by Article 3: "Everyone has a right to life, liberty and security of person"; and by Article 5: "No one shall be subjected to torture or to cruel, degrading treatment or punishment." Articles 3 to 18 may fall under this heading of human rights proper, pending certain questions of interpretation. Then there are human rights that are obvious implications of these rights. These are the extreme cases described by the special conventions on genocide (1948) and on apartheid (1973). These two classes comprise the human rights.

Of the other declarations, some seem more aptly described as stating liberal aspirations, such as Article 1 of the Universal Declaration of Human Rights of 1948: "All human beings are born free and equal in dignity and rights. They are endowed with reason and conscience and should act towards one another in a spirit of brotherhood." Others appear to presuppose specific kinds of institutions, such as the right to social security, in Article 22, and the right to equal pay for equal work, in Article 23.

47. Nardin, *Law, Morality and the Relations of States,* 240, citing Luban's "The Romance of the Nation-State," 396.

48. On this, see Ludwig Dehio, *The Precarious Balance* (New York: Knopf, 1962).

49. Robert Gilpin, "The Theory of Hegemonic War," in Rotberg and Rabb, eds., *The Origin and Prevention of Major Wars.*

50. See Kant, *Rechtslehre,* sections 44 and 61.

51. Beitz, *Political Theory and International Relations;* pt. III gives a sustained discussion. This principle is defined in my *A Theory of Justice,* section 13. I do not review the principle here because, as my text says, I believe all liberal distributive principles are unsuitable for the case we are considering.

52. With much of Beitz's view the law of peoples agrees. Thus it seems that he thinks of the difference principle between societies as "a resource redistribution principle that would give each society a fair chance to develop just political institutions and an economy capable of satisfying its members' basic needs" (141). And "It [the resource distribution principle] provides assurance to persons in resource-poor societies that their adverse fate will not prevent them from realizing economic conditions sufficient to support just social

institutions and to protect human rights" (142). The law of peoples accepts Beitz's goals for just institutions, securing human rights, and meeting basic needs. But, as I suggest in the next paragraph, persons' adverse fate is more often to be born into a distorted and corrupt political culture than into a country lacking resources. The only principle that does away with that misfortune is to make the political traditions and culture of all peoples reasonable and able to sustain just political and social institutions that secure human rights. It is this principle that gives rise to the duties and obligations of assistance. We do not need a liberal principle of distributive justice for this purpose.

53. That the insistence on human rights may help here is suggested by Amartya Sen's work on famines. He has shown in *Poverty and Famines* (Oxford: Clarendon Press, 1981), by an empirical study of four well-known historical cases (Bengal, 1943; Ethiopia, 1972–74; Sahel, 1972–73; and Bangladesh, 1974), that food decline need not be the main cause of famine, or even a cause, nor even present. But sometimes it can be an important cause of famine, for example, in Ireland in the 1840s and in China from 1959 to 1961. In the cases Sen studies, while a drop in food production may have been present, it was not great enough to lead to famine given a decent government that cares for the well-being of all of its people and has in place a reasonable scheme of backup entitlements provided through public institutions. For Sen "famines are economic disasters, not just food crises" (162). In the well-known historical cases they revealed faults of the political and social structure and its failure to institute appropriate policies to remedy the effects of shortfalls in food production. After all, there would be massive starvation in any modern Western democracy were there not schemes in place to remedy the losses in income of the unemployed. Since a government's allowing people to starve when this is preventable is a violation of their human rights, and if well-ordered regimes as we have described them will not allow this to happen, then insisting on human rights is exerting pressure in the direction of decent governments and a decent society of peoples. Sen's book with Jean Drèze, *Hunger and Public Action* (Oxford: Clarendon Press, 1989)

confirms these points and stresses the success of democratic regimes in coping with these problems. See their summary statement in chap. 13: 257–79. See also the important work of Partha Dasgupta, *An Inquiry into Well-Being and Destitution* (Oxford: Clarendon Press, 1993), chaps. 1–2, 5, and passim.

54. It might be asked why the law of peoples as here constructed is said to be liberal when it is also accepted by well-ordered hierarchical societies. I have called it liberal because the law of peoples is presented as an extension from liberal conceptions of domestic justice. I do not mean to deny, however, that a well-ordered hierarchical society may have conceptions of justice that can be extended to the law of peoples and that its content would be the same as that of liberal conceptions. For the present I leave this question open. I would hope that there are such conceptions in all well-ordered hierarchical societies, as this would widen and strengthen the support for the law of peoples.

55. Three egalitarian elements are the fair value of equal political rights and liberties, fair equality of opportunity, and the difference principle, all to be understood as specified in my *A Theory of Justice.*

56. In the domestic case we are led in parallel fashion to count many comprehensive doctrines reasonable that we would not, in our own case, regard as worthy of serious consideration. See my *Political Liberalism,* Lecture II, sec. 3.1 and the footnote.

Catharine A. MacKinnon: Crimes of War, Crimes of Peace

1. Oliver Wendell Holmes, *The Common Law* (Boston: Little, Brown, 1881), 1. ("The life of the law has not been logic, it has been experience.")

2. Center for Women's Global Leadership, *1991 Women's Leadership Institute Report: Women, Violence, and Human Rights* (New Brunswick, N.J.: 1992), Appendix C: "Statistics on Gender Violence Globally," 77–80.

3. For a discussion of the killing of women as a systematic practice, see Jill Radford and Diana E. H. Russell, *Femicide: The Politics of Woman Killing* (New York: Twayne, 1992).

4. For the most advanced of Amnesty's efforts, see Amnesty International, *Rape and Sexual Abuse: Torture and Ill Treatment of Women in Detention* (New York: Amnesty International, January 1993). The advance is that rape is noticed; the limitation remains that it is only noticed when women are in official custody, thus, in effect, raped by a state.

5. [Name Withheld] Letter to author, October 13, 1992. Most of this information has since been independently corroborated by international reports and published accounts. See *Mass Killing and Genocide in Croatia 1991/92: A Book of Evidence* (Zagreb: Hrvatska Sveučilišna Naklada, 1992) (documenting genocide); *Human Rights Watch Report* (August 1992) ("A policy of 'ethnic cleansing' has resulted in the summary execution, disappearance, arbitrary detention, deportation, and forcible displacement of hundreds of thousands of people on the basis of their religion or nationality"); Carl Gustaf Strohm, "Serben vergewaltigen auf obersten Befehl," *Die Welt,* October 1, 1992 (30,000 women pregnant from rape); *Večernji List,* September 11, 1992 (20 rape/death camps for non-Serb women); Ibrahim Kajan, *Muslimanski Danak U Krvi, Svjedočanstva zločina nad Muslimanima* (Zagreb: Preporod, 1992) (genocide of Muslims and rape camps documented); Women's Group "Trešnjevka": Report (Zagreb, September 28, 1992) ("The existence of rape/death camps must be understood as a . . . tactic of genocide, of a 'final solution' . . . a gender-specific onslaught that is systematic. . . . [T]he tortures include rapes, gang-rapes, forced incest, the draining of the blood of captives to provide blood for transfusions for the needs of the criminals, setting children ablaze and drowning babies"). Given these reports, it is inexcusable that Amnesty International's October 1992 report on human rights violations in this war documents only three rapes, and these from an English newspaper rather than firsthand, as other atrocities are documented. Edith Niehuis, Head of the German Parliamentary Committee for Women and Youth, called the "systematic mass rapes" in Bosnia an "extermination war against women." "Wir machen euch kleine Tschetniks," *die tageszeitung,* December 8, 1992.

6. Universal Declaration of Human Rights, General Assem-

bly Resolution 217 A (III) of December 10, 1948, Preamble ("Whereas disregard and contempt for human rights have resulted in barbarous acts which have outraged the conscience of mankind . . . ").

7. An example of formal condonation is the U.S. case in which pornography is recognized as promoting rape, battering, and unequal pay but is protected as free speech. *American Booksellers v. Hudnut,* 771 F.2d 323 (7th Cir. 1985), aff'd 475 U.S. 1001 (1986).

8. For documentation of the use of "reservations" to the major convention prohibiting sex discrimination, see Rebecca Cook, "Reservations to the Convention on the Elimination of All Forms of Discrimination Against Women," *Virginia Journal of International Law* 30 (1990): 632. A lawsuit may be brought to invalidate the ratifications of nations whose exceptions are said to be excessive, voiding their acceptance of the Committee on the Elimination of Discrimination Against Women (CEDAW). "Court Ruling Sought on Women's Convention," *Human Rights Tribune* 1 (1992): 21.

9. Amnesty International says that all parties succeed to the international agreements that Yugoslavia ratified. Amnesty International, *Bosnia-Herzegovina: Gross Abuses of Basic Human Rights, International Secretariat* (London: October 1992). Helsinki Watch says that Croatia and Yugoslavia (the latter apparently referring to Serbia/Montenegro) are parties to the Geneva Conventions and their Protocols, Croatia by contract on May 11, 1992, and Serbia and Montenegro implicitly, by expressing a wish to be recognized as the successor state to what was Yugoslavia. Ivana Nizich, *War Crimes in Bosnia-Herzegovina* (New York: Helsinki Watch, August 1992), 138–39. Bosnia-Herzegovina formally ratified the relevant provisions in 1992. Humanitarian law is customary law, with universal jurisdiction, but human rights provisions require affirmative submission to secure jurisdiction.

10. Addressing the Conference on Security and Cooperation in Europe, U.S. Secretary of State Lawrence Eagleburger said that Serbian leaders were guilty of war crimes against humanity and should be prosecuted, "exactly as Hitler's associates were at Nuremberg." "Legal Commission to Start Investigation of Mass

Graves in Former Yugoslavia," Agence France Presse, December 14, 1992. At the time they were publicly recognized, the atrocities had been going on for approximately a year. There is also some discussion of creating a permanent international war crimes court whose first task would be to try war criminals from this war. "U.S., France Discussing Permanent War Crimes Court," Reuters, December 15, 1992.

11. See generally Roy Gutman, "The Rapes of Bosnia," *Newsday,* August 23, 1992. A special mission of the European Council concluded, after a preliminary visit, that "the rapes [of Muslim women] are widespread and are part of a recognizable pattern. . . . The general view expressed by interlocutors whom the delegation considered responsible and credible was that a horrifying number of Muslim women had suffered rape and that this was continuing. . . . The most reasoned estimate suggested to the delegation indicated a figure in the region of 20,000 victims. . . . The indications are that at least some of the rapes are being committed in particularly sadistic ways. . . . The delegation also received information strongly suggesting that many women, and more particularly children, may have died during or after rape. . . . [T]he delegation frequently heard . . . that a repeated feature of Serbian attacks on Muslim towns and villages was the use of rape, or the threat of rape, as a weapon of war. . . . [D]ocuments from Serbian sources . . . very clearly put such actions in the context of an expansionist strategy. . . . [R]ape cannot be seen as incidental to the main purposes of the aggression but as serving a strategic purpose in itself." *Investigative Mission into the Treatment of Muslim Women in the Former Yugoslavia* (December 24, 1992), 2–4.

12. Among the scores of examples of this seemingly requisite equalizing of oppressor and oppressed, although it is among the least egregious, is Amnesty International's "Bosnia-Herzegovina: Rape and Sexual Abuse by Armed Forces" (January, 1993), 3: "Reports indicate . . . that all sides have committed these abuses, but that Muslim women have been the chief victims and the main perpetrators have been members of Serbian armed forces." World War II atrocities against Serbs by Croatians and Muslims are often cited by Serbs as historical justification for current Serbian "re-

venge." Nothing justifies genocide. There is also historical evidence that Serbian war losses have been greatly exaggerated and are being used as a pretext. Phillip J. Cohen, "Holocaust History Misappropriated," *Midstream: A Monthly Jewish Review* (November 1992), 18–20; Phillip J. Cohen, "Exploitation of the Holocaust as Propaganda: The Falsification of Serbian War Losses" (unpublished manuscript, July 18, 1992). See also War Crimes Investigation Bureau, *Fourth Exodus of the Jews: War in Bosnia-Herzegovina* (Sarajevo, September 1992). Alain Finkielkraut comments on this in his *Comment peut-on être croate?* (Paris: Gallimard, 1992), 50: "La Serbie falsifie le passé en disant que les Croates étaient tous nazis et les Serbes tous résistants, falsifie le présent en disant que les Croates restent un 'peuple génocidaire', et mène à l'abri de cette double falsification la première guerre raciale que l'Europe ait connu depuis Hitler. Pour le dire d'un mot: *les nazis de cette histoire ont voulu se faire passer pour les Juifs.*" ("Serbia falsifies the past by saying that the Croatians were all Nazis and the Serbs all resisters, falsifies the present by saying that the Croatians remain a 'genocidal people,' and carries out, in the shadow of this double falsification, the first racial war that Europe has known since Hitler. To put it in a word: *the Nazis of this story are trying to pass themselves off as the Jews.*")

13. A. Kaurin, *Večernji List,* "War Crimes Against Young Girls" (September 11, 1992) ("They are even conducting orgies on the dead bodies of the torture victims, who are after that thrown [out]").

14. In addition, when the dead are counted, their rapes are not. When raped women are counted, their rapes are not.

15. Asja Armanda, *The Women's Movement, Feminism, and the Definition of War* (Kareta Feminist Group, October 1992).

16. "A Pattern of Rape," *Newsweek,* January 4, 1992, 34: "In his own defense, one attacker told Rasema, 'I have to do it, otherwise they will kill me.' " According to *Die Welt,* a rapist told his victim: " 'We have to do it, because our commanders ordered it, and because you are Muslim—and there are too many of you Muslims. We have to destroy and exterminate you, so that the heroic Serbian people can take over the reins in this area again.' "

"Serben vergewaltigen auf obersten Befehl" (Serbs rape on highest orders), *Die Welt,* October 1, 1992.

17. Roy Gutman, "Mass Rapes in Bosnia," *Newsday,* August 23, 1992 (reports on rape as a tactic of war, where victims were told by Serbian forces they were under orders to rape them); John F. Burns, "A Serbian Fighter's Trail of Brutality," *New York Times,* November 27, 1992 (an indicted Serb terrorist says "he and other Serbian fighters were encouraged to rape women and then take them away to kill them").

18. S. Džombic, "Go and Give Birth to Chetniks," *Večernji List,* November 25, 1992.

19. The prior analysis and the facts underlying it are based on my reading of firsthand accounts provided by victims.

20. Many firsthand accounts report this. See Center for Anti-War Activities, *Save Humanity Report* (Sarajevo: July 7, 1992), 6; Roy Gutman, "Victims Recount Nights of Terror at Makeshift Bordello," *Newsday,* August 23, 1992. It is unclear whether the brothels simply organize serial rape or whether some men are being paid or receiving other benefits in exchange for access to the women.

21. Z. Džombic, "Go and Give Birth to Chetniks," *Večernji List,* November 25, 1992. My testimonies further support this.

22. Evidence indicates that Jewish babies born in concentration camps were drowned. See *The Trial of German Major War Criminals* (London: HMSO, 1946), Part 5, 188. No Jewish women were documented to have been impregnated, then released, to "bear German babies." However, the Nazis required special permission to be obtained before the fetuses of Eastern European women and German men could be aborted. For discussion of this, see *McRae v. Califano,* 491 F. Supp. 630, 759 (1980).

23. [Name Withheld] Letter to author, October 13, 1992. See also "Schwere Vorwürfe gegen UN-Soldaten in Bosnien," *Die Welt,* October 6, 1992.

24. "Investigation against General MacKenzie," *Večernji List,* November 25, 1992. According to an interview with Ragib Hadžic, head of the Center for Research on Genocide and War Crimes in Zenica, Bosnia, General MacKenzie visited the "Sonje" restaurant

in Dobrinja, which was a brothel and had become a wartime rape/death camp. He reportedly loaded four Muslim women in his UN-PROFOR truck, and drove away. The women have never been seen again. "Vergewaltigungen als eine Taktik des Krieges," *Die Welt,* December 2, 1992.

25. Nazis documented many atrocities with photographs, including those shown in *The Trial of German Major War Criminals,* Part 7; 99–101: "these naked women are being taken to the execution ground. Condemned to death, these women have been forced, by the same Obergruppenführer, to pose before the camera" (photographs presented by Soviet prosecution team). See also Helke Sander, *Befreier und Befreite* (Munich: Verlag Antje Kunstmann, 1992), 131–34 (German photographs of dead raped German and Russian women). On the point of media manipulation, my correspondent from Croatia ([Name Withheld] Letter to author, November 28, 1992) notes: "The manipulation of film documentation of atrocities in which Muslim and Croatian victims of Serb aggression have fallaciously been presented as Serb victims of Muslims and Croatians has been a notable strategy of the war against Croatia and Bosnia-Herzegovina." See also A. Kaurin, "War Crimes Against Young Girls," *Večernji List,* September 11, 1992 ("pictures and videotapes of the concentration camps exist"); *Mass Killing,* 234 (dead Croatian boy presented as dead Serbian boy); "Villages in Croatia Recount Massacre by Serbian Forces," *New York Times,* December 19, 1991; Ibrahim Kajan, *Muslimanski Danak U Krvi, Svjedočanstva zločina nad Muslimanima* (Zagreb: Preporod, 1992), 31–34, 51–52.

26. "MacKinnon's central point is that 'a woman' is not yet the name of a way of being human." Richard Rorty, "Feminism and Pragmatism," *Michigan Quarterly Review* 30 (1991): 234.

27. Isaiah Berlin, "Two Concepts of Liberty," in *Four Essays on Liberty* (Oxford: Oxford University Press, 1969).

28. *Belgian Linguistics Case,* ECHR, 1968, Series A, No. 6, 832.

29. Inter-American Court of Human Rights, *Velasquez-Rodriguez v. Honduras* Judgment of July 29, 1988, Series C, no. 4.

30. Lori Heise, quoted in Center for Women's Global Leadership, *Women, Violence, and Human Rights,* 17.

31. For illuminating background, see M. Tardu, *Human*

Rights: The International Petition System, vol. 1 (Dobbs Ferry, N.Y.: Oceana Publications, August, 1985), 45 ("The potential of [divisive postwar] UN debates for conflict escalation was so obvious that all governments became fiercely determined to keep the process under their own control through rejecting individual complaint systems"). See also Louis B. Sohn, "The New International Law: Protection of the Rights of Individuals Rather Than States," *American University Law Review* 1 (1982): 32.

32. For an example of the inability to see a violation of a woman's human rights to the degree the abuse is deemed "personal," see *Lazo-Majaro v. INS,* 813 F.2d 1432 (9th Cir. 1987) (dissent).

33. See Tardu, *Human Rights,* vol. 1 (German-speaking minorities used as a propaganda base in other countries by insisting on minority rights); Alessandra Luini del Russo, *International Protection of Human Rights* (Washington, D.C.: Lerner Law Book Co., 1971), 32 (nations realized that individual protections cannot be left solely to states).

34. Elizabeth Spelman, *Inessential Woman* (Boston: Beacon Press, 1988); Eva Kuehls, *The Reign of the Phallus* (New York: Harper & Row, 1985).

35. This is discussed further in my *Toward a Feminist Theory of the State* (Cambridge, Mass.: Harvard University Press, 1989), chap. 12.

36. John Stuart Mill and Harriet Taylor, "On the Subjection of Women," in Alice Rossi, ed., *Essays in Sex Equality* (Chicago: University of Chicago Press, 1970).

37. Susan Moller Okin, *Women in Western Political Thought* (Princeton, N.J.: Princeton University Press, 1980); John Locke, *The Second Treatise of Government,* ed. J. W. Gough (Oxford: Blackwell, 1966); Thomas Hobbes, *Leviathan,* ed. M. Oakeshott (Oxford: Blackwell, 1946).

38. This point is made unintentionally by Theodor Meron in his attack on CEDAW for conflicting with existing notions of human rights in various areas. Theodor Meron, *Human Rights Law-Making in the United Nations* (Oxford: Clarendon Press, 1986).

39. "Court Ruling Sought on Women's Convention," *Human Rights Tribune* 1 (1992): 21.

40. Art. 6, CEDAW; Convention for the Suppression of Traffic in Persons and the Exploitation of the Prostitution of Others, 1949. See also the draft, "U.N. Convention Against Sexual Exploitation," reported in *Ms.*, September/October 1991, 13.

41. In 1966, Thailand enacted the Service Establishments Act which gives specific legal status to "special service girls." The women had to turn to the establishments for protection from prosecution under prostitution laws, which exempt customers but not the women. Thanh-Dom Truong, *Sex, Money and Morality: Prostitution and Tourism in Southeast Asia* (London: Zed Books, 1990), 155. In another sense, wherever prostitution is legalized, the state is trafficking in women.

42. U.S. State Department, *Country Reports on Human Rights Practices for 1991* (Washington, D.C.: USGPO, 1992) ("Physical compulsion to submit to abortion or sterilization is not authorized, but continues to occur as officials strive to meet population targets. Reports of forced abortions and sterilizations continue, though well below the levels of the early 1980s. While recognizing that abuses occur, officials maintain that China does not condone forced abortion or sterilization, and that abuses by local officials are punished. They admit, however, that punishment is rare and have yet to provide documentation of any punishments" [818–19]).

43. An intelligent discussion of these provisions can be found in Karen Engle, "International Human Rights and Feminism: When Discourses Meet," *Michigan Journal of International Law* 13 (1992): 517.

44. E. M. Adams, *The Metaphysics of Self and World: Toward a Humanistic Philosophy* (Philadelphia: Temple University Press, 1991).

45. Simone de Beauvoir, *The Second Sex* (New York: Alfred A. Knopf, 1952).

46. Jacques Maritain, *The Rights of Man and Natural Law,* trans. Doris C. Anson (New York: Scribner, 1951; France, 1942). "[The] human person possess[es] rights because of the very fact that it is a person, a whole, a matter of itself and of its acts . . . by virtue of natural law, the human person has to have the right to be respected, is the subject of rights, possesses rights. These are things

which are owed to a man because of the very fact that he is a man" (65).

47. Herbert C. Kelman, *Crimes of Obedience* (New Haven: Yale University Press, 1989); M. McDougal, H. Lasswell, L. Chen, *Human Rights and World Public Order* (New Haven: Yale University Press, 1980).

48. Mortimer Adler, "Robert Bork: The Lessons to be Learned" (comments on Robert H. Bork, *The Tempting of America*) *New York University Law Review* 84 (1990): 1121.

49. Max Solomon, *Der Begriff der Gerechtigkeit bei Aristoteles* (Leiden: A. W. Sijthoff, 1937), 26; E. W. Vierdag, *The Concept of Discrimination in International Law* (The Hague: Nijhoff, 1973). See page 8 regarding Aristotle, and page 26 for the Third Reich and the proposition that "equality in the sense of complete equality is identity: one and the same thing." Illustrating equality thinking during the Nazi period, leading constitutional scholar Ulrich Scheuner states in 1939 that the substance of the equality right is "Artgleichheit" of Aryans (page 267). From the "völkisch" tenets of contemporary German law, see page 267, "[daraus] folgt notwendig die Absonderung der artfremden Elemente, insbesondere der Juden, aus dem deutschen Volkskörper, und ihre . . . differentielle Behandlung" ("follows necessarily the extraction of elements of alien blood, particularly Jews, from the body of the German people, and their . . . differential treatment"). How the Jews were treated is thus rendered "differential treatment." See also the use of the Aristotelian principle at page 260. Scheuner cites the U.S. Supreme Court with approval with regard to racial segregation and miscegenation laws, noting that this leads to "Benachteiligung" (disadvantage) of people of color, which is exactly what is intended, at pages 265–66. He also notices the Court beginning to weaken in its defense of segregation. "Der Gleichheitsgedanke in der volkischen Verfassungsordnung," *Zeitschrift für die Gesamte Staatswissenschaft* 99 (1939): 245.

50. Andrea Dworkin, *Right-Wing Women: The Politics of Domesticated Females* (New York: Putnam, 1983).

51. Art. 2, Universal Declaration of Human Rights, General Assembly Resolution 217 A (III) of December 10, 1948.

52. Part I, Art. 1, CEDAW, adopted December 18, 1979.

53. General Recommendation No. 19, Violence Against Women, Committee on the Elimination of Discrimination Against Women, CEDAW/C/1992/L/1/Add.15, January 29, 1992. This document goes very far in recognizing the scope of the problem and in adapting sex equality as a concept to addressing violence against women. For a useful discussion, see Charlotte Bunch, "Women's Rights as Human Rights: Toward a Re-Vision of Human Rights," *Human Rights Quarterly* 12 (1990): 483.

54. Many other human rights documents, notably Art. 3 and Art. 26 of the International Covenant on Civil and Political Rights, December 16, 1966, guarantee sex equality. This covenant stands out in allowing, through an Optional Protocol, complaints by individuals as well as state parties, but only applies to those who have accepted it specifically. Yugoslavia did not. Enforcement includes denunciation of violators.

55. These movements are well documented. See Robin Morgan, *Sisterhood Is Global: The International Women's Movement Anthology* (Garden City, N.Y.: Anchor Press/Doubleday, 1984); Center for Women's Global Leadership, *Women, Violence, and Human Rights*. See also Marilyn Waring, *If Women Counted* (New York: HarperCollins, 1990) (economic discrimination against women including exclusion of women's work from international accounting systems). The reference to Canada is to the "Montreal Massacre," in which fourteen young women were murdered by a man screaming he hated feminists. Jane Caputi and Diana E. H. Russell, "Femicide: Sexist Terrorism Against Women," in Radford and Russell, *Femicide,* 13–14.

56. In this sense, equality is derivative in virtually all legal systems. See Art. 14, Convention for the Protection of Human Rights and Fundamental Freedoms, 213 U.N.T.S. 221, E.T.S. 5, U.K.T.S. 71 (1953) (September 3, 1953), which has been held to permit no complaints on its own, but merely refers to equal access to other rights. *X and Y v. The Netherlands,* ECHR, 1985 Series A., No. 91, para. 32.

57. *The Law Society of British Columbia v. Andrews* [1989] 1 S.C.R. 143, 171–182.

58. *Jane Doe v. Board of Commissioners of Policy for the Municipality of Metropolitan Toronto* [1989] Ont. L.J. LEXIS 115.

59. *Janzen v. Platy Enterprises* [1959] 1 S.C.R. 1252 (sexual harassment is sex discrimination under the Manitoba human rights code).

60. *Brooks, Allen and Dixon v. Canada Safeway* [1989] 1 S.C.R. 1219 (pregnancy discrimination is sex discrimination).

61. *Norberg v. Wynrib* [1992] 2 S.C.R. 224.

62. *K.M. v. H.M.* (1992) 142 N.R. 321 (S.C.C.).

63. *Regina v. Lavallee*, 76 C.R. (3d) 329 (1990).

64. *The Queen v. Canadian Newspapers Co.* [1988] 2 S.C.R. 122.

65. *R. v. Seaboyer* (August 22, 1991) (S.C.C., Rep. Serv. 2nd ed. 1991 cases [Digest 1713]).

66. Less positive results occurred in the prostitution cases, *R. v. Skinner* [1990] 1 S.C.R. 1235, and in statutory rape, *R. v. Nguyen and Hess* [1990] 2 S.C.R. 906. No serious sex equality argument was made in either instance.

67. *Daigle v. Trembley* [1989] 2 S.C.R. 530.

68. On women's rights in childbirth: See *The Queen v. Sullivan and LeMay* (March 21, 1991), Doc. 21080, 21494 (S.C.C.).

69. *Keegstra v. The Queen* [1991] 2 W.W.R. 1; *The Queen v. Butler* [1992] 2 W.W.R. 557 (S.C.C.).

70. Women's Help Now and Kareta, "Who Are We? Where Are We?" (leaflet, October 2, 1992, Zagreb); Natalie Nenadic, "How do you get rid of the guns?" *Everywoman*, July–August 1991, 19; Katja Gattin for Kareta, "Where have all the feminists gone?" (unpublished paper, January 20, 1992, Zagreb). ("In 1991/1992, Croatia is a woman.")

71. A useful review is Yougindra Khushalani, *Dignity and Honour of Women as Basic and Fundamental Human Rights* (The Hague: Nijhoff, 1982).

72. Art. 76(1), Protocol I, Protocol Additional to the Geneva Conventions of August 12, 1949 (victims of international armed conflict protected against "rape, forced prostitution and any other form of indecent assault"); Art. 4(e), Protocol II, Protocol Additional to the Geneva Conventions of August 12, 1949 (victims of

noninternational armed conflicts protected against "outrages upon personal dignity, in particular humiliating and degrading treatment, rape, enforced prostitution and any form of indecent assault"). Murder and torture are prohibited under many international conventions, with additional protections against doing so on ethnic grounds.

73. *In re Yamashita,* 327 U.S. 1 (1945). Courtney Whitney, Brigadier General, U.S. Army, *The Case of General Yamashita: A Memorandum* (1950), 5–16, contains detailed excerpts from the record of the trial, revealing many rapes. The U.S. Supreme Court upheld the decision of the military tribunal. See also Richard L. Lael, *The Yamashita Precedent: War Crimes and Command Responsibility* (Wilmington: Scholarly Resources, 1982), 83–84; L. C. Green, *Essays on the Modern Law of War* (Dobbs Ferry, N.Y.: Transnational Publications, 1985), 227–28; Arnold Brackman, *The Other Nuremburg: The Untold Story of the Tokyo War Crimes Trials* (New York: Morrow, 1987), 179–80. Brackman discusses the death sentence of General Iwane Matsui, who was convicted of "failing to take adequate steps to secure the observance and prevent breaches of conventions and laws of war in respect of prisoners of war and civilian internees" in the mass rapes that were called the Rape of Nanking (419; see also 180 and 409).

74. Lael, *Yamashita Precedent,* 83. All that is distinguishable in the Japanese war accounts is the pornography and the intention to create pregnancies.

75. Joan Fitzpatrick, "The Use of International Human Rights Norms to Combat Violence Against Women" (unpublished manuscript, 1992). This is a lucid, informed treatment. On the rapes in Bangladesh, see Susan Brownmiller, *Against Our Will: Men, Women and Rape* (New York: Bantam, 1976), 78–87.

76. *The Trial of German Major War Criminals,* Part 6, 303 (evidence of Soviet prosecutors); Part 5, 159, 325–27 (evidence of French prosecutors).

77. *The Trial of German Major War Criminals,* Part 1, 24: "One hundred and thirty-nine women had their arms painfully bent backward and held by wires. From some their breasts had been cut off, and their ears, fingers and toes had been amputated. The bodies

bore the marks of burns." (Russian women's bodies in Stalingrad region after German expulsion).

78. Opening statement by Justice Jackson, *The Trial of German Major War Criminals,* 53. One exhibit of a Soviet official documenting "revolting acts of rape" by the German invaders observed this: "Unquestionable facts prove that the regime . . . did not consist of certain excesses of individual undisciplined military units, or individual German officers and soldiers. Rather does it point to a definite system, planned far in advance and encouraged by the German Government and the German Army Command, a system which intentionally unleashed within their army the lowest animal instincts among the officers and men." *The Trial of German Major War Criminals,* Part 7, 26 (notes of V. M. Molotov, National Commissar for Foreign Affairs in USSR, Exhibit USSR 51, dated as early as January 6, 1942). The Nuremberg trial was conducted under the common law of war, even though the violations of the Geneva Conventions under which the Nazi leadership was charged had not been made a specific penal offense. See Howard S. Levie, *The Code of International Armed Conflict* (London: Oceana Publications, 1986), 862.

79. "Consistent pattern of gross and reliably attested violations of human rights and fundamental freedoms" violate Resolution 1503 (XLVIII) of the Economic and Social Council authorizing the establishment of a subcommission on Prevention of Discrimination and Protection of Minorities. It is empowered to appoint a group to determine violations and bring them to the attention of the subcommission and it enables the U.N. to interfere in "domestic" matters. See Ermacora, "Human Rights and Domestic Jurisdiction," *Recueil des Cours* (1968): 124, 375, 436.

80. Bogdan Tirnanic, quoted by Michael Moorcock, "Working in the Ministry of Truth: Pornography and Censorship in Contemporary Britain," in C. Itzin, ed., *Pornography: Women, Violence, and Civil Liberties* (Oxford: Oxford University Press, 1992), 536. As Moorcock then asks, "Have sex crimes dropped in Serbia?" (550).

81. It should be noted that the Serbs consider the Serbian-occupied areas of Croatia and Bosnia-Herzegovina to be Serbian

states, parts of the United States of Serbia. So the Serbian military forces, in addition to being state actors under orders from Belgrade, function under color of official authority of the self-declared Serbian mini-states within and against the established governments of Croatia and Bosnia-Herzegovina. In addition, the local Serbian irregulars, termed *chetniks,* provide yet another layer of actual and apparent state authority.

Richard Rorty: Human Rights, Rationality, and Sentimentality

1. "Letter from Bosnia," *New Yorker,* November 23, 1992, 82–95.

2. "Their griefs are transient. Those numberless afflictions, which render it doubtful whether heaven has given life to us in mercy or in wrath, are less felt, and sooner forgotten with them. In general, their existence appears to participate more of sensation than reflection. To this must be ascribed their disposition to sleep when abstracted from their diversions, and unemployed in labor. An animal whose body is at rest, and who does not reflect must be disposed to sleep of course." Thomas Jefferson, "Notes on Virginia," *Writings,* ed. Lipscomb and Bergh (Washington, D.C.: 1905), 1: 194.

3. Geertz, "Thick Description" in his *The Interpretation of Culture* (New York: Basic Books, 1973), 22.

4. Rabossi also says that he does not wish to question "the idea of a rational foundation of morality." I am not sure why he does not. Rabossi may perhaps mean that in the past—for example, at the time of Kant—this idea still made a kind of sense, but it makes sense no longer. That, at any rate, is my own view. Kant wrote in a period when the only alternative to religion seemed to be something like science. In such a period, inventing a pseudoscience called "the system of transcendental philosophy"—setting the stage for the show-stopping climax in which one pulls moral obligation out of a transcendental hat—might plausibly seem the only way of saving morality from the hedonists on one side and the priests on the other.

5. The present state of metaethical discussion is admirably

summarized in Stephen Darwall, Allan Gibbard, and Peter Railton, "Toward *Fin de Siècle* Ethics: Some Trends," *The Philosophical Review* 101 (1992): 115–89. This comprehensive and judicious article takes for granted that there is a problem about "vindicating the objectivity of morality" (127), that there is an interesting question as to whether morals is "cognitive" or "non-cognitive," that we need to figure out whether we have a "cognitive capacity" to detect moral properties (148), and that these matters can be dealt with ahistorically.

When these authors consider historicist writers such as Alasdair MacIntyre and Bernard Williams, they conclude that they are "[meta] *théoriciens malgré eux*" who share the authors' own "desire to understand morality, its preconditions and its prospects" (183). They make little effort to come to terms with suggestions that there may be no ahistorical entity called "morality" to be understood. The final paragraph of the paper does suggest that it might be helpful if moral philosophers knew more anthropology, or psychology, or history. But the penultimate paragraph makes clear that, with or without such assists, "contemporary metaethics moves ahead, and positions gain in complexity and sophistication."

It is instructive, I think, to compare this article with Annette Baier's "Some Thoughts On How We Moral Philosophers Live Now," *The Monist* 67 (1984): 490. Baier suggests that moral philosophers should "at least occasionally, like Socrates, consider why the rest of society should not merely tolerate but subsidize our activity." She goes on to ask, "Is the large proportional increase of professional philosophers and moral philosophers a good thing, morally speaking? Even if it scarcely amounts to a plague of gad-flies, it may amount to a nuisance of owls." The kind of meta-philosophical and historical self-consciousness and self-doubt displayed by Baier seems to me badly needed, but it is conspicuously absent in *Philosophy in Review* (the centennial issue of *The Philosophical Review* in which "Toward *Fin de Siècle* Ethics" appears). The contributors to this issue are convinced that the increasing sophistication of a philosophical subdiscipline is enough to demonstrate its social utility, and are entirely unimpressed by murmurs of "decadent scholasticism."

6. Fichte's *Vocation of Man* is a useful reminder of the need that was felt, circa 1800, for a cognitive discipline called philosophy that would rescue utopian hope from natural science. It is hard to think of an analogous book written in reaction to Darwin. Those who couldn't stand what Darwin was saying tended to go straight back past the Enlightenment to traditional religious faith. The unsubtle, unphilosophical opposition, in nineteenth-century Britain and France, between science and faith suggests that most intellectuals had become unable to believe that philosophy might produce some sort of superknowledge, knowledge that might trump the results of physical and biological inquiry.

7. Some contemporary intellectuals, especially in France and Germany, take it as obvious that the Holocaust made it clear that the hopes for human freedom which arose in the nineteenth century are obsolete—that at the end of the twentieth century we postmodernists know that the Enlightenment project is doomed. But even these intellectuals, in their less preachy and sententious moments, do their best to further that project. So they should, for nobody has come up with a better one. It does not diminish the memory of the Holocaust to say that our response to it should not be a claim to have gained a new understanding of human nature or of human history, but rather a willingness to pick ourselves up and try again.

8. Nietzsche was right to remind us that "these same men who, amongst themselves, are so strictly constrained by custom, worship, ritual gratitude and by mutual surveillance and jealousy, who are so resourceful in consideration, tenderness, loyalty, pride and friendship, when once they step outside their circle become little better than uncaged beasts of prey." *The Genealogy of Morals,* trans. Golffing (Garden City, N.Y.: Doubleday, 1956), 174.

9. Colin McGinn, *Moral Literacy: or, How to Do the Right Thing* (London: Duckworth, 1992), 16.

10. Baier, "Hume, the Women's Moral Theorist?," in Eva Kittay and Diana Meyers, eds., *Women and Moral Theory* (Totowa, N.J.: Rowman and Littlefield, 1987), 40.

11. Baier's book on Hume is entitled *A Progress of Sentiments: Reflections on Hume's Treatise* (Cambridge, Mass.: Harvard University Press, 1991). Baier's view of the inadequacy of most attempts

by contemporary moral philosophers to break with Kant comes out most clearly when she characterizes Allan Gibbard (in his book *Wise Choices, Apt Feelings*) as focusing "on the feelings that a patriarchal religion has bequeathed to us," and says that "Hume would judge Gibbard to be, as a moral philosopher, basically a divine disguised as a fellow expressivist" (312).

12. Nietzsche's diagnosis is reinforced by Elizabeth Anscombe's famous argument that atheists are not entitled to the term "moral obligation."

13. See Jane Tompkins, *Sensational Designs: The Cultural Work of American Fiction, 1790–1860* (New York: Oxford University Press, 1985), for a treatment of the sentimental novel that chimes with the point I am trying to make here. In her chapter on Stowe, Tompkins says that she is asking the reader "to set aside some familiar categories for evaluating fiction—stylistic intricacy, psychological subtlety, epistemological complexity—and to see the sentimental novel not as an artifice of eternity answerable to certain formal criteria and to certain psychological and philosophical concerns, but as a political enterprise, halfway between sermon and social theory, that both codifies and attempts to mold the values of its time" (126).

The contrast that Tompkins draws between authors like Stowe and "male authors such as Thoreau, Whitman and Melville, who are celebrated as models of intellectual daring and honesty" (124), parallels the contrast I tried to draw between public utility and private perfection in my *Contingency, Irony and Solidarity* (Cambridge, England: Cambridge University Press, 1989). I see *Uncle Tom's Cabin* and *Moby Dick* as equally brilliant achievements, achievements that we should not attempt to rank hierarchically, because they serve such different purposes. Arguing about which is the better novel is like arguing about which is the superior philosophical treatise: Mill's *On Liberty* or Kierkegaard's *Philosophical Fragments*.

14. Technically, of course, Kant denied knowledge in order to make room for moral faith. But what is transcendental moral philosophy if not the assurance that the noncognitive imperative delivered via the common moral consciousness shows the existence of a "fact

of reason"—a fact about what it is to be a human being, a rational agent, a being that is something more than a bundle of spatio-temporal determinations? Kant was never able to explain how transcendental knowledge could be knowledge, but he was never able to give up the attempt to claim such knowledge.

On the German project of defending reason against Hume, see Fred Beiser, *The Fate of Reason: German Philosophy From Kant to Fichte* (Cambridge, Mass.: Harvard University Press, 1987).

15. I have discussed the relation between Derrida and feminism in "Deconstruction, Ideology and Feminism: A Pragmatist View," forthcoming in *Hypatia*, and also in my reply to Alexander Nehamas in *Lire Rorty* (Paris: Éclat, 1992). Richard Bernstein is, I think, basically right in reading Derrida as a moralist, even though Thomas McCarthy is also right in saying that "deconstruction" is of no political use.

Jean-François Lyotard: The Other's Rights

1. H. Arendt: *The Origins of Totalitarianism,* 10th ed. (New York, Medina, 1966), 300; rev. ed. (London: George Allen and Unwin, 1967), 300. "Fellow man" in French is *semblable,* implying likeness.

Agnes Heller: The Limits to Natural Law and the Paradox of Evil

1. See H. Arendt, *Eichmann in Jerusalem* (New York: Viking Press, 1964), 256.

2. Plato: *Republic,* 336b ff., and *Gorgias,* 482c ff.

3. See Arendt, *Eichmann in Jerusalem,* 256.

4. Dostoevsky, *The Brothers Karamazov* (Harmondsworth: Penguin, 1982), 284.

5. J. Shklar, *Legalism: Law, Morals and Political Trials* (Cambridge, Mass.: Harvard University Press, 1964).

6. See Nicolaus of Cusa, *On Learned Ignorance* (Minneapolis: Arthur J. Banning Press, 1981).

7. J. Derrida, "Deconstruction and the Possibility of Justice," *Cardoza Law Review* 11 (1990): 919.

8. Shakespeare, *Hamlet,* 5.2.79.

Jon Elster: Majority Rule and Individual Rights

1. When used without further qualification, "majority rule" in this paper always means "simple majority rule."

2. A similar story for Norway is told in F. Sejersted, "Democracy and the Rule of Law," in J. Elster and R. Slagstad, eds., *Constitutionalism and Democracy* (Cambridge, England: Cambridge University Press, 1988), 131–52.

3. References to the American proceedings will be cited from the three volumes of M. Farrand, ed., *Records of the Federal Convention* (New Haven, Conn.: Yale University Press, 1966). References to the French proceedings will be cited from volumes 8 through 30 of the *Archives Parlementaires. Série I: 1789–1799* (Paris: 1875–1888).

4. A good exposition is A. Sen, *Collective Choice and Social Welfare* (San Francisco: Freeman, 1970), chaps. 5 and 5*.

5. Here I draw on B. Barry, "Is Democracy Special?," reprinted in his *Democracy, Power and Justice* (New York: Oxford University Press, 1989), 24–60. For the idea of focal point, see T. C. Schelling, *The Strategy of Conflict* (Cambridge, Mass.: Harvard University Press, 1960), chap. 2.

6. Karl Marx, *The Eighteenth Brumaire,* in Marx and Engels, *Collected Works* (New York: International Publishers, 1979), vol. 11, 166.

7. Barry, "Is Democracy Special?," 56. The same idea underlies Tocqueville's *Democracy in America.*

8. For a survey, see E. Spitz, *Majority Rule* (Chatham, N.J.: Chatham House Publishers, 1984), chap. 8 and passim.

9. See, for instance, the essays in R. G. Frey, ed., *Utility and Rights* (Oxford: Blackwell, 1985).

10. For the idea of rights as trumps, see notably R. Dworkin, *Taking Rights Seriously* (London: Duckworth, 1977).

11. One might try to avoid the regress by fixed-point reasoning. Consider the proposal that x percent of the votes ($x \geq 50$) is sufficient for a law to be passed. The percentage of members of the assembly who agree with the proposal is some decreasing function $f(x)$. There must then exist some self-sustaining percentage of $x^\star$ such that $f(x^\star) = x^\star$. This is the percentage that should be adopted by the assembly. However, this procedure must itself be voted by simple majority.

12. Mounier, *Archives,* 8:555; Mirabeau, ibid., 8: 538; Clermont-Tonnerre, ibid., 8: 574; Robespierre, ibid., 26:124.

13. J. M. Thomson, *Robespierre* (Oxford: Blackwell, 1988), 134ff.

14. F. Furet, *La révolution 1770–1870* (Paris: Hachette, 1988), 104.

15. L. Fuller, *The Morality of Law* (New Haven, Conn.: Yale University Press, 1969), 79–81.

16. In fact, even when the government cannot choose the date of the election, it can still manipulate the economic conjectures so as to make them more favorable. To overcome this problem, one could time elections randomly, as proposed by A. Lindbeck, "Stabilization Policy in Open Economies with Endogenous Politicians," *American Economic Review: Papers and Proceedings* 66 (1976): 1–19. I note as a curiosum that in the debates of the Assemblée Constituante the proposal was made (30: 97) to have periodical constitutional conventions called in a quasi-random manner, namely, by linking them to the death of the monarch. However, in these cases, as in many others, the advantages of randomization are easily seen to be offset by its drawbacks. See generally chap. 2 of my *Solomonic Judgements* (Cambridge, England: Cambridge University Press, 1989). An important exception is randomization in the judiciary, as further discussed below.

17. Madison, *Records,* 1:135.

18. For an analysis of the distinction between interest and passion among the American founders, see M. White, *Philosophy, The Federalist, and the Constitution* (New York: Oxford University Press, 1987), chap. 7. For general discussions, see S. Holmes, "The Secret History of Self-Interest," in J. Mansbridge, ed., *Beyond Self-*

Interest (Chicago: University of Chicago Press, 1990), 267–86, and my *Sadder but Wiser? Studies in Rationality and the Emotions,* forthcoming from Cambridge University Press.

19. Madison, *Records,* 2:123.

20. Bergasse, *Archives,* 9:116. Strictly speaking, this example is out of place. It shows how certain solutions to the problem of majority rule might fail to work, rather than instantiating that problem itself.

21. When such short-sighted behavior is induced by passion rather than representing the permanent subjective interest of the actor, it belongs to the next category. For quotations in this paragraph: Randolph, *Records,* 1:51; Randolph, ibid., 1:59; Hamilton, ibid., 1:289; Madison, ibid., 1:421; Madison, ibid., 1:430; Morris, ibid., 1:512; Lally-Tollendal, *Archives,* 8:516; Grégoire, ibid., 8:567; Sieyès, ibid., 8:597; Robespierre, ibid., 9:81.

22. See, however, Madison's letter to Jefferson of October 24, 1787, for a discussion of religious sects as a threat to the freedom of worship.

23. See also chap. 6 of my *The Cement of Society* (Cambridge, England: Cambridge University Press, 1989).

24. See, for instance, G. Wood, *The Creation of the American Republic* (New York: Norton, 1972), 188–96.

25. See notably Sieyès, *Archives,* 8:595.

26. Spitz, *Majority Rule,* 149–52.

27. My mother tells me that when she was a girl, she and her friends were obsessed by the following hypothetical choice: given that you could only have two out of the three properties of intelligence, kindness, and beauty, which two would you choose? Similarly, the discussion in the text suggests that democracies can only have two out of the following three virtues: enabling deliberation, limiting passionate popular majorities, and limiting self-interested legislative majorities.

28. V. Bogdanov, "Britain: The Political Constitution", in V. Bogdanov, ed., *Constitutions in Democratic Politics* (London: Gower, 1988), 53–72. It has been argued, however, that the violations of the unwritten British constitution under Mrs. Thatcher have created the need for a formal bill of rights (L. Siedentop,

"Thatcherism and the Constitution," *Times Literary Supplement,* January 26, 1990).

29. M. J. C. Vile, *Constitutionalism and the Separation of Powers* (New York: Oxford University Press, 1967), 189.

30. G. Vedel, "The Development of the Conseil Constitutionnel," forthcoming in E. Smith, ed., *Constitutional Justice under Old Constitutions.*

31. For applications of the motive-opportunity distinction to political affairs see chaps. 9 and 10 of White, *Philosophy, The Federalist, and the Constitution,* and chap. 4 of my *Political Psychology* (Cambridge, England: Cambridge University Press, 1993).

32. A similar practice obtains in Great Britain: "Under the Parliament Act of 1911, as amended by the Parliament Act of 1949, a non-money bill can be passed into law over the opposition of the House of Lords if it has been passed by simple majority in two consecutive sessions of the House of Commons and one year has elapsed between the second reading of the Bill in the Commons in the first sessions and its third reading in the Commons in the second session." (J. Jaconelli, "Majority Rule and Special Majorities," *Public Law* [1989] 587–616, at 597.)

33. J. N. Eule, "Temporal Limits on the Legislative Mandate," *American Bar Foundation Research Journal* [1987] 379–459, at 394. Eule goes on to say, however, that "even in such a system . . . there remain moral and political restraints on the legislative alteration of constitutional doctrine."

34. John Potter Stockton in debates over the Ku Klux Klan Act of 1871, as cited in J. E. Finn, *Constitutions in Crisis* (New York: Oxford University Press, 1991), 5. On the general theme of self-binding, see chap. 2 of my *Ulysses and the Sirens,* rev. ed. (Cambridge, England: Cambridge University Press, 1984) and S. Holmes, *The Paradox of Democracy,* forthcoming from University of Chicago Press. On the theme of constitutional self-binding, see my "Intertemporal Choice and Political Theory," in G. Loewenstein and J. Elster, eds., *Choice over Time* (New York: Russell Sage Foundation, 1992). For a discussion of the putative paradoxes involved in self-binding, see P. Suber, *The Paradox of Self-Amendment* (New York: Peter Lang, 1990).

35. I simplify. The use of qualified majorities can also act as a restraint on momentary passions, because with a larger proportion

of people required for the decision, the chances are better that not all of them will be caught up in the collective frenzy. Unamendable clauses, in particular, offer a perfect protection against impulsive rashness.

36. Tocqueville warned against the excessively stringent amendment procedures proposed for the French 1848 constitution. "I have long thought that, instead of trying to make our forms of government eternal, we should pay attention to making methodical change an easy matter. All things considered, I find that less dangerous than the opposite alternative. I thought one should treat the French people like those lunatics whom one is careful not to bind lest they become infuriated by the constraint." See A. de Tocqueville, *Recollections: The French Revolution of 1848* (New Brunswick, N.J.: Transaction Books, 1990), 181. The implication, whether intended or not, is that by making change easier one reduces the desire for change. A similar motive was adduced by the government of East Germany in 1989: by making it clear that everybody could leave for the West, they hoped to ensure that nobody would want to do so. Also, it has been argued that the possibility of divorce makes marriages more stable rather than less: "We thought we were tying our marriage-knots more tightly by removing all means of undoing them; but the tighter we pulled the knot of constraint the looser and slacker became the knot of our will and affection. In Rome, on the contrary, what made marriages honoured and secure for so long a period was freedom to break them at will." (Montaigne, *Essays* 2:15.)

37. Mason, *Records*, 2:309.

38. See notably G. Ainslie, *Picoeconomics* (Cambridge, England: Cambridge University Press, 1992).

39. Sieyès, *Archives*, 8:596.

40. See my "Limits to Majority Rule: Alternatives to Judicial Review in the Revolutionary Epoch," forthcoming in E. Smith, ed., *Constitutional Justice under Old Constitutions*.

41. Gerry, *Records*, 1:97; King, ibid., 1:109.

42. Wilson, *Records*, 2:73; Madison, ibid., 2:74; Mason, ibid., 2:78.

43. Madison, *Records*, 3:424, italics added.

44. I am indebted to Cass Sunstein for pressing this point on me.

45. I am indebted to Justice Suetens of the Belgian Cour d'Arbitrage for this point.

46. For a review of this case, see G. R. Stone et al., *Constitutional Law*, 2d ed. (Boston: Little, Brown, 1991), 568–81.

47. The Constitution of the United States says only that their compensation "shall not be diminished during their continuance in office." At the Convention, however, Madison argued (2:45) that one should also make it impossible to bribe judges by *increasing* their salary.

48. W. Nordhaus, "The Political Business Cycle," *Review of Economic Studies* 42 (1975): 169–90, at 188.

49. Mounier, *Archives,* 8:555.

50. Clermont-Tonnerre, *Archives,* 8:574; Malouet, ibid., 8:591.

51. *Records,* 1:421–22.

52. Dickinson, *Records,* 2:429; Mason, ibid., 1:254; Lally-Tollendal, *Archives,* 8:515.

53. Gerry, *Records,* 2:286; Wilson, ibid., 2:522; Madison, ibid., 1:218–19.

54. Morris, *Records,* 2:52.

55. Recall here that the same two procedures—qualified majorities and delays—are also used as constraints on constitutional amendments.

56. Madison, *Records,* 1:108; Morris, ibid., 2:52, 2:76; Mason, ibid., 2:78.

57. Some of the interventions quoted in this paragraph may seem to refer to majoritarian interests rather than passions; see however, note 21 above.

58. I am indebted to Bernard Manin and Pasquale Pasquino for help in understanding the motivations of the *constituants* on this issue.

59. LaSalle, *Archives,* 8:529; Lameth, ibid., 8:552; Grégoire, ibid., 8:567; LaSalle, ibid., 8:534; Pétion, ibid., 8:581.

60. Lally-Tollendal, ibid., 8:517–18; Mirabeau, ibid., 8:538; Malouet, ibid., 8:535–36; Duport, ibid., 28:263 ff.; Barnave, ibid., 28:326 ff.; Duport, ibid., 28:265.

61. Wilson, *Records,* 2:301.

62. Morris, ibid., 2:299–300.

63. d'Antraigues, *Archives,* 8:544; Mirabeau, ibid., 8:539; Mounier, ibid., 8:561; Lanjuinais, ibid., 8:588.

64. Sherman, *Records,* 1:60; Morris, ibid., 1:29; Madison, ibid., 2:109.

65. Morris, ibid., 2:585; Gerry, ibid., 2:586.

66. The following applies to the situation at the time of writing (April 1993). I do not discuss developments in the former Soviet Union, partly because I know less about them and partly because they appear to be less advanced. The total lack of references to Albania is due to the very fluid nature of the constitutional process in that country, together with the difficulty of obtaining accurate information. For obvious reasons I do not consider the new constitution of the rump Yugoslavia (Serbia and Montenegro) that was adopted on April 13, 1992.

67. For details, see W. Osiatynski, "The Roundtable Negotiations in Poland," working paper from the Center for Study of Constitutionalism in Eastern Europe, University of Chicago Law School.

68. For Poland, see A. Rapaczynski, "Constitutional Politics in Poland," *University of Chicago Law Review* 58 (1991): 595–632, at 615.

69. For a discussion, see L. Cutler and H. Schwartz, "Constitutional Reform in Czechoslovakia," *University of Chicago Law Review* 58 (1991): 511–53, at 536.

70. For a discussion see E. Klingsberg, "Judicial Review and Hungary's Transition from Communism to Democracy," *Brigham Young University Law Review* 41 (1992): 41–144. Klingsberg concludes that this clause was intended not only to protect rights from being limited by statute, but "to entrench fundamental rights in the Constitution beyond the reach of the amendment process."

71. To see the potentially illiberal implications of this clause, the following characterization of Communist Bulgarian practices may be useful: "There are . . . public campaigns directed at two religious practices which, though phrased in terms of their public health implications, could easily be seen as connecting the campaign against Turkish names with an anti-Islam campaign. The

government has directly called for an end to the Ramadan feast and ritual circumcision, calling the former 'A Means of Crippling the Individual,' while describing the latter as 'Criminal Interference with Children's Health.' " R. J. McIntyre, *Bulgaria: Politics, Economics and Society* (London: Pinter, 1988), 73.

72. I was told by a judge on the Slovenian constitutional court that the greatest weakness of their constitution, in his opinion, is that rights are limited only by the rights of others, with no room for public-interest limitations.

73. For a survey, see H. Schwartz, "The New Eastern European Constitutional Courts," *Michigan Journal of International Law* 13 (1992): 741–85.

74. For details, see Klingsberg, "Judicial Review."

75. Constitutional Court Decisions No. 21/1990, No. 16/1991, and No.28/1991. For discussions, see Klingsberg, "Judicial Review," and P. Paczolay, "Judicial Review of the Compensation Law in Hungary," *Michigan Journal of International Law* 13 (1992): 806–31.

76. Constitutional Court Decision No.11/1992.

77. Decision rendered on April 22, 1992.

78. Here is a brief summary. In Slovenia, parliament appoints ordinary judges as well as judges to the constitutional court. In Croatia, ordinary judges are appointed by an independent judicial body, whereas judges to the constitutional court are appointed by parliament. A similar system obtains in Poland. In Romania and Bulgaria, ordinary judges are appointed by independent judicial bodies, whereas the power to appoint judges to the constitutional court is divided among the three powers of state. In Hungary, parliament appoints judges to the constitutional court, whereas the president (de facto the government) appoints ordinary judges.

CONTRIBUTORS

JON ELSTER is Edward L. Ryerson Distinguished Science Professor of Political Science and Philosophy at the University of Chicago.

AGNES HELLER is Hannah Arendt Professor of Philosophy at the New School for Social Research, New York City.

SUSAN HURLEY is a Fellow and Tutor in Philosophy at St. Edmund Hall, University of Oxford. She has been elected to a chair in Political and Ethical Theory at the University of Warwick.

STEVEN LUKES is Professor of Political and Social Theory at the European University Institute, Florence.

JEAN-FRANÇOIS LYOTARD is Emeritus Professor at the Université de Paris VIII and Distinguished Professor at the University of California, Irvine.

CATHARINE A. MACKINNON is Professor of Law at the University of Michigan, Ann Arbor.

JOHN RAWLS is Emeritus Professor of Philosophy at Harvard University.

RICHARD RORTY is University Professor of Humanities at the University of Virginia.

STEPHEN SHUTE is a Fellow and Tutor in Law at Corpus Christi College, University of Oxford.

INDEX

259

Index

Fairness, justice as, 46–47, 51, 62, 63, 65, 67
Federal Convention, 176, 183, 184, 186, 189, 190–91, 198–99, 200–201, 203
Foucault, Michel, 131
Foundationalism, 116, 122–23, 128
France, 153
France, Anatole, 33
Franco, Francisco, 163
Free speech, 62
French Revolution, 94, 96, 121
Freud, Sigmund, 146

Galileo, 120
Geertz, Clifford, 113
Germany, 101, 152–53, 211
Gerry, Eldridge, 190
Gewirth, Alan, 116
Goebbels, Joseph, 171
Gramsci, Antonio, 26
Guatemala, 59
Gypsies, 206, 211

Hegel, Georg, 14, 69–70, 121, 132
Heidegger, Martin, 131
Heise, Lori, 92
Heller, Agnes, 11, 14–16, 149–73
Helsinki Declaration, 120
Helsinki Watch, 20, 116
Herder, Johann, 121
Himmler, Heinrich, 171
Hitler, Adolf, 92, 99, 155, 171
Holocaust, 88, 99, 126, 246n7
Honduras, 92
Honecker, Erich, 152
Humanism, 3, 17
Human rights: absence of women and, 9–10, 85–86, 92–93, 97; experiences of men and violations of, 10, 92–93; fables for imagining a world with, 5, 31–37; fables for imagining a world without, 4–5, 21–31; law of peoples and, 68–71; liberalism and theory of, 3–4; list of rights included as, 38–39; regarding victims as human in violations of, 11, 113–15; right to equality for women and, 10, 100–107; states acting against states and, 93–94; theory and practice of, 1–18; universality of, 20, 70–71, 227n46
Human rights culture, 11–12, 115–16
Hume, David, 128, 129, 133, 134

Hungary, 165, 188, 205, 207, 209–10, 211, 212, 214
Hurley, Susan, 1–18

Immigration, 57, 223n17
India, 101, 102
Individualism, 69
International Covenant on Civil and Political Rights, 240n54
International law: crimes against women and, 10, 87, 91–92; human rights and, 70; law of peoples distinct from, 50–51; sex equality under, 97–98; sovereignty of the state and, 49
Iran, 59
Ireland, 101
Italy, 101, 214

Jackson, Robert, 189
Japan, 101, 107
Japanese-Americans, internment of, 183
Jefferson, Thomas, 112, 197
Judicial review, 17, 186–87, 189–93, 209–11
Justice: domestic, and law of peoples, 48–49, 50; as fairness, 46–47, 51, 62, 63, 65, 67; hierarchical societies and conceptions of, 64–65; political conception of, 42, 44–45, 220n2
Just war, 42

Kant, Immanuel, 15, 54, 73, 117, 118, 119, 120, 122, 123, 124–25, 128, 130, 131–32, 134, 150, 156, 166, 222n12, 247n14
King, Rufus, 190
Kulcsár, Kálmán, 211
Kurds, 30

Language, interlocutory nature of, 13, 137–39, 143
Law, and the experience of women, 84–85
Law of peoples, 41–82; extension to hierarchical societies of, 8, 60–68; extension to liberal societies of, 7–8, 51–59; human rights and, 68–71; law of nations distinct from, 50–51; meaning and use of term, 42, 220n1; noncompliance and, 71–74; public opinion of governments and, 50; relations between societies and, 44; society's

260